RAILS CRASH COURSE

RAILS CRASH COURSE

A No-Nonsense Guide to Rails Development

by Anthony Lewis

no starch press

San Francisco

Printed in USA

First printing

18 17 16 15 14   1 2 3 4 5 6 7 8 9

ISBN-10: 1-59327-572-2
ISBN-13: 978-1-59327-572-3

Text stock is SFI certified

Publisher: William Pollock
Production Editor: Serena Yang
Cover Illustration: W. Sullivan
Interior Design: Octopod Studios
Developmental Editor: Jennifer Griffith-Delgado
Technical Reviewer: Xavier Noria
Copyeditor: LeeAnn Pickrell
Compositor: Susan Glinert Stevens
Proofreader: James Fraleigh
Indexer: Nancy Guenther

For information on distribution, translations, or bulk sales, please contact No Starch Press, Inc. directly:

No Starch Press, Inc.
245 8th Street, San Francisco, CA 94103
phone: 415.863.9900; info@nostarch.com
www.nostarch.com

Library of Congress Cataloging-in-Publication Data

Lewis, Anthony, 1975- author.
  Rails crash course : a no-nonsense guide to Rails development / by Anthony Lewis.
      pages cm
  ISBN 978-1-59327-572-3 -- ISBN 1-59327-572-2
 1. Ruby (Computer program language) 2. Ruby on rails (Electronic resource) I. Title.
 TK5105.8885.R83L49 2015
 006.7'54--dc23
                                          2014034816

BRIEF CONTENTS

CONTENTS IN DETAIL

PART I
RUBY ON RAILS FUNDAMENTALS

1
RUBY FUNDAMENTALS   3

2
RAILS FUNDAMENTALS   19

PART II
BUILDING A SOCIAL NETWORKING APP

7
ADVANCED RUBY   89

8
ADVANCED ACTIVE RECORD   105

FOREWORD

Ruby on Rails turned web development upside down. By abstracting the core of web programming in an unparalleled way, this unique piece of technology changed the game forever. With Rails, you can write web applications quickly without compromising quality. You can be very productive, write little code, deal with almost no configuration, and adapt to changes in specifications with agility, all while keeping a well-organized and elegant code base.

With Ruby on Rails, you feel empowered. Want to explore something with a quick prototype? Delivered in no time. Need to develop a solid production-ready website? Presto!

A decade later, the fundamental principles underlying the Rails breakthrough still permeate and drive the design of the framework and the way Rails applications are developed. You'll learn about these fundamental aspects of the Rails culture explicitly in the second chapter of *Rails Crash Course* and implicitly by example throughout the book.

While the foundational ideas behind Ruby on Rails remain key, the framework has evolved. Ruby on Rails has been extended here, shrunk there, iterated, and refined. The world in which Rails applications live has also evolved. *Rails Crash Course* presents the most modern and idiomatic Ruby on Rails.

But first things first. Ruby on Rails is a web framework written in the Ruby programming language. Think about Rails as a huge Ruby library: A Rails application is written in Ruby and uses the classes and core support provided by Ruby on Rails. Therefore, you definitely have to know some Ruby in order to write Ruby on Rails applications! The first chapter of *Rails Crash Course* introduces Ruby in case you are not familiar with it. Ruby is a powerful programming language, but it is easy to learn, and with that quick introduction, you'll know enough to begin. Later, more advanced Ruby is explained.

Once you know some Ruby, you're going to learn Rails. All aspects of the framework are covered, including how to write models that get persisted easily in a database, how to validate data, how to handle web requests, how to serve HTML, and so on.

Rails Crash Course covers all sides of Ruby on Rails, but then it takes you beyond the basics. For example, you'll learn some advanced Active Record, authentication, and how to write an application that provides a REST API, but you'll also learn about testing, security, performance, debugging, and other practical concerns of writing real-world web applications.

Further, *Rails Crash Course* guides you step-by-step all the way through uploading your application to production platforms and seeing it run on the Internet. That's an amazing experience. You'll learn how to deploy to Heroku and how to deploy to a computer in the Amazon cloud. While the servers needed to run an application for learning are small and free, they are the real thing: You'll upload to the exact same services big companies are deploying their applications to. *Rails Crash Course* is a superb introduction to Ruby on Rails, and by reading it, you'll get a solid understanding of Ruby on Rails and its ecosystem in a broad sense.

Welcome, and enjoy!

Xavier Noria
Cubelles, Spain
July 2014

ACKNOWLEDGMENTS

First, I'd like to thank everyone at No Starch Press for giving me the opportunity to write this book. Jennifer Griffith-Delgado guided me through the process of writing this book. As a first-time author, I found her corrections and suggestions invaluable. Serena Yang managed the production of the book and kept everything moving forward even as I dragged my feet at times.

Xavier Noria did an outstanding job as the technical reviewer. Not only did he make sure the code samples were correct and followed best practices, he also pointed out several places where my explanations could be better. If there are any mistakes left in this book, I'm sure it's only because I didn't correct them when he pointed them out.

I am grateful to Tim Taylor for introducing me to programming by teaching me BASIC on a Commodore 64 in the 7th grade. We've come a long way since then. I'd also like to thank a few more of my friends from the Paris Independent School District who convinced me that I could teach even though I'm not really a teacher: Karol Ackley, Paula Alsup, Denise Kornegay, Dee Martin, and Frances Reed.

Thanks to everyone in the amazing Austin technology community. Special thanks to Austin on Rails and its founder Damon Clinkscales. Thank you to everyone who attended one of my Rails classes or conference sessions. This book grew out of the curriculum I developed for those classes. Your questions and comments helped clarify the material in this book.

Finally, my most heartfelt thanks to my family: my wife, Paige, and our sons, Matthew and Wyatt. The book is finally done; let's go play!

INTRODUCTION

The Ruby on Rails framework emphasizes developer productivity, making it possible to implement sites that would once have taken months to build in a matter of weeks—or even days! Thanks to the Ruby programming language and principles such as *convention over configuration* and *don't repeat yourself*, Rails developers spend less time configuring their applications and more time writing code.

Ruby on Rails is also a *full-stack* web framework, meaning it handles everything from accessing data in a database to rendering web pages in the browser. As a full-stack framework, Rails is made up of a seemingly endless list of different components, such as Active Record, the asset pipeline, CoffeeScript, Sass, jQuery, turbolinks, and a variety of testing frameworks.

This book aims to cut through that list and explain exactly what you need to know to develop your own Ruby on Rails applications. After you gain some experience with the fundamentals of Rails, I'll introduce and explain new components of the framework as needed.

By the end, you'll know how to build your own Rails application from scratch. You'll add tests to ensure features work as expected, protect your application and your users from security vulnerabilities, optimize your application's performance, and finally deploy your application to your own server.

Who This Book Is For

I assume you have some experience with web development before starting this book. You should be familiar with HTML and CSS. You should know what an H1 element is and how to add images and links to a web page. Some knowledge of object-oriented programming is helpful but not required.

You'll use your computer's terminal (or command prompt) to enter commands, but you don't need much prior experience with terminal commands to follow the examples. In addition to the terminal, you'll also need a text editor for writing Ruby code. Many Rails developers use a vintage editor, such as Vim or Emacs.

If you don't already have a preferred text editor, I recommend Sublime Text. A free trial of Sublime Text is available online at *http://www.sublimetext .com/*. The free trial version never expires, but it does occasionally prompt you to purchase a license.

Overview

This book is divided into two parts. The first part covers the fundamentals of the Ruby language and the Ruby on Rails framework. The second covers advanced topics in both Ruby and Ruby on Rails. There are exercises at the end of every chapter, and solutions for them appear at the end of the book.

Chapter 1: Ruby Fundamentals covers the basics of Ruby, including datatypes, control flow, methods, and classes.

Chapter 2: Rails Fundamentals covers the basics of Ruby on Rails. Topics include Rails principles, the directory structure used by Rails applications, and common Rails commands. You'll create your first Rails application at the end of this chapter!

Chapter 3: Models, **Chapter 4: Controllers**, and **Chapter 5: Views** describe the three parts of the model-view-controller architecture used by Rails.

Chapter 6: Deployment covers creating a Git repository to store your application and deploying your application to the web using Heroku.

Once you understand the fundamentals of Ruby and Ruby on Rails, you're ready for more advanced topics.

Chapter 7: Advanced Ruby covers Ruby modules, the Ruby object model, and even a bit of metaprogramming.

Chapter 8: Advanced Active Record covers more advanced Active Record associations. You'll also build the data model for a new application at the end of this chapter.

Chapter 9: Authentication covers the authentication system used by your new application. This system allows users sign up for an account, log in to your application, and log off.

Chapter 10: Testing covers automated testing for each part of your application using the MiniTest framework included with Ruby. This chapter also discusses test-driven development.

Chapter 11: Security covers common web application security vulnerabilities and explains how to make sure your application is secure.

Chapter 12: Performance covers performance optimizations for Rails applications. Topics include the optimization features already built in to Rails, SQL query optimizations, and caching.

Chapter 13: Debugging explains several ways to track down bugs. Learn how to add to the log files generated by your application and how to use the interactive debugger for really tough bugs.

Chapter 14: Web APIs explains how to use the GitHub API and then covers the process of creating your own API for your application.

Finally, **Chapter 15: Custom Deployment** explains the process of setting up your own server on the Amazon cloud and deploying your application using Capistrano.

Installation

To follow the examples and complete the exercises in this book, you'll need the Ruby programming language, the Ruby on Rails framework, the Git version control system, and the Heroku Toolbelt.

The Ruby language website provides installation instructions at *https://www.ruby-lang.org/en/installation/*. Rails is distributed as a collection of Ruby gems, which you'll download and install with a single command that depends on your operating system. (The Ruby on Rails website also provides instructions at *http://rubyonrails.org/download/*.) You can download Git at *http://git-scm.com/downloads/*.

Once you've installed Ruby, Rails, and Git, install the latest version of the Heroku Toolbelt, which you'll use to deploy your applications to Heroku. Download the Heroku Toolbelt installer from *https://toolbelt.heroku.com/*, and then follow the instructions there to complete the installation.

Ruby, Rails, and Git

The sections below contain detailed installation instructions for Ruby, Rails, and Git on Mac OS X, Linux, and Windows. If you're using Mac OS X or Linux, also see "Multiple Ruby Versions" on page xxiii for an alternative way to install Ruby. There's a tool called pik for managing multiple Ruby versions on Windows, but it hasn't been updated since 2012, so I won't cover it here.

Mac OS X

Check your current version of Ruby with `ruby --version`. If you have Mac OS X Mavericks, you should already have Ruby version 2.0.0. Otherwise, you need to install a newer version.

Even if you already have Ruby 2.0.0, I recommend using the Homebrew package manager on Mac OS X. Homebrew is an easy way to install and update common development tools on Mac OS X. Instructions for downloading and installing Homebrew are online at *http://brew.sh/*. Once you install Homebrew, open a terminal and enter the command `brew install ruby` to install the latest version of Ruby.

Next, install Ruby on Rails with the command `gem install rails`. Then use Homebrew again to install Git by entering the command `brew install git`.

Linux

Installation instructions for Linux differ slightly based on which Linux distribution you are using. First, check your package manager; it may have a recent version of Ruby. If so, just install that package as you would any other.

If not, you'll need to install Ruby from source. Download the current stable version from *https://www.ruby-lang.org/en/downloads/*. Unpack the file and then enter the following commands in a terminal:

```
$ ./configure
$ make
$ sudo make install
```

Once the installation is complete, install Ruby on Rails by entering the command `sudo gem install rails`.

Every Linux distribution includes Git. Install Git with your package manager if it's not already installed on your system.

Windows

You'll use RubyInstaller to install Ruby. Download the RubyInstaller and the matching Development Kit from *http://rubyinstaller.org/downloads/*.

First, click the latest Ruby version on the RubyInstaller download page to download the installer; at the time of writing, it's *2.0.0-p484*. Then scroll down to the section labeled Development Kit and click the link under your version of Ruby to download the Development Kit. As of this writing, for Ruby 2.0, you'd choose *DevKit-mingw64-32-4.7.2-20130224-1151-sfx.exe*. If you are using a 64-bit version of Windows, then download the 64-bit version of the installer and the matching 64-bit Development Kit, currently *DevKit-mingw64-64-4.7.2-20130224-1151-sfx.exe*.

Once these downloads finish, double-click the RubyInstaller file and then follow the prompts on your screen to install Ruby. Once that is complete, double-click the *DevKit* file and follow the prompts to install the Development Kit.

Once you've installed Ruby and the Development Kit, install Rails by opening a command prompt and entering **gem install rails**. This will connect to the RubyGems server. Then download and install the various packages that make up the Ruby on Rails framework.

Finally, download the latest version of Git and double-click the file to complete the installation.

Multiple Ruby Versions

Several third-party tools exist to make it easier to install and manage multiple versions of Ruby on a single computer. This can be useful if you maintain several different applications or if you want to test an application on a different version of Ruby.

The Ruby on Rails website recommends managing your Ruby installation with `rbenv` and the `ruby-build` plugin. The `rbenv` command switches between Ruby versions and `ruby-build` provides the `rbenv install` command that you use to install different versions of Ruby.

Installing rbenv

If you're using Mac OS X, both `rbenv` and `ruby-build` can be installed using Homebrew. Instructions for installing Homebrew are online at *http://brew.sh/*.

Open a Terminal, enter **brew install rbenv ruby-build**, and skip to "Installing Ruby" on page xxiv.

On Linux, install `rbenv` and `ruby-build` by cloning the code from GitHub as shown below. Complete installation instructions are available online at *https://github.com/sstephenson/rbenv/*.

First, make sure you have the proper development tools installed. The `ruby-build` wiki at *https://github.com/sstephenson/ruby-build/wiki/* contains a suggested build environment for most popular Linux distributions. For example, on Ubuntu, enter the following command to install everything you need to compile Ruby.

```
$ sudo apt-get install autoconf bison build-essential git \
                  libssl-dev libyaml-dev libreadline6 \
                  libreadline6-dev zlib1g zlib1g-dev
Reading package lists... Done
Building dependency tree
--snip--
Do you want to continue? [Y/n]
```

Type the letter **y** to install these packages, and press ENTER. Packages needed for other Linux distributions are listed on the wiki page above.

Next, enter the following command to clone the `rbenv` git repository into your home directory.

```
$ git clone https://github.com/sstephenson/rbenv.git ~/.rbenv
Cloning into '/home/ubuntu/.rbenv'...
--snip--
Checking connectivity... done.
```

Then, add the *~/.rbenv/bin* directory to your $PATH and add a line to your *.bashrc* file to initialize rbenv each time you log on.

```
$ echo 'export PATH="$HOME/.rbenv/bin:$PATH"' >> ~/.bashrc
$ echo 'eval "$(rbenv init -)"' >> ~/.bashrc
$ source ~/.bashrc
```

Finally, install ruby-build by cloning its git repository into the rbenv plugins directory with the following command.

```
$ git clone https://github.com/sstephenson/ruby-build.git \
        ~/.rbenv/plugins/ruby-build
Cloning into '/home/ubuntu/.rbenv/plugins/ruby-build'...
--snip--
Checking connectivity... done.
```

Once you have rbenv and ruby-build installed, you're ready to install Ruby.

Installing Ruby

Enter the command **rbenv install -l** to list the currently available Ruby versions.

```
$ rbenv install -l
Available versions:
  1.8.6-p383
  1.8.6-p420
  1.8.7-p249
  1.8.7-p302
  --snip--
```

Ignore the versions with words such as *jruby*, *rbx*, and *ree* at the beginning. For now, just focus on the version numbers. The latest version as of this writing is 2.1.1. If there is a newer version when you install rbenv, replace 2.1.1 with the correct version number in the command below.

```
$ rbenv install 2.1.1
Downloading yaml-0.1.6.tar.gz...
--snip--
Installed ruby-2.1.1 to /home/ubuntu/.rbenv/versions/2.1.1
```

Once this completes, enter **rbenv global 2.1.1** to set your system's global default Ruby version. Now install Ruby on Rails by entering **gem install rails**. Finally, update rbenv by entering **rbenv rehash**. You can learn more about how rbenv lets you switch Ruby versions at the rbenv website *https://github.com/sstephenson/rbenv/*.

PART I

RUBY ON RAILS FUNDAMENTALS

1

RUBY FUNDAMENTALS

In 1993, Yukihiro "Matz" Matsumoto combined parts of his favorite languages (Perl, Smalltalk, Eiffel, Ada, and Lisp) to create his own ideal language, which he called Ruby.

Ruby is a dynamic, object-oriented programming language that also supports imperative and functional programming styles. It focuses on simplicity, productivity, and developer happiness. The Ruby website refers to it as "A Programmer's Best Friend," and developers with experience in other languages usually find Ruby easy to write and natural to read.

A solid foundation in Ruby is essential to understanding Ruby on Rails, so I'll cover Ruby fundamentals in this chapter. As we progress through the language features, I'll demonstrate common idioms used by experienced Ruby developers, so you can use them in your own programs later.

Interactive Ruby

My favorite way to explore the Ruby language is through the *Interactive Ruby interpreter (IRB)*. Most of the time, I develop applications in a text editor, but I still keep an IRB session open to test ideas quickly.

To start IRB, open a terminal (or command prompt on Windows), type **irb**, and press ENTER. You should see a prompt similar to this:

```
irb(main):001:0>
```

If you see an error message after entering irb, then you probably don't have it installed. Check out the Introduction, and follow the Ruby installation instructions to get IRB set up.

IRB is a type of program called a *read-eval-print loop (REPL)*. IRB reads your input, evaluates it, and displays the result. It repeats this process until you press CTRL-D or enter quit or exit.

Try out IRB by typing a few words surrounded by quotation marks:

```
irb(main):001:0> "Hello, Ruby"
=> "Hello, Ruby"
```

Ruby evaluates the expression you entered and displays the result. A simple string evaluates to itself, but this isn't the same as printing the string. To output something on the screen, use the Ruby method puts, as shown here:

```
irb(main):002:0> puts "Hello, Ruby"
Hello, Ruby
=> nil
```

Now Ruby outputs the string to the screen and displays nil, which is the result of evaluating the puts method. In Ruby, every method returns something. The puts method doesn't have anything useful to return, so it returns nil.

As you work through the rest of this chapter, you'll find more examples that you can enter into IRB. I encourage you to try them out and explore what you can do with IRB and Ruby.

NOTE *If IRB stops evaluating what you're typing, you may have "confused" it by forgetting a closing quotation mark or some other syntax it was expecting. If this happens, press CTRL-C to cancel the current operation and return to a working prompt.*

Now, let's take a look at the data types available in Ruby.

Data Types

Ruby has six main data types: number, string, symbol, array, hash, and Boolean. In this section, I'll briefly discuss each of these data types and how to use them.

Numbers

Ruby supports the math operations you learned in school, plus a few you may not have seen before. Type an expression into IRB and press ENTER to see the result:

```
irb(main):003:0> 1 + 1
 => 2
```

We asked Ruby to evaluate the expression 1 + 1, and it responded with the result, which is 2. Try out a few more math operations. Everything should work as expected, at least until you try division, as shown here:

```
irb(main):004:0> 7 / 3
 => 2
```

Ruby performs *integer division* by default. In other words, it drops the remainder. You can find that remainder with the modulus operator (%). If you'd rather get a fractional answer, however, you need to tell Ruby explicitly to use floating-point math by including a decimal point and zero after at least one of the numbers. Here, you can see examples of both the modulus operator and floating-point division in IRB:

```
irb(main):005:0> 7 % 3
 => 1
irb(main):006:0> 7.0 / 3
 => 2.3333333333333335
```

This concept is important to understand: although these appear to be simple math operators, they are actually methods in Ruby. You can even call methods on data types that other languages consider primitives.

```
irb(main):007:0> 1.odd?
 => true
```

Here, we ask the number 1 if it is odd and IRB responds with true.

Strings

You can create strings by surrounding characters with single or double quotes, as in this example:

```
irb(main):008:0> 'A String!'
 => "A String!"
```

You can also combine strings in Ruby to create larger ones. The language understands both adding strings and multiplying a string by a number. Let's look at an example of each:

```
irb(main):009:0> "Hello" + "World"
 => "HelloWorld"
irb(main):010:0> "Hi" * 3
 => "HiHiHi"
```

Notice that Ruby doesn't automatically put spaces between words when adding or multiplying. You are responsible for that detail.

Until now, I haven't differentiated between single- and double-quoted strings, but double-quoted strings actually allow you to combine strings in more complex ways. For example, they support a feature called *string interpolation*, in which Ruby evaluates an expression surrounded by #{ and }, converts the result to a string, and inserts it into the string automatically, as shown here:

```
irb(main):011:0> x = 10
 => 10
irb(main):012:0> "x is #{x}"
 => "x is 10"
```

In this case, #{x} evaluates to 10, so Ruby converts the number 10 to a string and returns "x is 10".

Double-quoted strings also support special characters such as newlines and tabs. These special characters consist of a backslash followed by a letter Type \n to create a newline (shown next) or \t to create a tab. To add a literal backslash in a double-quoted string, type two backslashes.

```
irb(main):013:0> puts "Line one\nLine two"
Line one
Line two
 => nil
```

You've already seen a few string methods, but many others are handy, including length and empty?. (Yes, methods in Ruby can end with question marks and even exclamation marks.) Let's look at those two methods in action:

```
irb(main):014:0> "Hello".length
 => 5
```

```
irb(main):015:0> "Hello".empty?
=> false
```

The length method returns the number of characters in a string, whereas empty? tells you whether a string contains any characters.

NOTE *A question mark at the end of method name, as in empty?, indicates that it is a predicate, and it will return a true or false value. An exclamation mark (!) usually signifies that the method does something dangerous such as modifying the object in place.*

Symbols

Ruby has a data type not often seen in other programming languages, and that's the symbol. Symbols are similar to strings in that they are made of characters, but instead of being surrounded by quotes, symbols are prefixed with a colon, like this:

```
irb(main):016:0> :name
=> :name
```

Symbols are typically used as identifiers. They are created only once and are unique. This means they are easy for programmers to read as a string, but also memory efficient. You can see this for yourself by creating a few strings and symbols and then calling the object_id method on them.

```
irb(main):017:0> "name".object_id
=> 70156617860420
irb(main):018:0> "name".object_id
=> 70156617844900
irb(main):019:0> :name.object_id
=> 67368
irb(main):020:0> :name.object_id
=> 67368
```

Notice that the two strings here have the same content, but different object ids. These are two different objects. The two symbols have the same content and the same object id.

When Ruby compares two strings for equality, it checks each individual character. Comparing two symbols for equality requires only a numeric comparison, which is much more efficient.

Arrays

An array represents a list of objects in Ruby. You create an array by surrounding a list of objects with square brackets. For example, let's make an array of numbers:

```
irb(main):021:0> list = [1, 2, 3]
=> [1, 2, 3]
```

Ruby arrays can contain any kind of object, even other arrays. You can access individual elements of an array by passing a numeric index to the array's [] method. The first element is at index zero. Try examining the first element in the array just created:

```
irb(main):022:0> list[0]
=> 1
```

Entering list[0] tells Ruby to fetch the first number in the array, and the method returns 1.

NOTE   *If you try to access an element that isn't in the array, the [] method will return nil.*

You can also pass two numbers to the [] method to create an array *slice*, as shown next. The first number you provide specifies the starting index, whereas the second tells it how many elements you want in your array slice:

```
irb(main):023:0> list[0, 2]
=> [1, 2]
```

Here, the [] method starts at index zero and returns the first two numbers in list.

Like strings, you can also add arrays to create a new one using the + operator. If you just want to add elements to the end of an existing array, you can use the << operator. You can see an example of each operation here:

```
irb(main):024:0> list + [4, 5, 6]
=> [1, 2, 3, 4, 5, 6]
irb(main):025:0> list << 4
=> [1, 2, 3, 4]
```

Though the + operator returns a new array, it doesn't modify the existing array. The << operator does modify the existing array. You can also use an index to reassign an existing element or add a new element to the array.

Hashes

A hash is a set of key-value pairs. In Ruby, hashes are enclosed in curly braces. Unlike an array index, a hash key can be of any data type. For example, symbols are frequently used as hash keys. When you need to access a value in a hash, just pass the corresponding key to the [] method, as shown next. Attempting to access a key that does not exist returns nil.

```
irb(main):026:0> some_guy = { :name => "Tony", :age => 21 }
=> {:name=>"Tony", :age=>21}
irb(main):027:0> some_guy[:name]
=> "Tony"
```

The combination of an equal sign and a greater-than sign (=>) between the key and value is commonly referred to as a *hash rocket*. Because symbols are used as hash keys so often, Ruby 1.9 added a shorthand syntax specifically for them. You can take the colon from the front of the symbol, put it at the end, and then leave out the hash rocket. Here's an example:

```
irb(main):028:0> another_guy = { name: "Ben", age: 20 }
 => {:name=>"Ben", :age=>20}
```

Although you can create a hash with this shorthand, Ruby seems to be sentimental as it still uses the old syntax when displaying the hash.

You can also use the keys method to get an array of all keys in a hash. If you need an array of all the values in the hash, use the method values instead. The code here shows an example of each method, using the same hash just created:

```
irb(main):029:0> another_guy.keys
 => [:name, :age]
irb(main):030:0> another_guy.values
 => ["Ben", 20]
```

Hashes are frequently used to represent data structures, as in these examples. They are also sometimes used to pass named parameters to a method. If a hash is the last (or only) argument to a method call, you can even leave off the curly braces.

For example, the merge method combines two hashes. The code here merges the hash named another_guy with a new hash containing { job: "none" }.

```
irb(main):031:0> another_guy.merge job: "none"
 => {:name=>"Ben", :age=>20, :job=>"none"}
```

Because the only argument to this method call is the new hash, you can leave off the curly braces. Rails has many other examples of this type of method call.

Booleans

A Boolean expression is anything that evaluates to true or false. These expressions often involve a Boolean operator, and Ruby supports familiar operators including *less than* (<), *greater than* (>), *equal* (==), and *not equal* (!=). Try these Boolean expressions at the IRB prompt:

```
irb(main):032:0> 1 < 2
 => true
irb(main):033:0> 5 == 6
 => false
```

Ruby also provides *and* (&&) and *or* (||) operators for combining multiple Boolean expressions, as shown next:

```
irb(main):034:0> 1 < 2 || 1 > 2
 => true
```

```
irb(main):035:0> 5 != 6 && 5 == 5
=> true
```

Both of these operators *short circuit*. That is, && is only true if the expressions on both sides evaluate to true. If the first expression is false, then the second expression is not evaluated. Likewise, || is true if either expression is true. If the first expression is true, then the second expression is not evaluated.

The || operator is also sometimes used with assignment. You might do this when you want to initialize a variable only if it is currently nil and keep the current value otherwise. Ruby provides the ||= operator for this case. This is referred to as *conditional assignment*, and you can see an example here:

```
irb(main):036:0> x = nil
=> nil
irb(main):037:0> x ||= 6
=> 6
```

If the variable x had not been a false value, then the conditional assignment would have returned the value of x instead of setting it to 6.

NOTE *Any expression in Ruby can be evaluated as a Boolean expression. In Ruby, only nil and false are considered false. Every other value is considered true. This differs from some other languages, where things like empty strings, empty collections, and the number zero are considered false.*

Constants

A *constant* gives a name to a value that doesn't change. In Ruby, the name of a constant *must* begin with a capital letter. Constants are typically written in uppercase, like this one:

```
irb(main):038:0> PI = 3.14
=> 3.14
irb(main):039:0> 2 * PI
=> 6.28
```

Ruby won't actually stop you from assigning a new value to a constant, but it does display a warning if you do.

Variables

In Ruby, you don't need to declare a variable in advance or specify a type. Just assign a value to a name as shown here:

```
irb(main):040:0> x = 10
=> 10
```

The variable x now refers to the number 10. Variable names are typically written in *snake case*, that is, all lowercase with underscores between words.

```
irb(main):041:0> first_name = "Matthew"
 => "Matthew"
```

Variable names can include letters, numbers, and underscores, but they must start with either a letter or underscore.

Control Flow

The examples we've looked at so far have all been linear. Real programs usually include statements that only execute when a certain condition is met and statements that are repeated multiple times. In this section, I cover Ruby's conditional statements and iteration.

Conditionals

Conditional statements let your program choose between one or more branches of code to execute based on an expression you provide. As such, making a decision in code is also called *branching*. For example, the following conditional prints the word *Child* only if the expression age < 13 evaluates to true.

```
irb(main):042:0> age = 21
 => 21
irb(main):043:0> if age < 13
irb(main):044:1>   puts "Child"
irb(main):045:1> end
 => nil
```

The variable age is set to 21, so age < 13 will evaluate to false, and nothing will be printed.

You can also use elsif and else to make more complicated conditionals. Let's look at a code example that has to check multiple conditions:

```
irb(main):046:0> if age < 13
irb(main):047:1>   puts "Child"
irb(main):048:1> elsif age < 18
irb(main):049:1>   puts "Teen"
irb(main):050:1> else
irb(main):051:1>   puts "Adult"
irb(main):052:1> end
Adult
 => nil
```

This code can take three different branches depending on the value of age. In our case, it should skip the code inside the if and elsif statements and just print *Adult*.

All of the previous conditional examples checked for true expressions, but what if you want to execute a block of code when an expression is false instead? Like other languages, Ruby has a logical *not* operator (either not or !), which is useful here. The following example will print the value of name if it is not an empty string.

```
irb(main):053:0> name = "Tony"
=> "Tony"
irb(main):054:0> if !name.empty?
irb(main):055:1>   puts name
irb(main):056:1> end
=> nil
```

When `name.empty?` is false, the ! operator should reverse the result to true so the code inside the if statement executes. A more natural way to say this conditional might be "unless name is empty, print its value." Unlike an if statement, Ruby's unless statement executes code when the expression evaluates to false.

```
irb(main):057:0> name = "Tony"
=> ""
irb(main):058:0> unless name.empty?
irb(main):059:1>   puts name
irb(main):060:1> end
=> nil
```

That still seems a little wordy to me. For one-line expressions such as this, Ruby lets you put the conditional at the end of the line:

```
irb(main):061:0> name = "Tony"
=> ""
irb(main):062:0> puts name unless name.empty?
=> nil
```

This example is concise and readable. To me, this code says "print name unless it's empty." This code is also a great example of Ruby's flexibility. You can write conditional expressions using the style that makes the most sense to you.

Iteration

When you're working with a collection of objects, such as an array or hash, you'll frequently want to perform operations on each item. In addition to the for loops seen in other languages, Ruby collections provide the each method.

The each method accepts a block of code and executes it for every element in the collection. A block in Ruby usually starts with the word do and ends with the word end. A block can also accept one or more parameters, which are listed inside a pair of pipe characters. The each method returns the value of the entire collection.

This next example iterates over each element in the array list, which we created earlier in this chapter as [1, 2, 3, 4]. It assigns the element to the variable number and then prints the value of number.

```
irb(main):063:0> list.each do |number|
irb(main):064:1>    puts number
irb(main):065:1> end
1
2
3
4
 => [1, 2, 3, 4]
```

Simple blocks like this are often written on one line in Ruby. Instead of writing do and end to indicate a block, you can use opening and closing curly braces, which are common in one-line blocks. Like the previous example, this one iterates over the list and prints each element, but it does everything in a single line of code.

```
irb(main):066:0> list.each { |n| puts n }
1
2
3
4
 => [1, 2, 3, 4]
```

You can also use the each method to iterate over a hash. Because a hash is a collection of key-value pairs, the block will take two parameters. Let's try using each with one of our earlier hashes:

```
irb(main):067:0> some_guy.each do |key, value|
irb(main):068:1>    puts "The #{key} is #{value}."
irb(main):069:1> end
The name is Tony.
The age is 21.
 => {:name=>"Tony", :age=>21}
```

Blocks are useful for more than just iteration. Any method can potentially accept a block and use the code it contains. For example, you can pass a block to the File.open method. Ruby should pass the file handle as a variable to the block, execute the code within the block, and then close the file automatically.

Methods

A *method* is a named block of reusable code. Defining your own methods in Ruby is simple. A method definition starts with the word def, followed by a name, and continues until end. This method will print "Hello, World!" each time it is called:

```
irb(main):070:0> def hello
irb(main):071:1>   puts "Hello, World!"
irb(main):072:1> end
 => nil
```

As you can see in the example, a method definition should return nil.

NOTE *If you're using Ruby 2.1, method definitions return the name of the method as a symbol.*

Once you've defined a method, you can call it by entering its name at the IRB prompt:

```
irb(main):073:0> hello
Hello, World!
 => nil
```

Ruby methods always return the value of their last statement; in this case, the last statement was puts, which returns nil. You can use return to return a value explicitly, or you can just add the value you wish to return as the last line of the method.

For example, if you want the hello method to return true, you can modify it like this:

```
irb(main):074:0> def hello
irb(main):075:1>   puts "Hello, World!"
irb(main):076:1>   true
irb(main):077:1> end
 => nil
```

Now call the method as before:

```
irb(main):078:0> hello
Hello, World!
 => true
```

Because the last line of the method is the value true, the method returns true when called.

In Ruby, you specify method parameters by adding them after the method name, optionally enclosed in parentheses, as shown in the next example. Parameters can also have default values.

```
irb(main):079:0> def hello(name = "World")
irb(main):080:1>   puts "Hello, #{name}!"
irb(main):081:1> end
 => nil
```

This example redefines the `hello` method to accept a parameter called name. This parameter has a default value of `"World"`. This method can be called as before to display "Hello, World!", or you can pass a value for the name parameter to greet someone else.

```
irb(main):082:0> hello
Hello, World!
 => nil
irb(main):083:0> hello "Tony"
Hello, Tony!
 => nil
```

The parentheses around method arguments are also optional. Include them if the intention is not clear; otherwise, feel free to omit them.

Classes

In an object-oriented programming language such as Ruby, a *class* represents the state and behavior of a distinct type of object. In Ruby, an object's state is stored in instance variables, and methods define its behavior. A Ruby class definition starts with the word `class`, followed by a capitalized name, and continues to the matching `end`.

Class definitions can include a special method called `initialize`. This method is called when a new instance of the class is created. It is typically used to assign values to the instance variables needed by the class. In Ruby, instance variables start with an `@`, as shown in the following class definition:

```
irb(main):084:0> class Person
irb(main):085:1>   def initialize(name)
irb(main):086:2>     @name = name
irb(main):087:2>   end
irb(main):088:1>   def greet
irb(main):089:2>     puts "Hi, I'm #{@name}."
irb(main):090:2>   end
irb(main):091:1> end
 => nil
```

This code defines a new class called `Person`. The `initialize` method takes one parameter and assigns the value of that parameter to the instance variable `@name`. The greet method prints a friendly greeting. Let's write some code that uses this new class.

```
irb(main):092:0> person = Person.new("Tony")
 => #<Person:0x007fc98418d710 @name="Tony">
irb(main):093:0> person.greet
Hi, I'm Tony.
 => nil
```

You can create an instance of the `Person` class by calling `Person.new` and passing the required parameters. The previous example creates an instance of `Person` with the name Tony.

The return value of `Person.new` is a string representation of the object. It consists of the class name followed by a reference to the object in memory and a list of instance variables. Calling the greet method should display the friendly greeting we expect.

Instance variables, like `@name`, are not accessible outside of the class. Try to access `person.name` from the IRB prompt, and you should see an error.

```
irb(main):094:0> person.name
NoMethodError: undefined method 'name'
```

If you need to access or change `@name` outside of the class, you need to write a *getter* and a *setter*. These are methods that *get* or *set* the value of an instance variable. Fortunately, Ruby classes provide the method `attr_accessor`, which writes getters and setters for you.

You would normally include `attr_accessor :name` in your definition of the `Person` class. Rather than retype the entire class definition, you can reopen the class and add this line:

```
irb(main):095:0> class Person
irb(main):096:1>   attr_accessor :name
irb(main):097:1> end
 => nil
```

This code adds the `attr_accessor` call to the `Person` class and updates all objects of the class automatically. And this is another example of the Ruby's flexibility. You can reopen a class, even at runtime, and add new methods as needed.

Now, if we want to change the name of our person, we can just set it equal to something else, as shown here:

```
irb(main):098:0> person.name
 => "Tony"
irb(main):099:0> person.name = "Wyatt"
 => "Wyatt"
irb(main):100:0> person.greet
Hi, I'm Wyatt.
 => nil
```

The attr_accessor method uses the symbol :name to define the getter name and the setter name=. You can now get and set the value of the instance variable as needed. If you only want a getter, include a call to attr_reader instead of attr_accessor. Doing this lets you read the value of @name, but not change it.

Class Methods

The attr_accessor method is different from the methods I've discussed so far. Note that attr_accessor is called inside the body of the class definition. The methods you've seen so far, such as the greet method, are called on an instance of a class.

In Ruby, methods called on an instance of a class are called *instance methods*. Methods called on the class itself are called *class methods*. Another example of a class method is new. When you typed Person.new("Tony") before, you were calling the class method new of the class Person.

Inheritance

In Ruby, you can define a new class that builds on the state and behavior of an existing class, and the new class will inherit variables and methods from the existing one. *Inheritance* defines an *is-a* relationship between those two classes. For example, a student is a person. We can define the class Student like this:

```
irb(main):101:0> class Student < Person
irb(main):102:1>   def study
irb(main):103:2>     puts "ZzzzZzzz"
irb(main):104:2>   end
irb(main):105:1> end
 => nil
```

The < Person on the first line indicates that the Student class inherits from the Person class. The variables and methods defined by Person are now available to Student:

```
irb(main):106:0> student = Student.new("Matt")
#<Student:0x007fd7c3ac4d90 @name="Matt">
❶ irb(main):107:0> student.greet
Hi, I'm Matt.
 => nil
irb(main):108:0> student.study
ZzzzzZzzzz
=> nil
```

Because we created greet on Person earlier in the chapter, we can have any Student call this method ❶ without defining it in our new class.

Ruby only supports *single inheritance*, which means that one class can't inherit from multiple classes at the same time. You can, however, work around this limitation by using *modules*. A module is a collection of methods and constants that cannot be instantiated but can be included in other classes to provide additional behavior. We discuss modules and other advanced features of Ruby in Chapter 7.

Summary

You are now well on your way to becoming a great Ruby on Rails programmer. The Ruby knowledge you gained in this chapter will make understanding the Rails framework much easier.

I recommend working with IRB as much as you need to feel comfortable with Ruby. When you're ready to start exploring Rails, enter exit to leave IRB, and continue on to Chapter 2.

Exercises

1. You can read plaintext files in Ruby with the File.read method. Create a file containing a paragraph or two from a blog post or book, and name it *test.txt* in the current directory. This next code sample reads a file named *test.txt* into the variable file and displays the contents of the file:

    ```
    file = File.read("test.txt")
    puts file
    ```

    As you can see, file contains a string. Use file.split to convert the string into an array of words. You can now use Ruby's built-in array methods to operate on the contents of the file. For example, use file.split.length to count words in the file. file.split.uniq.length tells you how many *unique* words are in the file.

2. Using the array of words from Exercise 1, count how many times each word appears in the file. One way to do this is by iterating over the array and storing the count for each word in a hash where the key is the word and the value is the count.

3. Create a WordCounter class to perform the operations from Exercises 1 and 2. The class should accept a filename to read when it is initialized and include methods named count, uniq_count, and frequency for performing the operations from the previous two exercises. The following class definition should help you get started:

    ```
    class WordCounter
      def initialize(file_name)
        @file = File.read(file_name)
      end

      # your code here...
    end
    ```

2

RAILS FUNDAMENTALS

Ruby on Rails is an open source web framework. Like the Ruby language, it emphasizes programmer happiness and productivity. As you'll see, it includes sensible defaults that allow you to spend less time dealing with configuration and more time writing code. It also creates a directory structure for your application with a place for every file you need.

Rails was created by David Heinemeier Hansson. He extracted the framework from the project management application Basecamp that he built for 37signals. It was first released as open source in July 2004.

Rails is also a *full-stack* web framework. This means it contains everything you need to build web applications that accept user requests, query databases, and respond with data rendered in templates.

Enter the following command in a terminal to ensure that Rails is installed:

```
$ rails --version
```

This should display Rails 4.0.0 or greater. If not, check the installation instructions for Rails in "Ruby, Rails, and Git" on page xxi.

Your First Rails Application

Rails makes getting started easy, so let's dive right in. You're only five commands away from having a running Rails web application.

Just like Jedi Knights build their own lightsabers, I think web developers should build their own personal websites, so that's where we'll start. I use my website as a playground for testing new ideas. In the fast-moving world of Ruby on Rails, keeping your own site up-to-date also helps you learn to use new features as they are released.

Open a terminal window and create a directory for your Rails projects. I call mine *code*, but you can use any name you like.

```
$ mkdir code
$ cd code
```

Now use the `rails new` command to create a new application. Our first application will be a simple weblog, so let's just call it *blog*.

```
$ rails new blog
```

This command creates all of the files your new application needs and then runs the `bundle install` command to download and install any other gems needed by Rails. (*Gems* are packaged Ruby applications or libraries.) Depending on your connection speed, this may take a few minutes. When the install is complete, use the `cd` command to move to the newly created *blog* directory:

```
$ cd blog
```

Finally, use the `rails server` command to launch a server so you can see your new application. When you created this application, a directory called *bin* was also created inside *blog*. The *bin* directory is where you'll find `rails` and other commands you'll need later.

```
$ bin/rails server
```

This command starts the WEBrick server that is built in to Ruby. Once the server has started, open your web browser and go to this address: *http://localhost:3000*. If everything worked correctly, you should see a web page like the one in Figure 2-1.

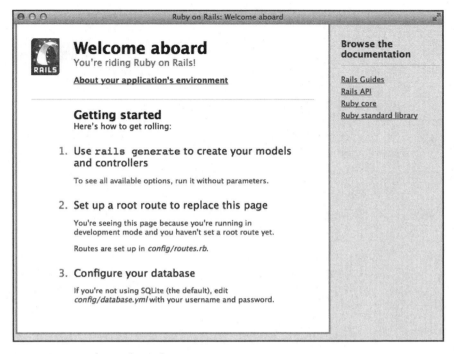

Figure 2-1: Your first Rails application

Congratulations! You're officially a Ruby on Rails developer. The page you just created includes some tips for getting started with your application, but before we get into that, let's learn a little more about Rails.

Rails Principles

The Rails framework is based on two well-known software engineering principles. Understanding these principles will help you understand the "Rails way" of building applications.

Convention over Configuration

You didn't have to configure anything to get a basic Rails application up and running. In Rails, this concept is known as *convention over configuration.* As long as you follow the Rails conventions, everything should just work.

Rails makes many choices for you when you create an application. Those choices include which web server and database server to run in development mode and which JavaScript library and testing library your application will use. Even the names of your application's database tables and models are chosen automatically based on convention. You can certainly break convention and change those settings if you'd like, but then you'll have to configure some things for yourself.

Don't Repeat Yourself

The other key principle in Rails is *don't repeat yourself*, often abbreviated *DRY*. In Rails, you avoid duplicating knowledge within your application. Specifying the same information in more than one place can lead to errors when you change one instance and not the other.

You'll see several examples of the DRY principle as we work our way through the Rails architecture and directory structure. There is a single, specific place for each part of a Rails application. Things that can be inferred from another source, such as the names of columns in a database table, don't need to be specified anywhere.

Rails Architecture

Rails applications are structured around the *model-view-controller (MVC)* software engineering pattern. The MVC pattern is designed to separate an application's data from a user's interaction with it. This separation of concerns usually results in an application that is easier to understand and maintain.

Model

The *model* represents your application's data and the rules for manipulating that data. The application's data is sometimes referred to as the application's *state*. The rules for manipulating this data are also known as *business logic*. All changes to your application's state must pass through the model layer.

Rails models contain code for data validation and associations between models. Most of the code you write will be inside of a Rails model, unless it is directly involved with the user's view of the data.

View

The *view* is the user interface for your application. Because we are building web applications, the view will consist mainly of HTML. Rails uses a template system called *Embedded Ruby (ERB)* by default.

Embedded Ruby allows you to include Ruby code for accessing data within an HTML template. When the user requests a page, the Ruby code in the template is evaluated by the server, and the resulting HTML page is sent to the user.

The ability to embed Ruby code inside a view can sometimes lead programmers to include too much code inside a view. Doing this is problematic because if you add another view, then that code will need to be duplicated. Code used only by the view can be moved to a *helper*, which is a method meant specifically for use in the view. In general, a view should never contain code more complex than a simple conditional statement.

NOTE *In addition to HTML pages, Rails can also generate JSON and XML. Ruby has built-in support for generating CSV files, and gems are available for generating other types of output, such as PDF documents and Excel spreadsheets.*

Controller

The *controller* is like the glue that holds together the model and the view. The controller is responsible for accepting a request from the user, gathering the necessary data from the model, and rendering the correct view. This sounds like a lot of work, but thanks to the conventions used in Rails applications, the process happens almost automatically.

In Rails, the controller is simply a Ruby class with methods that correspond to the various actions in your application. For example, in your blog application, you have a method named show for displaying a blog post and a method named new for adding a new post.

Rails Application Structure

Now that you're familiar with the principles and architecture used by Rails, let's see where these pieces live within the directory structure created by the rails new command. Inside the blog directory, you should find 10 subdirectories.

The app Directory

The *app* directory is where you'll spend most of your time while building your application. It contains subdirectories for each part of the MVC architecture discussed previously, as well as *assets*, *helpers*, and *mailers*.

The *assets* directory holds the images, JavaScript files, and CSS stylesheets used by your application. The *helpers* directory contains Ruby files with methods used by your views. The *mailers* directory is for Ruby classes used to send email.

The bin Directory

The *bin* directory holds simple Ruby scripts for accessing the *bundle, rails,* and *rake* command-line programs used while building your application. These scripts ensure that the three programs run in the context of the current Rails application. You can have multiple versions of these programs installed at the same time, which can lead to errors if you don't use the scripts in *bin* to access them.

The config Directory

Rails makes heavy use of convention over configuration, but sometimes configuration is unavoidable. In those cases, look to the *config* directory.

The *environments* subdirectory contains configuration files for the three different environments created automatically by Rails. An environment is a collection of settings used for a specific purpose such as development or testing. These settings are stored in *development.rb* (used while developing your application), *test.rb* (used while running automated tests), and *production.rb* (used after your application is deployed and running in production).

The file *application.rb* contains the settings for all environments. Information in one of the specific environment files just mentioned will, however, take precedence over settings here.

The file *database.yml* holds database configuration for each of the three environments. Rails creates a SQLite database, by default, when you run `rails new`, so the default settings in *database.yml* are for that SQLite database This database is a single file that you will use during development. You usually want to specify a different database server to use in production.

The file *routes.rb* maps the web address entered by the user to a specific controller and action in your application. As you add resources and actions to your application, you need to update this file to reflect the changes. I cover resource-based routing during the discussion of controllers in Chapter 4.

The db Directory

The *db* directory initially contains only a single file called *seeds.rb*. Use this file to create your application's default data. For example, in an application with user accounts, you may want to include a special "admin" user here.

As you build your application, you will create *database migrations*, Ruby scripts that create and modify the tables in your database. A directory named *migrate* is created to hold these database migration files. The file *schema.rb*, which shows the current state of your application's database, is created as well. If you use the default SQLite database in your application, the database itself is also placed in this folder.

The lib Directory

The *lib* directory is the place to put any reusable library code you write. This directory is initially empty except for two subdirectories: assets and tasks. *Assets* are images, CSS stylesheets, and JavaScript files. *Tasks* are Ruby scripts used to automate actions such as managing your application's database, clearing log and temporary files, and running tests. These tasks are executed using the rake command.

The log Directory

As your application runs, data is written to a file in the *log* directory. When you run your code in the development environment, this file is named *development.log*. Separate files will be created for the test and production environments.

The public Directory

Files in the *public* directory are sent to users as if the files were in the root directory of your application. For example, three files in this directory are for error messages—*404.html*, *422.html*, and *500.html*. You can see one of these files in your browser by adding its name to your address bar. If you visit *http://localhost:3000/404.html*, for example, you should see the default "page does not exist" error page.

This directory also holds a default *favicon.ico*, the image that appears in the address bar of most browsers, and a *robots.txt* file that controls how search engines index your application. You can modify all of these files for your application. You'll probably want to customize the error pages with your own branding and add a custom favicon for your site.

The test Directory

The *test* directory contains subdirectories with automated tests for each part of your application. It also holds the script *test_helper.rb*, which loads the test environment settings in *config/environments/test.rb* and adds helper methods used in your tests.

Some Rails developers practice *test-driven development (TDD)*. In TDD, you first write an automated test describing a new feature; then you add just enough code to make the test pass; and finally you *refactor*, or restructure, the code as needed to improve readability and reduce complexity.

The tmp Directory

The *tmp* directory contains ephemeral files. Here, you find cached copies of your application's assets, process id files (pids) for running programs (such as your web server), user sessions, and files representing sockets being used by your application.

NOTE *Because these files usually do not need to be saved, version control systems ignore them.*

The vendor Directory

Finally, the *vendor* directory holds assets needed by third-party gems that you add to your application. Its purpose is similar to the *lib* directory, except it is used by libraries that you did not write yourself.

Rails Commands

You use four different command-line programs when building Rails applications. These can sometimes be confusing to new Rails developers.

The gem Command

The gem command installs Ruby gems. The Rails framework is actually distributed as a collection of gem files.

Your newly created Rails application is made up of over 40 gems. Maintaining the correct versions of these gems and dependencies between them can get complicated. For this reason, you rarely use the gem command directly; instead, you usually rely on a tool called Bundler to manage gems and keep your dependencies up to date. You interact with Bundler using the bundle command.

The bundle Command

The bundle command is used to install and update the gems needed by your application. It installs gems by reading the *Gemfile* that was automatically created by the rails new command in the root directory of your Rails application. It stores the version numbers of gems you're using and their dependencies in the file *Gemfile.lock*.

The bundle list command displays the names and versions of all gems currently being used by your application:

```
$ bin/bundle list
```

As mentioned earlier, we are using the copy of bundle inside the *bin* directory.

The rake Command

The rake command is an automated build tool used to run tasks related to your application. (If you are familiar with the make command, rake is the Ruby version.) Enter this command to obtain a list of the available tasks for your application:

```
$ bin/rake --tasks
```

This command prints a list of tasks your application can use along with a short description of each to your terminal. Some gems add tasks to your application, and you can also add your own tasks by writing Ruby scripts and saving them in the *lib/tasks* directory.

The rails Command

You used the rails command earlier to create an application and start the server. You can also use this command to generate new code and launch the console. Enter the rails command by itself to list the available options:

```
$ bin/rails
```

In addition to the new command that you used to build your application and the server command that starts a web server, Rails also provides several other helpful commands. These include the generate command (generates new code), the console command (starts an interactive Ruby console with your Rails application preloaded), and the dbconsole command (starts a command-line interface for the currently configured database).

Now that you've seen some Rails command-line tools, let's use a few of them to add some functionality to the blog application we created.

Rails Scaffold

We're going to use a Rails feature known as *scaffolding*. Rails scaffolding is a sometimes-controversial feature that generates application code for you. This single command creates a model, a set of views, and a controller automatically.

Many developers believe that you should write all of your own code. I agree with them, but Rails scaffolding is helpful for bootstrapping an application, especially for developers new to Ruby on Rails. We will explore the generated code over the next few chapters. By the end, you will understand each file and be able to write those files by hand.

Open a new terminal window (or a new tab in your current one). Change to your *code/blog* directory if necessary. Then, use the `rails generate` command to add posts to the blog:

```
$ bin/rails generate scaffold Post ❶title:string ❷body:text
```

Here, we've asked Rails to generate a scaffold for a blog Post. We specified that a Post should have a title ❶ and a body ❷.

The title will be a string, and the body will be a text field in the database. As this command runs, you should see a flurry of activity in your terminal as files are generated and placed in the correct folders.

The previous command should have generated a database migration. Use the rake command to run that migration:

```
$ bin/rake db:migrate
```

This command should create a table named *posts* with fields named `id`, `title`, `body`, `created_at`, and `updated_at`. The `title` and `body` fields will store data entered by the user. Rails adds the `id`, `created_at`, and `updated_at` fields automatically. The `id` field is a unique, auto-incrementing integer that represents each row in the database. The `created_at` and `updated_at` fields are timestamps representing when the row was created and when it was last updated. Rails keeps track of these values automatically.

To see the results, go to *http://localhost:3000/posts* in your web browser. You should see a page like the one in Figure 2-2.

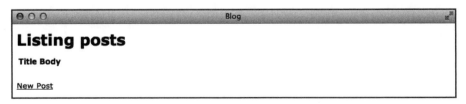

Figure 2-2: The Rails Post scaffolding

This page certainly won't win any awards for design, but it is functional. Click the *New Post* link to see a form for adding a new blog post. After you add a post, click the *Back* link to return to the home page.

By default, Rails shows your data in a table with links for *Show, Edit,* and *Destroy.* Feel free to try these links and verify that the application is working.

As you play with the application, be sure to look at the output in the terminal window where the server is running. This is a copy of the development log generated by your application. You'll find a wealth of information here, such as the URL requested, the Ruby method being run, and the SQL commands being executed.

Summary

This chapter covered the basic principles, architecture, directory structure, and commands used to build Rails applications. In the next chapter, we'll dig in to the Rails code we just generated, starting with models, and you'll learn to write your own code.

Exercises

1. Explore the functionality of your new blog. Create, edit, and destroy posts. View the list of posts and individual posts. Note how the URL in the address bar changes as you move around the application.

2. Get used to moving around the various files in the blog application in your editor of choice. If you're using Sublime Text 2, you can open the blog directory itself and then use the sidebar to open individual files.

3

MODELS

In Rails, models represent the data in your application and the rules to manipulate that data. Models manage interactions between your application and a corresponding database table. The bulk of your application's business logic should also be in the models.

This chapter covers Active Record, the Rails component that provides model persistence (that is, storing data in the database), as well as data validations, database migrations, and model associations. *Validations* are rules to ensure that only valid data is stored in the database. You create database *migrations* to change the schema of the database, and *associations* are relationships between multiple models in your application.

The Post Model

In the previous chapter, we used the Rails scaffold generator to build a simple blog with models, views, and controllers for blog posts. Look at the post model created by the scaffold generator by opening the file *app/models/post.rb* in your favorite text editor.

```
class Post < ActiveRecord::Base
end
```

There's not much to see here. Right now, the file just tells us that the class Post inherits from ActiveRecord::Base. Before I talk about what you can actually do with Post, let's begin our discussion with Active Record.

Active Record

Active Record is an implementation of the object-relational mapping (ORM) pattern described, using the same name, by Martin Fowler in *Patterns of Enterprise Application Architecture* (Addison-Wesley Professional, 2002). It's an automated mapping between classes and tables as well as attributes and columns.

Each table in your database is represented by a class in your application. Each row of that table is represented by an instance (or object) of the associated class, and each column of that row is represented by an attribute of that object. The example in Table 3-1 demonstrates this structure. If you could look inside your database, this is what you would see.

Table 3-1: The Posts Table

id	title	body	created_at	updated_at
1	Hello, World	Welcome to my blog...	...	...
2	My Cat	The cutest kitty in the...	...	...
3	Too Busy	Sorry I haven't posted...	...	...

Table 3-1 holds three example blog posts. This table is represented by the Post class. The post with an id of 1 can be represented by a Post object. Let's call our object post.

You can access the data associated with a single column by calling an attribute method on the object. For example, to see the post's title, call post.title. The ability to access and change database values by calling attribute methods on an object is known as *direct manipulation*.

Create, Read, Update, and Delete

Let's explore Active Record further by entering a few commands in the Rails console. The Rails console is the IRB that you used in Chapter 1 with your Rails application's environment preloaded.

To start the Rails console, go to your *blog* directory and enter **bin/rails console**. You might notice that the console takes a little longer to start than the IRB. During that slight pause, your application's environment is being loaded.

As with the IRB, you can enter exit to quit the console when you're done.

The four major functions of database applications are *create, read, update,* and *delete,* usually abbreviated as *CRUD.* Once you know how to perform these four actions, you can build any type of application you need.

Rails makes these actions easy for you. In most cases, you can accomplish each with a single line of code. Let's use them now to work with posts on our blog.

Create

We'll start by adding a few records to the database. Enter these commands in the Rails console as you work through this section. The remaining examples in this chapter use these records.

The easiest way to create a record in Rails is with the appropriately named create method, as shown here:

```
2.1.0 :001 > Post.create title: "First Post"
❶    (0.1ms) begin transaction
   SQL (0.4ms) INSERT INTO "posts" ("created_at"...
   (1.9ms) commit transaction
=> #<Post id: 1, title: "First Post", ...>
```

The Rails console displays the SQL being sent to the database as commands are run ❶. In the interest of brevity, I'm going to omit these SQL statements in the rest of the samples.

The create method accepts a hash of attribute-value pairs and inserts a record into the database with the appropriate values. In this case, it's setting the title attribute to the value "First Post". When you run this example, the values for id, created_at, and updated_at are set for you automatically. The id column is an auto-incrementing value in the database, whereas created_at and updated_at are timestamps set for you by Rails. The body column is set to NULL since no value was passed for it.

The create method is a shortcut for instantiating a new Post object, assigning values, and saving it to the database. If you don't want to take the shortcut, you could also write a separate line of code for each action:

```
2.1.0 :002 > post = Post.new
 => #<Post id: nil, title: nil, ...>
2.1.0 :003 > post.title = "Second Post"
 => "Second Post"
2.1.0 :004 > post.save
 => true
```

We had to use multiple commands this time, but just like before, we've created a brand new Post object. Two posts are now stored in the database. In both examples, we only assigned values to the post's title attribute, but you would assign values to the post body in exactly the same way. Rails assigns values to id, created_at, and updated_at automatically. You shouldn't change these.

Read

Once you have a few posts in your database, you'll probably want to read them back out for display. First, let's look at all of the posts in the database with the all method:

```
2.1.0 :005 > posts = Post.all
 => #<ActiveRecord::Relation [#<Post id: 1, ...>, #<Post id: 2, ...>]>
```

This returns an Active Record *relation*, which contains an array of all posts in your database, and stores it in posts. You can chain additional methods onto this relation, and Active Record combines them into a single query.

Active Record also implements the first and last methods, which return the first and last entries in an array. The Active Record version of these methods returns only the first or last record in the database table. This is much more efficient than fetching all of the records in the table and then calling first or last on the array. Let's try fetching a couple of posts from our database:

```
2.1.0 :006 > Post.first
 => #<Post id: 1, title: "First Post", ...>
2.1.0 :007 > Post.last
 => #<Post id: 2, title: "Second Post", ...>
```

This example returns the first and last posts, as ordered by id. You'll learn how to order records by a different field in the next section. Sometimes however, you'll know exactly which record you want, and it might not be the first or last one. In that case, you can use the find method to retrieve a record by id.

```
2.1.0 :008 > post = Post.find 2
 => #<Post id: 2, title: "Second Post", ...>
```

Just don't ask find to fetch a record that doesn't exist. If a record with the specified id isn't in your database, Active Record will raise an ActiveRecord::RecordNotFound exception. When you know a specific record exists but you don't know its id, you can use the where method to specify an attribute that you do know:

```
2.1.0 :009 > post = Post.where(title: "First Post").first
 => #<Post id: 1, title: "First Post", ...>
```

The where method also returns a relation. If more than one record matches, you can chain the all method after where and tell Rails to retrieve all matching records on demand when they are needed.

If you know the database has only one matching record, you can chain the first method after where to retrieve that specific record as in the previous example. This pattern is so common that Active Record also provides the find_by method as a shortcut:

```
2.1.0 :010 > post = Post.find_by title: "First Post"
 => #<Post id: 1, title: "First Post", ...>
```

This method takes a hash of attribute-value pairs and returns the first matching record.

Update

Updating a record is as easy as reading it into a variable, changing values via direct manipulation, and then saving it back to the database:

```
2.1.0 :011 > post = Post.find 2
 => #<Post id: 2, title: "Second Post", ...>
2.1.0 :012 > post.title = "2nd Post"
 => "2nd Post"
2.1.0 :013 > post.save
 => true
```

Rails also provides the update method, which takes a hash of attribute-value pairs, updates the record, and saves to the database all on one line:

```
2.1.0 :014 > post = Post.find 2
 => #<Post id: 2, title: "2nd Post", ...>
2.1.0 :015 > post.update title: "Second Post"
 => true
```

The update method, like the save method, returns true when successful or false if it has a problem saving the record.

Delete

Once you have read a record from the database, you can delete it with the destroy method. But this time don't type in these commands. You don't want to delete the posts you created earlier!

```
2.1.0 :016 > post = Post.find 2
 => #<Post id: 2, title: "Second Post", ...>
2.1.0 :017 > post.destroy
 => #<Post id: 2, title: "Second Post", ...>
```

The destroy method can also be called on the class to delete a record by id, which has the same effect as reading the record into a variable first:

```
2.1.0 :018 > Post.destroy 2
 => #<Post id: 2, title: "Second Post", ...>
```

You can also delete records based on a relation:

```
2.1.0 :019 > Post.where(title: "First Post").destroy_all
=> [#<Post id: 1, title: "First Post", ...>]
```

This example deletes all records with a title of "First Post". Be careful with the destroy_all method, however. If you call it without a where clause, you'll delete all records of the specified class!

More Active Record Methods

If you're familiar with SQL or other methods of accessing records in a database, you know there's much more to working with a database than simple CRUD. Active Record provides methods for more database operations, such as ordering, limiting, counting, and other calculations.

Query Conditions

In addition to the simple where conditions you've seen so far, Active Record also has several methods to help refine your queries. The order method specifies the order of returned records; limit specifies how many records to return; and offset specifies the first record to return from a list.

The limit and offset methods are often used together for pagination. For example, if you want to show 10 blog posts per page, you can read the posts for the first page like this:

```
2.1.0 :020 > posts = Post.limit(10)
=> #<ActiveRecord::Relation [#<Post id: 1, ...>, #<Post id: 2, ...>]>
```

To read the posts for the second page of your site, you'll need to skip the first 10 posts:

```
2.1.0 :021 > posts = Post.limit(10).offset(10)
=> #<ActiveRecord::Relation []>
```

Entering this returns an empty set since we only have two posts in our database. When you combine offset with limit in this way, you can pass offset multiples of what you passed limit to view different pages of your blog.

You can also change how the entries in a relation are ordered. When using limit, the order of records returned is undefined, so you need to specify an order. With the order method, you can specify a different order for the set of records returned:

```
2.1.0 :022 > posts = Post.limit(10).order "created_at DESC"
=> #<ActiveRecord::Relation [#<Post id: 2, ...>, #<Post id: 1, ...>]>
```

Using DESC tells order to return the posts from newest to oldest. You could also use ASC to order them the opposite way. If you would rather see posts alphabetized by title, try replacing "created_at DESC" with "title ASC". The order method defaults to ascending order if you don't specify ASC or DESC, but I always give an order so my intention is clear.

Calculations

Databases also provide methods for performing calculations on records. We could read the records and perform these operations in Ruby, but the methods built in to the database are usually optimized to be faster and use less memory.

The count method returns the number of records matching a given condition:

```
2.1.0 :023 > count = Post.count
 => 2
```

If you don't specify a condition, count counts all records by default, as in this example.

The sum, average, minimum, and maximum methods perform the requested function on a field. For example, this line of code finds and returns the date on the newest blog post:

```
2.1.0 :024 > date = Post.maximum :created_at
 => 2014-03-12 04:10:08 UTC
```

The maximum created_at date you see should match the date for your newest blog post, not necessarily the date you see in the example.

Migrations

Database migrations are used any time you need to change your database's structure. When we used the scaffold generator to create blog posts, it generated a migration for us, but you can also create migrations yourself. As you build your application, your database migrations contain a complete record of the changes made to your database.

Migration files are stored in the *db/migrate* directory and start with a timestamp that indicates when they were created. For example, you can see the migration created by the scaffold generator by editing the file *db/migrate/*_create_posts.rb*. (Because the timestamps on your files will surely be different from mine, I'll use an asterisk from now on to refer to the date part of the filename.) Let's look at that file now:

```
   class CreatePosts < ActiveRecord::Migration
❶    def change
       create_table :posts do |t|
         t.string :title
         t.text :body

         t.timestamps
```

```
      end
    end
  end
```

Database migrations are actually Ruby classes. The change method is called ❶ when the migration is run. In this case, the method creates a table named posts with fields for title, body, and timestamps. The timestamps field refers to both the created_at and updated_at fields. Rails also automatically adds the id column.

You can run migrations as tasks with the rake command. For example, you enter bin/rake db:migrate to run all pending migrations and bring your database up-to-date.

Rails keeps track of which migrations have been run by storing the timestamps in a database table called schema_migrations.

If you make a mistake in a database migration, use the db:rollback task to undo it. After you correct the migration, use db:migrate to run it again.

The Schema

In addition to the individual migration files, Rails also stores your database's current state. You can see this by opening the file *db/schema.rb*. Ignoring the comment block at the top of the file, it should look like this:

```
--snip--
ActiveRecord::Schema.define(version: 20130523013959) do

  create_table "posts", force: true do |t|
    t.string   "title"
    t.text     "body"
    t.datetime "created_at"
    t.datetime "updated_at"
  end

end
```

This file is updated whenever you run a database migration. You should not edit it manually. If you are moving your application to a new computer and would like to create a new, empty database all at once instead of by running the individual migrations, you can do that with the db:schema:load rake task:

```
$ bin/rake db:schema:load
```

Running this command resets the database structure and removes all of your data in the process.

Adding a Column

Now that you know more about migrations, let's create one and run it. When we created our blog post model, we forgot that posts need authors. Add a string column to the posts table by generating a new migration:

```
$ bin/rails g migration add_author_to_posts author:string
```

The Rails generator (g is short for generate) looks at the name of your migration, in this case, add_author_to_posts, and tries to figure out what you want to do. This is another example of convention over configuration: name your migration in the format add_*ColumnName*_to_*TableName*, and Rails will parse that to add what you need. Based on the name, we clearly want to add a column named author to the posts table. We also specified that author is a string, so Rails has all the information it needs to create the migration.

NOTE *You can name a migration anything you want, but you should follow the convention so you don't have to edit the migration manually.*

Enter **bin/rake db:migrate** to run the migration and add the author column to your database. If you still have a Rails console open, you'll need to **exit** and restart with **bin/rails console** for your changes to take effect. You can also look at the *db/schema.rb* file to see the new column in the posts table.

Inside the Author Migration

The code you just generated for adding a column is simple. Edit the file *db/migrate/*_add_author_to_posts.rb* to see how it works.

```
class AddAuthorToPosts < ActiveRecord::Migration
  def change
    add_column :posts, :author, :string
  end
end
```

Like *_create_posts.rb*, this migration is a class containing a change method. The add_column method is called with the table name, column name, and column type. If you want to add multiple columns, you could create separate migrations for each, or you could call this method multiple times.

Active Record migrations also provide the rename_column method for changing a column's name, the remove_column method for removing a column from a table, and the change_column method for changing a column's type or other options, such as default value.

Validations

Remember that models have rules for manipulating application data. Active Record *validations* are sets of rules created to protect your data. Add validation rules to ensure that only good data makes it into your database.

Adding a Validation

Let's look at an example. Because we're making a blog, we should ensure that all posts have a title so readers don't get confused, and we can do that with a validation rule.

Validations are implemented as class methods in Rails. Open the post model (*app/models/post.rb*) in your editor and add this line:

```ruby
class Post < ActiveRecord::Base
  validates :title, :presence => true
end
```

This validates the presence of text in the title field. Attempting to create a blog post with a blank title should now result in an error.

OTHER COMMON VALIDATIONS

Rails provides a variety of other validations in addition to the :presence validation. For example, you can use the :uniqueness validation to ensure that no two posts have the same title.

The :length validation accepts a hash of options to confirm that the value is the correct length. Adding this line to your post model confirms that all titles are at least five characters:

```ruby
validates :title, :length => { :minimum => 5 }
```

You can also specify a :maximum value instead of a :minimum, or you can use :is to set an exact value.

The :exclusion validation ensures the value does not belong to a given set of values. For example, adding this validation prohibits blog posts with the title *Title*:

```ruby
validates :title, :exclusion => { :in => [ "Title" ] }
```

You can think of :exclusion as a blacklist for values you don't want to allow. Rails also provides an :inclusion validation for specifying a whitelist of accepted values.

Testing Data

Validations are automatically run before data is saved to the database. Attempt to store invalid data, and save returns false. You can also test a model manually with the valid? method:

```
2.1.0 :025 > post = Post.new
 => #<Post id: nil, title: nil, ...>
2.1.0 :026 > post.valid?
 => false
2.1.0 :027 > post.errors.full_messages
 => ["Title can't be blank"]
```

In this example, the valid? method should return false because you didn't set a value for the title. Failing validations add messages to an array called errors, and calling full_messages on the errors array should return a list of error messages generated by Active Record based on your validations.

Use validations freely to keep bad data out of your database, but also consider your users when you create those validations. Make it clear which values are valid, and display error messages if invalid data is given so the user can correct the mistake.

Associations

Only the simplest of applications contain a single model. As your application grows, you'll need additional models, and as you add more, you'll need to describe the relationships between them. Active Record *associations* describe the relationships between models. For example, let's add comments to our blog posts.

Posts and comments are associated. Each post *has many* comments, and each comment *belongs to* a post. This *one-to-many* relationship is one of the most commonly used associations, and we'll explore it here.

Generating the Model

A blog comment should have an author, a body, and a reference to a post. You can easily generate a model using that information:

```
$ bin/rails g model Comment author:string body:text post:references
```

NOTE *Remember to run database migrations after generating this new model!*

The post:references option tells the Rails generator to add a foreign key to the comments database table. In this case, the foreign key is named post_id because it refers to a post. The post_id field contains the id of this comment's post. The migration created the column we need in the database, so now we need to edit our models to finish setting up the association.

Adding Associations

First, open *app/model/post.rb* again to add the comments association. Earlier I said that each post has many comments, and that's the association we need here:

```
class Post < ActiveRecord::Base
  validates :title, :presence => true
  has_many :comments
end
```

Rails uses a class method called has_many to create this association in a readable way. Now, edit *app/model/comment.rb*, and you'll see that the Rails generator already added the matching belongs_to statement for you automatically:

```
class Comment < ActiveRecord::Base
  belongs_to :post
end
```

The post to comments association should now work as intended. If your Rails console was still running while you made these changes, you'll need to restart it to see the effects.

Using Associations

When you create an association in a model, Rails automatically defines several methods for that model. Use these methods, and you won't have to worry about keeping the post_id updated. They maintain this relationship for you automatically.

The has_many Methods

The has_many :comments statement you saw inside Post defines several methods:

comments Returns an Active Record relation representing the array of comments for this post

comments< Adds an existing comment to this post

comments= Replaces the existing array of comments for this post with a given array

comment_ids Returns an array of the comment ids associated with this post

comment_ids= Replaces the existing array of comments for this post with the comments corresponding to the given array of ids

Because the comments method returns a relation, it is commonly used with other methods. For example, you can create new comments associated with a post with post.comments.build, which builds a new comment belonging to this post, or post.comments.create, which creates a new comment belonging to this post and saves it to the database. Each of these methods automatically assigns the post_id of the newly created comment. This example creates a new comment associated with your first post. You should see the new comment in the output from post.comments:

```
2.1.0 :028 > post = Post.first
 => #<Post id: 1, title: "First Post", ...>
2.1.0 :029 > post.comments.create :author => "Tony", :body => "Test comment"
 => #<Comment id: 1, author: "Tony", ...>
2.1.0 :030 > post.comments
 => #<ActiveRecord::Relation [#<Comment id: 1, author: "Tony", ...>]>
```

If you want to check if any comments are associated with a post, use comments.empty?, which returns true if there are none. You might also find it helpful to know how many comments are associated with a particular post; in that case, you use comments.size:

```
2.1.0 :031 > post.comments.empty?
 => false
2.1.0 :032 > post.comments.size
 => 1
```

When you know a post has comments associated with it, you can look for a particular comment by passing post.comments.find a comment id. This method raises an ActiveRecord::RecordNotFound exception if a matching comment cannot be found belonging to this post. Use post.comments.where instead if you would rather not raise an exception. This method just returns an empty relation if a matching comment is not found.

The belongs_to Methods

The belongs_to :post statement inside the Comment model defines five methods. Because belongs_to is a singular association (a comment can only belong to one post), all of these methods have singular names:

post   Returns an instance of the post that this comment belongs to

post=   Assigns this comment to a different post

build_post   Builds a new post for this comment

create_post   Creates a new post for this comment and saves it to the database

create_post!   Creates a new post for this comment but raises ActiveRecord::RecordInvalid if the post is not valid

These methods are the inverse of the methods defined in the Post model. Use them when you have a comment and you would like to manipulate its post. For example, let's fetch the post associated with our first comment:

```
2.1.0 :033 > comment = Comment.first
 => #<Comment id: 1, author: "Tony", ...>
2.1.0 :034 > comment.post
 => #<Post id: 1, title: "First Post", ...>
```

Calling post on the first comment, which is also our only comment so far, should return our first post. This confirms the association works both ways. Assuming you still have more than one post in your database, you can also assign this comment to a different post:

```
2.1.0 :035 > comment.post = Post.last
 => #<Post id: 2, title: "Second Post", ...>
2.1.0 :036 > comment.save
 => true
```

Assigning a comment to another post updates the comment's post_id, but does not write that to the database. Don't forget to call save after updating the post_id! If you make this common mistake, the comment's post_id won't actually change.

Summary

This chapter has been a whirlwind tour of Active Record, so play around in the console until you're comfortable with these ideas. Add more posts, update the existing posts with body text, and create comments associated with these posts. Focus on the CRUD operations and association methods in particular. These methods are commonly used in all Rails applications.

The next chapter covers Rails controllers. There, you'll see all of these methods in use as you work your way through the various controller actions.

Exercises

1. It might be nice to contact the people leaving comments on our blog. Generate a new migration to add a string column to the comments table to store an email address. Run this migration, and use the Rails console to verify that you can add an email address to comments now.

2. We need to ensure that users actually enter some text when they create a comment. Add validations to the comments model for the author and body fields.

3. Write a query to determine the number of comments belonging to each post. You can't do this with a single query, but you should be able to find the answer by iterating over a collection of posts as if it were an array.

4

CONTROLLERS

Rails *controllers* connect your application's models and
views. Any web requests that your application receives
are routed to the appropriate controller. The controller gets data from the model and then renders the
appropriate view or redirects to a different location.

In this chapter, we continue working on our blog. Along the way, you'll
learn about controllers in detail. I'll cover resource representation with
REST, routing resources, and the types of actions a controller can take.

Representational State Transfer

Representational State Transfer, or *REST*, is a client-server software architecture introduced in 2000 by Dr. Roy Fielding, one of the authors of the
HTTP specification. REST deals with the representation of resources,
and in Rails, resources correspond to models. In RESTful architectures,
clients initiate requests to servers. Servers process those requests and return

responses to the clients. In a Rails application, the server that processes requests and returns responses is the controller. The controller interacts with the client through a collection of common URLs and HTTP verbs.

You're probably already familiar with at least two of these HTTP verbs. A request for a web page is sometimes called a *GET* request. A GET request doesn't change the state of the application; it simply returns data. When you submit form data on a web page, the result is usually a *POST* request. In an application using REST, a POST request is used to create a record on the server.

During our discussion of models in the last chapter, you learned about CRUD (create, read, update, and delete). REST uses the four HTTP verbs in Table 4-1, which correspond to each of those actions.

Table 4-1: Mapping Database Actions to HTTP Verbs

Database Action	HTTP Verb
Create	POST
Read	GET
Update	PATCH
Delete	DELETE

Your application determines how to handle a request based on the HTTP verb used. A GET request for a resource returns the data from the corresponding model; a PATCH request updates the model with new information; and a DELETE request destroys the model. All three of these actions use the same URL. Only the HTTP verb is different.

Rails applications add three more actions in addition to the four CRUD actions in Table 4-1. The index action displays a list of all resources; the new action displays a form for creating a new resource; and the edit action displays a form for editing an existing resource.

Each of these actions has a corresponding method in a Rails controller. These seven methods are summarized in Table 4-2.

Table 4-2: Default RESTful Actions

Action	Description	HTTP Verb
index	List all records	GET
show	Show one record	GET
new	Show form to create a record	GET
edit	Show form to edit a record	GET
create	Create a new record	POST
update	Update an existing record	PATCH
destroy	Delete a record	DELETE

We'll cover each of these actions in this chapter, but first let's see how URLs are generated.

Routing

Setting up all of these URLs and mapping actions to verbs might sound pretty complicated, but luckily, Rails routing handles all of this for you. *Routes* connect URLs to the code that comprises an application. First, let's look at the most common type of route, the resource route.

Resources

Your application's routes are stored in the file *config/routes.rb*. Open that file in your text editor.

Ignore all of the comments. Your file should only have three lines right now:

```
Rails.application.routes.draw do
  resources :posts
end
```

Rails applications use REST by default. The blog application currently has only one resource (blog posts), and the single line `resources :posts` builds a set of routes for your application. Use the rake command to display your application's routes:

```
$ bin/rake routes
Prefix Verb  URI Pattern          Controller#Action
 posts GET   /posts(.:format)     posts#index
       POST  /posts(.:format)     posts#create
--snip--
```

This command outputs the route helper prefix, HTTP verb, URL pattern, and controller action for each of the seven default RESTful actions.

For example, a GET request to */posts* calls the `PostsController#index` method. As you make changes to the routes file, run this command again to see how your application's routes also change.

Nested Resources

When one resource belongs to another resource, you can add it as a *nested resource*. In the blog, comments belong to posts. Here's how you represent that in *config/routes.rb*:

```
resources :posts do
  resources :comments
end
```

Add a block after `resources :posts` with a do, end pair. Then add `resources :comments` inside that block. This tells Rails that comments are only available inside of posts.

Restricted Resources

Adding `resources :comments` as you just saw creates routes for each of the seven default RESTful actions for comments. For now, let's only worry about creating new comments. You can restrict the set of routes generated for a resource by adding an only clause to that resource in *config/routes.rb*:

```
resources :posts do
  resources :comments, only: :create
end
```

Now, only the comment create action is mapped to a URL. You should only provide routes to actions that you plan to implement.

Custom Routes

Some actions in your application may not correspond to any of the seven default actions. For example, your application may include a search action that returns a list of posts containing a specific term. In cases such as this, Rails lets you manually configure *custom routes*.

Custom routes are also useful for mapping old URLs to a new Rails application or simplifying URLs for complex actions. For example, imagine your application allows users to log in by creating a new session and log out by destroying their session. Adding `resources :user_session` creates paths like *user_session/new*. If you would rather use different paths, you can create custom routes for *login* and *logout*.

```
Rails.application.routes.draw do
  resources :posts do
    resources :comments, :only => :create
  end

  get 'login'    => 'user_sessions#new'
  post 'login'   => 'user_session#create'
  delete 'logout' => 'user_sessions#destroy'
end
```

Now your application's login page should be at the path */login*. When a user visits the login page, his or her browser sends a GET request for this path. The controller displays the login form in response to that GET request. When the user submits the form, the browser sends a POST request to the same path with the contents of the form. The controller then creates a new session for the user in response to the POST request. When the user clicks the log out button, a DELETE request to the path */logout* destroys the user's session.

We aren't adding authentication to the blog application, but you can still add these routes to *config/routes.rb* if you want to see the routes created. Remove them before moving on because accessing a path that doesn't correspond to a controller action results in an error.

The Root Route

Finally, let's create a *root route* so we don't have to add */posts* to the browser's address bar every time. The root route sets the home page for your application. Add root 'posts#index' near the end of *config/routes.rb*:

```
Rails.application.routes.draw do
  resources :posts do
    resources :comments, :only => :create
  end
  root 'posts#index'
end
```

Now, accessing your server without a path should display the posts index page. You should always include a root route for your application.

Paths and URLs

Adding a route also automatically creates helpers for your controllers and views. You can use these helpers, shown in Table 4-3, instead of manually typing URLs in your application. That way, if you decide to change your application's URLs in the future, you won't have to search for and update all of the old URLs in your code.

Table 4-3: Rails Path and URL Helpers

Path Helpers	URL Helpers
posts_path	posts_url
new_post_path	new_post_url
edit_post_path(id)	edit_post_url(id)
post_path(id)	post_url(id)

The *path helpers* include only the path, whereas the *URL helpers* also include the protocol, server, and port (if not standard). Rails applications generally use path helpers. The URL helpers are useful for situations in which the full URL is needed, such as to generate URLs for inclusion in emails.

The first part of each method name matches the prefix displayed by the bin/rake routes command.

You can test these helpers in the Rails console like this:

```
2.1.0 :001 > app.posts_path
 => "/posts"
2.1.0 :002 > app.post_path(1)
 => "/posts/1"
2.1.0 :003 > app.new_post_path
 => "/posts/new"
2.1.0 :004 > app.root_path
 => "/"
```

Testing these helpers is a useful sanity check when working with Rails routes. If you forget which helper to use to create a path, you can type it in the console to see the result.

Controller Actions

The convention in Rails is to have a controller corresponding to each resource. That controller includes methods for each action. (Remember the principle from Chapter 2: convention over configuration.) The Rails scaffold generator created a controller for posts. Open the file *app/controllers/posts_controller.rb* to see the Ruby code behind these methods. I recommend running the Rails server as you work your way through the rest of this chapter:

```
$ bin/rails server
```

Now, let's look at each controller method in turn, starting with `index` and working our way down to `destroy`.

The `index` action retrieves all posts from the database:

```
def index
  @posts = Post.all
end
```

You see the familiar `@post = Post.all` in that method. You may be surprised that this is the *only* line of code in the `index` method. By default, Rails renders a view file matching the action name, in this case *app/views/posts/index.html.erb*. (We'll discuss views in the next chapter.)

Go to *http://localhost:3000/posts* in your browser to see the results of the index action.

The `show` action retrieves a single post from the database, but the `show` method contains no code at all:

```
def show
end
```

This method relies on a Rails `before_action`, which you should see on line two of the controller:

```
before_action :set_post, only: [:show, :edit, :update, :destroy]
```

The `before_action` is a class method that automatically calls the `set_post` method, shown next, before the methods `show`, `edit`, `update`, and `destroy`. This eliminates duplicate code in these methods. (Remember DRY: Don't repeat yourself.)

```
def set_post
  @post = Post.find(params[:id])
end
```

The set_post method is defined near the bottom of the controller under the keyword private. It calls the Post.find method to retrieve the post with an id corresponding to a parameter passed to the controller. Parameters are covered in more detail in the next section, so for now, let's continue examining these controller methods.

The new action displays a form for adding a new post:

```
def new
  @post = Post.new
end
```

The form uses data from a newly created post. Click the *New Post* link at the bottom of the post index page to see this form.

The edit action displays a form for editing an existing post. Like the show method, this method contains no code:

```
def edit
end
```

This form uses data retrieved by the set_post method discussed previously.

A Brief Detour from Actions

Before discussing create, update, and destroy, let's talk about a few key Rails topics that you need to know to understand those methods. In this section, we'll explore parameters, render/redirect, response formats, and the flash.

Parameters

Parameters generally represent part of the URL used to request a page or values from a form, and they're accessible in the controller as a hash named params. For example, the set_post method you saw earlier retrieved the id of the requested post from the params hash, like this:

```
@post = Post.find(params[:id])
```

You can see the parameters passed with each request in the output from the rails server command in your terminal. For example, go to *http://localhost:3000/posts/1* and then look at the Rails server output in your terminal:

```
Started GET "/posts/1" for 127.0.0.1 at 2014-03-31 20:30:03 -0500
Processing by PostsController#show as HTML
❶   Parameters: {"id"=>"1"}
  Post Load (0.3ms)  SELECT "posts".* FROM "posts"
    WHERE "posts"."id" = ? LIMIT 1  [["id", "1"]]
  Rendered posts/show.html.erb within layouts/application (233.9ms)
Completed 200 OK in 274ms (Views: 245.5ms | ActiveRecord: 26.2ms)
```

In this case, the 1 in the URL represents the `id` of the requested post ❶. Because we requested a single post, the `show` method is called, and this `id` is used to find the post in `set_post`.

Form data is represented by a nested hash with values. For example, editing this post results in a `params` hash more like this:

```
{
  "utf8"=>"✓",
  "authenticity_token"=>"...",
❶  "post"=>{"title"=>"First Post", "body"=>""},
  "commit"=>"Update Post",
❷  "id"=>"1"
}
```

You still access `params[:id]` ❷ to find the correct post, and you can also access `params[:post]` ❶ to see the new values submitted by the user. Because these are user-submitted values, you should ensure that your application only accepts data for the appropriate attributes. Malicious users could send requests with invalid parameters in an attempt to attack your application.

For blog posts, you only want users to be able to edit the `title` and `body` attributes. Rails includes a feature called *Strong Parameters*, which makes specifying which attributes your application accepts easy. You can see the feature in action in the `post_params` method:

```
def post_params
  params.require(:post).permit(:title, :body)
end
```

This method first requires the `params` hash to contain a nested hash with the key `:post`. It then returns only the permitted values (`:title` and `:body`) from this nested hash. Using the earlier example `params` hash, `post_params` returns a hash like this:

```
{"title" => "First Post", "body" => ""}
```

Other values in the `params[:post]` hash are silently ignored. Remember, always use the `post_params` method when accessing the parameters for a newly created or updated post.

Render or Redirect

Every action must either *render* a view or *redirect* to another action. By default, an action renders a file matching the action name. For example, the `show` method in the posts controller looks for a file named *app/views/posts/show.html.erb* and uses that file to build the HTML response that is sent back to the user.

You can tell Rails to render the response for a different action with the render method like this:

```
render action: "edit"
```

The ability to specify actions is helpful if you need to render a different view based on user input. This example is from the update method. If the post could not be updated with the data provided by the user, this method renders the edit view again, giving the user a chance to correct the data.

Sometimes you need to send the user to a page other than the one he or she requested. Use the redirect_to method to take care of this. For example, if the user enters valid data while creating or updating a post, the controller action redirects the user to that post:

```
redirect_to @post
```

When you call redirect_to, the address in the user's browser changes to reflect the new page, and another request is made. You can see this by watching the address bar as you submit form data and by looking at the output from rails server in your terminal.

To see this in action, first go to *http://localhost:3000/posts/new* in your browser. This is the new post form. Enter a title for the new post, and then click the *Create Post* button. Watch the address bar closely after clicking the button.

The form makes a POST request to *http://localhost:3000/posts*. This request is routed to the create method. After creating the post, you are redirected to *http://localhost:3000/posts/3*, assuming that your new post has an id of 3. The address is changed automatically by the redirect_to method.

Response Formats

Rails can generate responses in several formats, though all I've discussed so far is HTML. Scaffold-generated controllers can also include JavaScript Object Notation (JSON) responses, which are useful for creating application programming interfaces (APIs). Other formats include XML and even PDF.

You can try another response type in your web browser by visiting this URL: *http://localhost:3000/posts.json*. This URL is the same as the posts index URL used earlier, except it has *.json* added to the end. Rails recognizes this as a JSON request and renders the collection of posts as JSON, as in Figure 4-1.

Figure 4-1: Posts in JSON format

You specify the formats an action accepts and the responses to each format with a call to the `respond_to` method. This method accepts a block with a single parameter representing the requested format. Here is an example from the `destroy` method:

```
respond_to do |format|
  format.html { redirect_to posts_url }
  format.json { head :no_content }
end
```

This method is called right after a post is destroyed. If the client requests HTML data, this block redirects to `posts_url`, the index page. If the client requests JSON data, by adding *.json* to the end of the URL, this block responds with an empty header to indicate the post no longer exists.

The Flash

Flash messages are alerts to the user that are only valid for a single request. Flash messages are stored in the user's session, typically in a cookie. They are usually styled differently to stand out. For example, the stylesheet included with Rails scaffolding uses green text for flash messages.

Flash messages are helpful for sending error messages or other notifications to the user. They are generally set on a redirect. Here's an example from the `create` method in the posts controller:

```
redirect_to @post, notice: 'Post was successfully created.'
```

When a post is successfully created, the user is redirected to the new post and a flash message like the one in Figure 4-2 is shown.

Figure 4-2: A flash message

The create flash message is the green text, and it matches the message added earlier.

Back to Controller Actions

Now you should know everything you need to understand the `create`, `update`, and `destroy` actions. The methods written by the scaffold generator respond to requests for both HTML and JSON data with messages indicating success or errors, but let's focus on the HTML responses for now. I'll cover JSON responses in depth when I talk about building your own APIs.

The formatting in each method has been adjusted slightly to better fit this page.

The create method is responsible for creating a post using the `params` from the new post form:

```ruby
def create
  @post = Post.new(post_params)

  respond_to do |format|
    if @post.save
      format.html { redirect_to @post,
                    notice: 'Post was successfully created.' }
      format.json { render action: 'show',
                    status: :created, location: @post }
    else
      format.html { render action: 'new' }
      format.json { render json: @post.errors,
                    status: :unprocessable_entity }
    end
  end
end
```

The first line of the method `@post = Post.new(post_params)` uses Strong Parameters to ensure only the accepted parameters are allowed into the call to `new`. Inside the `respond_to` block, the return value of `@post.save` is checked. If it's true, then the user is redirected to the newly created post. If it is `false`, then the `new` action is rendered again so the user can correct any errors.

The `update` method is similar to the `create` method. The main difference is that the code checks the return value of `@post.update` instead of `@post.save`.

```ruby
def update
  respond_to do |format|
    if @post.update(post_params)
      format.html { redirect_to @post,
                    notice: 'Post was successfully updated.' }
      format.json { render action: 'show',
                    status: :ok, location: @post }

    else
      format.html { render action: 'edit' }
      format.json { render json: @post.errors,
                    status: :unprocessable_entity }
    end
  end
end
```

If `@post.update` returns true, the code redirects the user to the updated post; otherwise, it renders the edit form so the user can correct the errors.

The `destroy` method is simpler than the `create` and `update` methods because it doesn't check the return value of `@post.destroy`.

```
def destroy
  @post.destroy
  respond_to do |format|
    format.html { redirect_to posts_url }
    format.json { head :no_content }
  end
end
```

After the post is destroyed, the code redirects the user back to the index page, `posts_url`.

Adding Comments

You added a route to the create comment action earlier, so now let's add a simple controller for that action. You'll add the form for entering new comments in the next chapter.

Generate a new controller for comments using the Rails generator:

```
$ bin/rails generate controller comments
❶   create  app/controllers/comments_controller.rb
    invoke  erb
❷   create    app/views/comments
    invoke  test_unit
    create    test/controllers/comments_controller_test.rb
    invoke  helper
    create    app/helpers/comments_helper.rb
    invoke    test_unit
    create      test/helpers/comments_helper_test.rb
    invoke  assets
    invoke    coffee
    create      app/assets/javascripts/comments.js.coffee
    invoke    scss
    create      app/assets/stylesheets/comments.css.scss
```

Note that I specified only a controller, not scaffolding. This code generates an empty controller ❶ and an empty *views* directory ❷, as well as files for helpers, tests, and assets. We'll have to fill in the details ourselves. Start by opening the file *app/controllers/comments_controller.rb* in your editor:

```
class CommentsController < ApplicationController
end
```

Because you're implementing the create action, the first thing you need is a create method. You can model it after the create method in the posts controller. Assume that users won't be adding comments via an API, so it isn't necessary to generate JSON responses.

```
class CommentsController < ApplicationController
  def create
❶    @post = Post.find(params[:post_id])

❷    if @post.comments.create(comment_params)
❸      redirect_to @post,
                   notice: 'Comment was successfully created.'
     else
       redirect_to @post,
                   alert: 'Error creating comment.'
     end
  end
end
```

This code first finds the correct post ❶ using the post_id in the params hash. It then uses the comments association to create a new comment ❷ and redirects back to the post ❸. Each call to redirect_to sets a flash message to indicate success or failure.

Because you're using Strong Parameters in your application, you also need to add the comment_params method to specify the parameters you want to accept.

```
class CommentsController < ApplicationController
  --snip--

  private

  def comment_params
    params.require(:comment).permit(:author, :body)
  end
end
```

In the case of comments, you only accept an author and a body. Any other parameters are ignored. In the next chapter, you'll update the post show view to display existing comments and include a form for creating new comments.

Summary

This chapter introduced many important Rails concepts—REST, routing, and controllers. I also discussed parameters, render versus redirect, response formats, and the flash.

We started at the database in the last chapter and worked our way forward in this chapter. In the next chapter, we'll get all the way to the user and cover the last piece of the MVC puzzle: views.

Exercises

1. Good error messages are important for any application. If something goes wrong, your users need to know what the problem is and how to correct it. Currently, if a comment can't be created, users see the message "Error creating comment." Update the `CommentsController` `create` method to also show a list of error messages in the alert.

2. In Exercise 1 at the end of Chapter 3, you added an `email` field to the `Comment` model. Update the `comment_params` method in `CommentsController` to also accept this field.

5

VIEWS

A *view* is the user interface to your application. Typically, views include web pages for displaying database records and forms for creating and updating those records. Views also sometimes take the form of responses to API requests.

This chapter covers the most common Rails view template type, called *Embedded Ruby*, as well as view-specific helpers and layouts. You'll also learn how to avoid duplication in your HTML code with partials and how to generate forms to accept user input.

Enter `bin/rails server` to start the Rails server now. And keep it running in a terminal window as you work through the examples in this chapter, so you can see the changes you make to the application in your web browser and watch the server output.

Embedded Ruby

Embedded Ruby (ERB), the default template type in Rails, is used to build view templates. An Embedded Ruby template contains a mixture of Ruby code and HTML that is similar to ASP, JSP, or PHP.

Templates are stored in a subdirectory of *app/views* named after the controller. For example, you'll find the templates for the posts controller in *app/views/posts*. The Rails convention is to name templates after the action they represent, with the file extension *.html.erb*. The default template for the index action is *index.html.erb*.

Embedded Ruby contains three special tags for executing Ruby code. These tags are used for output, control flow, and comments. Let's take a look at each of these.

Output

The `<%= %>` tag (also called the *output tag*) executes the code it contains and prints the return value on the page. Open the file *app/views/posts/show.html.erb* in your editor to see several examples of this tag.

For instance, this tag prints the title of the current post:

```
<%= @post.title %>
```

Note that any HTML in the title is escaped by default. That is, any reserved characters are converted to character references and displayed on the page instead of being interpreted as HTML. This safeguard prevents malicious users from entering HTML code on your page that could cause a page to break or even a cross-site scripting attack. Cross-site scripting attacks and other security concerns are covered in Chapter 11.

Control Flow

The `<% %>` tag executes the code it contains without printing anything on the page. This tag is useful for control flow statements such as loops or conditionals. Open the file *app/views/posts/index.html.erb* to see this tag in action.

This example uses the each method to loop over an array of posts:

```
<% @posts.each do |post| %>
  <tr>
    <td><%= post.title %></td>
    <td><%= post.body %></td>
    <td><%= link_to 'Show', post %></td>
    <td><%= link_to 'Edit', edit_post_path(post) %></td>
    <td><%= link_to 'Destroy', post, method: :delete,
              data: { confirm: 'Are you sure?' } %></td>
  </tr>
<% end %>
```

Output tags are used inside the loop to print the values of post.title and post.body. This example also shows three instances of the link_to helper. These helpers create links to the show, edit, and destroy actions for each post. We'll discuss helpers in the next section.

Comments

Finally, the <%# %> tag is used to enter comments. *Comments* are usually notes to yourself or other programmers describing what your code does. Unlike HTML comments (which start with <!-- and end with -->), ERB comments will not appear in the HTML source. Use ERB comments for notes that you don't want to be visible in the HTML generated by the view template.

The ERB templates you've looked at so far were generated by the Rails scaffold when we first created our blog. They're uncommented, but you can easily add your own comments. Here's one:

```
<%# This code is crazy %>
```

In addition to notes to the programmer, you can also use ERB comments to remove code temporarily from the page. Add a hash sign (#) after the first percent sign (%) in any other ERB tag, and the code inside that tag will not be executed.

Helpers

Helpers are Ruby methods that simplify the code inside your views, making it easier to read. Rails includes helpers for creating links to resources, formatting numbers, and other common tasks. You can also easily write your own helper methods.

By using helpers, you can avoid placing too much logic in your view. If it takes more than a single line of code to display a value, then that code should probably be in a helper method.

URL Helpers

Create links with the link_to helper method:

```
link_to 'Show', post
```

This example generates an HTML link like this: <a href="/posts/1">Show</a>, assuming post has an id of 1.

You can also use the URL and path helpers you saw in the last chapter to create links:

```
link_to 'Edit', edit_post_path(post)
```

This example generates a link like this: <a href="/posts/1/edit">Edit</a>.

You can also include the HTTP verb to use for the link as well as additional data attributes. Use this for links that change state on the server, such as a link to destroy a resource. Remember that GET requests should not be used to change state.

```
link_to 'Destroy', post, method: :delete,
  data: { confirm: 'Are you sure?'}
```

This example generates a link with `data-method="delete"` and `data-confirm="Are you sure?"`. Rails includes the jQuery unobtrusive Java-Script library (`jquery_ujs.js`) by default. This library uses the `method` and `confirm` attributes to build a hidden form at run-time that creates a confirmation window and then submits the destroy link using a proper DELETE request. Aren't you glad you don't have to do that yourself?

NOTE *Web browsers are only able to issue GET and POST requests. Rails fakes the DELETE request by passing a parameter named _method with the value* delete. *When you update a record, the PATCH request is handled the same way.*

Number Helpers

Rails includes several handy methods for displaying numbers:

```
number_to_currency
number_to_human
number_to_human_size
number_to_percentage
number_with_delimiter
number_with_precision
```

Each method accepts a number and returns a string representing that number with some formatting applied. That formatting is related to the word at the end of the method.

The `number_to_currency` method, shown next, rounds the given number to two decimal places and prepends a dollar sign:

```
number_to_currency 100
```

So this example returns `"$100.00"`.

The methods `number_to_human` and `number_to_human_size` convert numbers into easy-to-read string representations.

```
number_to_human 1000000
number_to_human_size 1024
```

So these examples return `"1 million"` and `"1 KB"`, respectively.

Format percentages with `number_to_percentage`. This method rounds the number to three decimal places, by default, and appends a percent sign. You can specify a precision as an option.

```
number_to_percentage 12.345
number_to_percentage 12.345, precision: 1
```

These examples return `"12.345%"` and `"12.3%"`, respectively.

In addition to URL and number helpers, Rails also has built-in helpers for working with dates and assets such as images, CSS files, and JavaScript files. Later in this chapter, I cover helpers for creating forms and form fields.

I can't cover all of the helpers in Rails here, so for now, let's see how to add your own helper methods.

Your Own Helpers

You can easily create your own helpers by adding methods to the appropriate file in the *app/helpers* directory. The Rails scaffold generator has created a couple of mostly empty files in that directory for you automatically.

Add helpers that are only needed in a single controller to the helper file for that controller. For example, helpers that are only used in posts views should be added to the `PostsHelper` module in *app/helpers/posts_helper.rb*.

Add helpers used throughout the application to the `ApplicationHelper` module in *app/helpers/application_helper.rb*. Open this file and let's see how it works:

```ruby
module ApplicationHelper
  def friendly_date(d)
    d.strftime("%B %e, %Y")
  end
end
```

This code defines a new helper method called `friendly_date`. You can use this method in any view in your application to format a date for display.

```ruby
friendly_date Time.new(2014, 12, 25)
```

This example returns `"December 25, 2014"`. If you later decide to display dates in a different format throughout your application, you only have to change this method instead of changing all of your views.

The Posts Index Page

Now that you know more about how views work in Rails, let's update the index view to look more like a blog. Go to *http://localhost:3000/posts* in your browser to see the index page, shown in Figure 5-1.

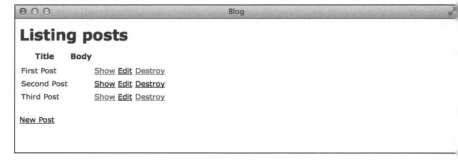

Figure 5-1: The posts index page

Your blog posts are currently displayed in a table. Open the file *app/views/posts/index.html.erb* in your editor:

```erb
<h1>Listing posts</h1>

❶ <table>
  <thead>
    <tr>
      <th>Title</th>
      <th>Body</th>
      <th></th>
      <th></th>
      <th></th>
    </tr>
  </thead>

  <tbody>
❷    <% @posts.each do |post| %>
      <tr>
        <td><%= post.title %></td>
        <td><%= post.body %></td>
        <td><%= link_to 'Show', post %></td>
        <td><%= link_to 'Edit', edit_post_path(post) %></td>
        <td><%= link_to 'Destroy', post, method: :delete,
                  data: { confirm: 'Are you sure?' } %></td>
      </tr>
    <% end %>
  </tbody>
</table>

<br>

<%= link_to 'New Post', new_post_path %>
```

This template first creates an HTML table ❶ and adds a table header to the page. It then loops over each post ❷ and displays that post's attributes in a table row.

A proper blog would display each post title as a heading followed by the post body in a paragraph. Update the index view to look like this:

```
<h1>Listing posts</h1>

❶  <% @posts.each do |post| %>
❷    <h2><%= link_to post.title, post %></h2>
❸    <p><i><%= friendly_date post.created_at %></i></p>
     <p><%= post.body %></p>
❹    <p>
       <%= link_to 'Edit', edit_post_path(post) %>
       <%= link_to 'Destroy', post, method: :delete,
             data: { confirm: 'Are you sure?' } %>
     </p>
   <% end %>

<br>

<%= link_to 'New Post', new_post_path %>
```

The template still loops over each post ❶ as before. Instead of display-ing the post attributes in table cells, however, it now shows the title ❷ in a second-level heading and uses the friendly_date helper ❸ you added in the previous section to format the created_at date. The links ❹ to edit and destroy the post are now at the bottom, and the link to show the post is now around the post title. Refresh the page in your browser to see the changes, shown in Figure 5-2.

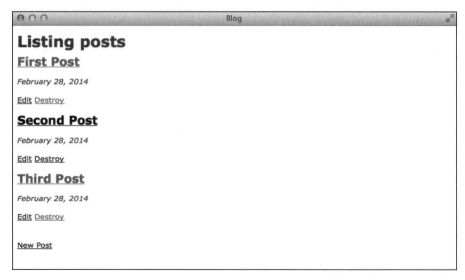

Figure 5-2: The updated posts index page

Our blog still won't win any design awards, but it's looking better!

Layouts

You may have noticed that the views you've seen so far only include the contents of the web page without the other required elements such as html, head, and body. These elements are the basic structure of all web pages.

Check the server output in your terminal to see what's happening when you load the index page:

```
--snip--
❶ Started GET "/posts" for 127.0.0.1 at 2014-03-09 18:34:40 -0500
❷ Processing by PostsController#index as HTML
    Post Load (0.2ms)  SELECT "posts".* FROM "posts"
❸   Rendered posts/index.html.erb within layouts/application (62.5ms)
Completed 200 OK in 92ms (Views: 91.2ms | ActiveRecord: 0.2ms)
--snip--
```

Here, we have a GET request ❶ for the path */posts*. It is processed by the index method ❷ in PostsController. Finally, the server renders posts/index.html.erb within layouts/application ❸.

In Rails, a *layout* is a file containing the basic HTML required for every page on your site. Rather than repeat the same HTML in every view, you only write it once inside the layout file. This is another way that Rails removes needless duplication.

Let's jump right in and dissect the layout for your blog. The server output calls it layouts/application, so open *app/views/layouts/application.html.erb* to see the layout for your application:

```
❶ <!DOCTYPE html>
  <html>
  <head>
    <title>Blog</title>
    <%= stylesheet_link_tag 'application', media: 'all',
❷       'data-turbolinks-track' => true %>
    <%= javascript_include_tag 'application',
❸       'data-turbolinks-track' => true %>
❹   <%= csrf_meta_tags %>
  </head>
  <body>

❺ <%= yield %>

  </body>
  </html>
```

This file contains the basic HTML for every page on your site: the HTML5 doctype ❶ followed by the head section and body section.

The head section sets the title of the page. It then includes Rails helpers for linking to your site's CSS ❷ and JavaScript ❸ files. It also includes a helper ❹ that protects your application from *cross-site request forgery (CSRF)* attacks, which I'll cover in Chapter 11. The body section includes the yield statement ❺.

The rest of this section covers these helper methods and the `yield` statement.

Asset Tag Helpers

In a Rails application, files such as CSS, JavaScript, and images are called *assets*. Assets are external files needed by the web browser accessing your application. These files are stored in subdirectories of the *app/assets* directory.

As your application grows, you may need several CSS and JavaScript files to control your site's appearance and client-side functionality. The Rails server output also lists the CSS and JavaScript files your application is already using:

```
--snip--
❶ Started GET "/assets/scaffolds.css?body=1" for 127.0.0.1 at ...

❶ Started GET "/assets/application.css?body=1" for 127.0.0.1 at ...

❷ Started GET "/assets/turbolinks.js?body=1" for 127.0.0.1 at ...

❷ Started GET "/assets/jquery.js?body=1" for 127.0.0.1 at ...

❷ Started GET "/assets/posts.js?body=1" for 127.0.0.1 at ...

❷ Started GET "/assets/jquery_ujs.js?body=1" for 127.0.0.1 at ...

❷ Started GET "/assets/application.js?body=1" for 127.0.0.1 at ...

❶ Started GET "/assets/posts.css?body=1" for 127.0.0.1 at ...
```

As you can see, our simple blog is already using three different CSS files ❶ and five JavaScript files ❷. Rather than list each of these files separately in the layout, Rails uses CSS and JavaScript files called *manifests* to require individual CSS and JavaScript files. A manifest file is simply a list of other files needed by your application.

A Rails feature known as the *asset pipeline* combines these CSS and JavaScript files together into two files and compresses them when your application is running in the production environment. These files are named *application.css* and *application.js*. By combining these files, your application receives fewer requests from users, which should improve its performance.

The head section of the layout contains ERB tags for adding the CSS and JavaScript manifest files that your application needs.

stylesheet_link_tag

The stylesheet_link_tag method adds an HTML link tag for the default CSS manifest, *application.css*, and each of the CSS files referenced in the manifest. Open the file *app/assets/stylesheets/application.css* to see how it works.

```
/*
--snip--
*
❶ *= require_tree .
❷ *= require_self
*/
```

This file starts with a block of comments explaining its purpose as well as the lines starting with require_tree ❶ and require_self ❷. The require_tree . statement includes all other CSS files in the *app/assets/stylesheets* directory and subdirectories. The require_self statement means the contents of this CSS file are included at the bottom.

javascript_include_tag

The javascript_include_tag method adds a script tag for the default JavaScript manifest, *application.js*, and each of the JavaScript files listed in the manifest. Now open the JavaScript manifest *app/assets/javascript/application.js*.

```
--snip--
//
//= require jquery
//= require jquery_ujs
//= require turbolinks
//= require_tree .
```

This file is similar to the CSS manifest. It starts with a block of comments explaining its purpose and then includes the JavaScript libraries, jquery, jquery_ujs, and turbolinks by default, as well as any other JavaScript files in the *app/assets/javascript* directory and subdirectories.

NOTE *The asset pipeline, turbolinks, and other performance issues are discussed in more detail in Chapter 12.*

CSRF Meta Tags Helper

The csrf_meta_tags method adds two meta tags to the head of each web page. These tags are designed to protect your application from CSRF attacks.

If you view the source on any page of your application, you should see a meta tag named csrf-token that contains a long string of random hexadecimal digits. This token is unique to your current session and is passed to your application any time a form is submitted.

```
<meta content="authenticity_token" name="csrf-param" />
<meta content="..." name="csrf-token" />
```

In a CSRF attack, a trusted user of your application visits a malicious site. The malicious site then attempts to submit requests to your application as that trusted user. Because the malicious site has no way of knowing this secret token, these requests fail. CSRF and other security concerns are covered in Chapter 11.

Yield

In a layout, the yield statement identifies where content from the view should be inserted. In this case, the HTML generated by *app/views/posts/index.html* is inserted between the body tags to form the complete web page that is sent to the user.

The yield statement is not required to be the only statement in the body element. You can add other elements to the body as needed. For example, you might add a common header or footer here that appears on each page of your application.

Partials

Like helpers, *partials* are used to extract code into meaningful units and to avoid duplicating code that is common to multiple views. The difference is that whereas helpers contain shared Ruby code, partials contain shared HTML code.

Partials are stored in view templates with filenames that begin with an underscore. For example, *app/views/posts/_form.html.erb* is a partial that renders a post form.

Code that is repeated across multiple pages is commonly separated out into partials to make the template code easier to follow. If you look at the new post and edit post templates, *app/views/posts/new.html.erb* and *app/views/posts/edit.html.erb*, respectively, you'll see they both render the same form partial with this line of code:

```
<%= render 'form' %>
```

Here, the partial is named *_form.html.erb* but is referred to simply as form when rendered.

If you find yourself repeating the same HTML code on more than one page, or in more than one place on a single page, you should copy that code into a partial and replace it with a render statement.

Collections

Partials can also be used to eliminate loops in view templates. When you use the :collection option, a corresponding partial is inserted into the template for each member of the collection. Using :collection doesn't necessarily remove code duplication entirely, but it can simplify the template.

For example, you could move the code inside the `<% @posts.each ... %>` block in *index.html.erb* into a new file named *app/views/posts/_post.html.erb*. You could then replace the block with a single line of code like this one:

```
<%= render :partial => 'post', :collection => @posts %>
```

In this example, Rails understands that `@posts` is an array of post objects, so it looks for a partial named *app/views/posts/_post.html.erb* and renders it on the page once for each object in the array. Because this action is so common, you can simplify even further to this:

```
<%= render @posts %>
```

Let's get some hands-on experience with partials by adding comments to the post show page.

Showing Comments

You added a model for comments in Chapter 3 and a controller in Chapter 4, but you still can't see them on the page. Nearly every post should have comments, and you don't want to repeat that code in every single page, so this is a perfect opportunity to put partials to work.

To get started, open *app/views/posts/show.html.erb* in your editor:

```
<p id='notice'><%= notice %></p>

<p>
  <strong>Title:</strong>
  <%= @post.title %>
</p>

<p>
  <strong>Body:</strong>
  <%= @post.body %>
</p>

<%= link_to 'Edit', edit_post_path(@post) %> |
<%= link_to 'Back', posts_path %>
```

Let's first clean up this page a bit like we did the posts index page by wrapping the title in a heading tag and the body in a paragraph, as shown here:

```
<p id='notice'><%= notice %></p>

<h2><%= @post.title %></h2>

<p><%= @post.body %></p>

<%= link_to 'Edit', edit_post_path(@post) %> |
<%= link_to 'Back', posts_path %>
```

Now add a heading and a render statement for the comments at the bottom of the page:

```
--snip--

<h3>Comments</h3>

<%= render @post.comments %>
```

This code shows the comments under the heading by rendering the @post.comments collection with a partial. For this to work, you'll also need to create a partial for rendering a single comment. Create a new file named *app/views/comments/_comment.html.erb* containing this:

```
<p><%= comment.author %> said:</p>

<blockquote>
  <%= comment.body %>
</blockquote>
```

If you added any comments earlier using the Rails console, you should now see them at the bottom of the page. Of course, you can't ask your users to add comments using the console; they expect a comment form. Let's see how forms are created in a Rails application.

Forms

Accepting input from users can be one of the more difficult parts of building a web application. Rails includes an elegant system for generating forms.

Rails provides helper methods for the various form controls. When bound to a model, these helper methods generate the correct HTML markup for passing values back to the controller automatically.

Go to *http://localhost:3000/posts/new* in your browser to see the New Post form created by the Rails scaffold generator, as shown in Figure 5-3.

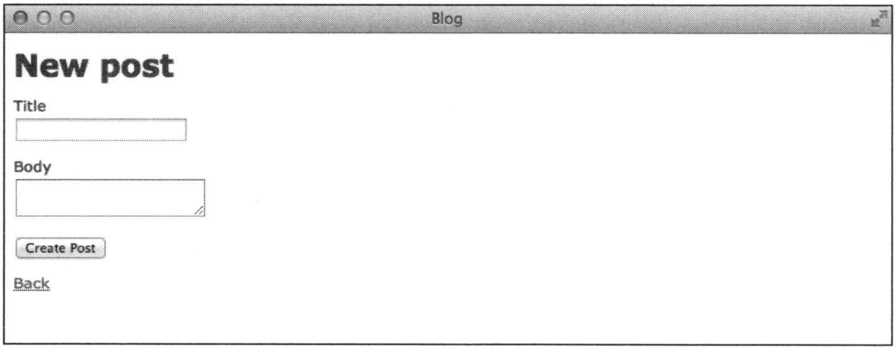

Figure 5-3: The New Post form

This simple form consists of a text box for the post title, a text area for the post body, and a button labeled Create Post to submit the form.

Form Helpers

You can use helpers to generate a form and all of the necessary fields and labels. Open the file *app/views/posts/_form.html.erb* to see an example of a Rails form:

```
❶ <%= form_for(@post) do |f| %>
❷   <% if @post.errors.any? %>
❸     <div id="error_explanation">
        <h2><%= pluralize(@post.errors.count, 'error') %>
          prohibited this post from being saved:</h2>

        <ul>
        <% @post.errors.full_messages.each do |msg| %>
          <li><%= msg %></li>
        <% end %>
        </ul>
      </div>
    <% end %>

❹   <div class='field'>
      <%= f.label :title %><br>
      <%= f.text_field :title %>
    </div>
    <div class='field'>
      <%= f.label :body %><br>
      <%= f.text_area :body %>
    </div>
    <div class='actions'>
      <%= f.submit %>
    </div>
    <% end %>
```

This partial is used when creating a new post and editing an existing post. The form begins with a call to the form_for method ❶ with a block that contains the rest of the form. Next an if statement ❷ checks to see if the post contains any errors. If the form has errors, the error_explanation div ❸ appears before the rest of the form. Otherwise, nothing is shown here. Finally, you'll see the form controls ❹.

Form Errors

Let's first look at the code for displaying errors like the one shown in Figure 5-4. Remember from our discussion of controllers that if a create or update action fails, the form will be rendered again. Try creating a new post with a blank title to see the error.

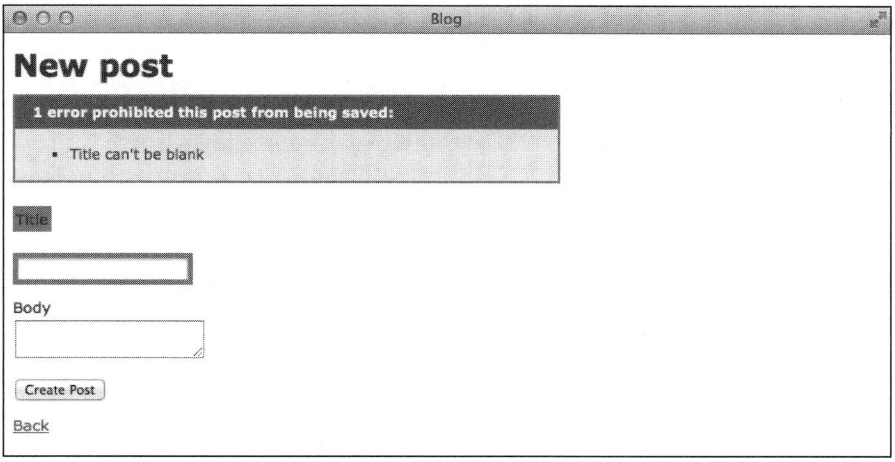

Figure 5-4: Post creation error

Figure 5-4 shows the error_explanation div with the number of errors in a heading followed by a bulleted list of the actual errors. Also, the label for the title field now has a red background and the text box for the title is outlined in red. Rails does this by wrapping these elements in a div with class field_with_errors.

Now that you know how to display errors, let's look at the form_for method and other helper methods for creating form controls.

Form Controls

Use the form_for block to create a form bound to a model. For example, this particular form is bound to the model stored in @post:

```
<%= form_for(@post) do |f| %>
```

Within this block, you have access to helper methods to add controls such as labels, text fields, and buttons to the form. Use the *form builder object* (in this case f) to call these methods.

```
<%= f.label :title %>
```

The label helper is used to create a label tag for the specified field. The previous statement will generate this HTML: <label for="post_title"> Title</label>. Rails converts the field name to a string and capitalizes the first letter. Your users can click this label to focus the cursor in the text field for the title. Of course, you still have to create that text field, and Rails has a helper for that, too.

```
<%= f.text_field :title %>
```

The text_field helper generates the following HTML: `<input id= "post_title" name="post[title]" type="text" />`. Note that the id of this input (post_title) matches the for value of the label tag in the previous paragraph. Also notice the name of this field. Rails sets names on form fields to indicate both the model (post) and the attribute to modify (title).

The next few lines of code add a label for the post body followed by a text_area for entering the body text. These controls work the same as the title fields. The text_area helper generates this HTML: `<textarea id= "post_body" name="post[body]"></textarea>`.

Besides controls for entering the title and body text, you need a button to submit the form:

```
<%= f.submit %>
```

The submit helper generates a submit button. The button's label is based on the class name of the current model and whether the model has been saved to the database. In the case of a new post, the value will be "Create Post" and the HTML looks like this: `<input name="commit" type="submit" value="Create Post" />`. If the post has already been saved to the database, the value is "Update Post".

Rails includes form helpers for every field you need, and you can always add your own helpers to create custom fields. Built-in examples include check_box, hidden_field, password_field, radio_button, and text_area.

Helper methods for HTML5 field types, such as email_field, phone_field, and url_field, are also included. These fields look like regular text fields, but on mobile devices, you'll see an alternate keyboard. Use these field types to ensure that your application is mobile-friendly.

Comment Form

Now let's put your new form knowledge to work and add the comment form First, add another heading to the end of the post show page at *app/views/ posts/show.html.erb*:

```
<h4>New Comment</h4>
```

Add the form for creating a comment underneath that new heading, as shown next. The array being passed to the form_for method contains both @post and @post.comments.build. Because every comment belongs to a post, you must pass the post and comment to the method. In this case, you're using the current post and a new comment created by @post.comments.build.

```
<%= form_for [@post, @post.comments.build] do |f| %>
  <div class='field'>
    <%= f.label :author %><br>
    <%= f.text_field :author %>
  </div>
```

```
  <div class='field'>
    <%= f.label :body %><br>
    <%= f.text_area :body %>
  </div>
  <div class='actions'>
    <%= f.submit %>
  </div>
<% end %>
```

The rest of the comment form should look similar to the post form; even the field names are the same. Refresh the page in your browser and make sure the form renders like the one shown in Figure 5-5.

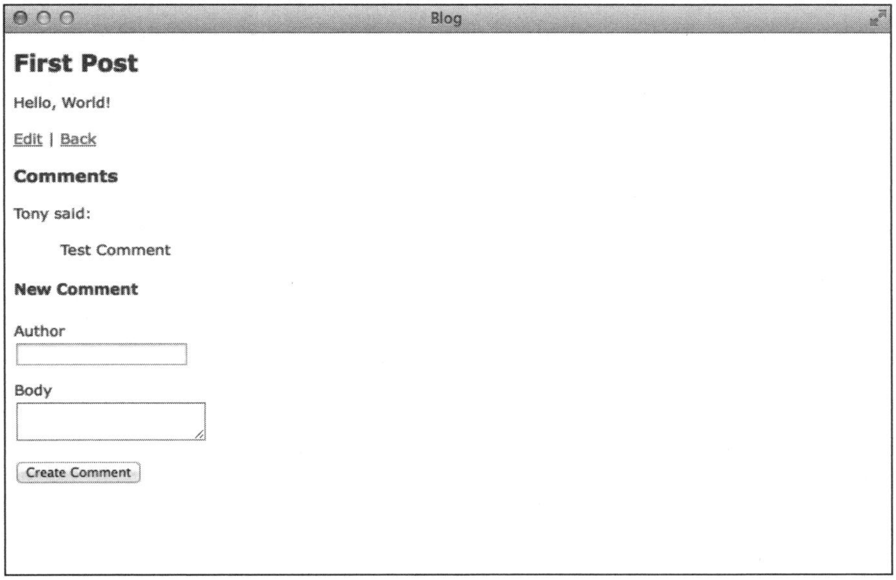

Figure 5-5: The New Comment form

Now enter an author name and comment body and click the **Create Comment** button. Submitting the form should display your new comment and add a flash message to the top of the page that says "Comment was successfully created."

Check the output of the rails server command in your terminal to see exactly what happened. Assuming your post has an id of 1, you should first see a POST to the path /posts/1/comments. This calls the CommentsController#create method.

You added this controller and method in the last chapter; recall that the create method builds and saves a new comment and then redirects the user back to the post. You should see this redirect as a GET request for /posts/1 in the output. This happens when the user is redirected back to the post show page.

Summary

Spend some time working on your application's views. We cleaned up the index page a little, but I recommend you improve it further. The other pages could also use some work. The following exercises should give you some ideas.

In the next chapter, you'll set up Git for version control and deploy your application to the web for everyone to see.

Exercises

1. Our blog's heading only appears on the index page. Move the h1 element from the posts index page to the application layout. While you're at it, come up with something a little more interesting to call it than "Listing posts." Also, change the h1 headings on the New Post and Edit Post pages to h2 headings.

2. In Chapter 3, you added an author field to the posts table. Add a text field for author to the post form and update the post_params method in PostsController to permit author as a parameter.

3. Users can create comments now, but you have no way to remove them. You need to be able to remove the inevitable spam posts! First, update the comment resource in *config/routes.rb* to add a route for the destroy action. The :only option should be :only => [:create, :destroy]. Next, add the destroy action in the CommentsController, similar to the destroy action for posts. Finally, add a link to this action at the bottom of *app/views/comments/_comment.html.erb*:

```
<%= link_to 'Destroy', [comment.post, comment],
  method: :delete, data: { confirm: 'Are you sure?' } %>
```

6

DEPLOYMENT

Now that you've built an application, let's put it on the Web for everyone to see. Rails applications can be deployed in many ways. Rails runs on everything from simple shared hosting to dedicated servers to virtual servers in the cloud.

The cloud application platform known as Heroku is one of the easiest ways to deploy your application, and I cover it in this chapter. Heroku uses the Git version control system to deploy applications, so we need to talk about version control systems first.

Version Control

A *version control system (VCS)* records changes to files over time so you can easily go back to a specific version later. The *repository* is the data structure, usually stored on a server, that holds a copy of the files in the VCS and a historical list of changes to those files. With a VCS, you can make changes to your source code knowing that you can always go back to the last working version.

Originally, version control systems were *centralized*. That is, the source code repository was stored on a single server. Developers could connect to that server and check out files to make changes to the code. But centralized systems also have a single point of failure. Examples of centralized version control systems include the Concurrent Version System (CVS) and Subversion.

The most popular type of version control system today is *distributed*. With a distributed version control system, each client stores a complete copy of the source code repository. That way, if a single client fails, everyone else can continue to work with no loss of data.

In a distributed system, a central server is still commonly used. Developers *push* their changes to this server and *pull* changes made by other developers. Popular distributed version control systems include Git and Mercurial. Because Heroku uses Git to deploy applications, I'll focus on Git.

Git

Git was originally developed by Linus Torvalds in 2005 for use with the Linux kernel. The word *git* is British slang for a despicable person. Torvalds once joked that he names all of his projects after himself.

Git quickly spread beyond the Linux community, and most Ruby projects now use Git, including Ruby on Rails. If you don't already have Git, installation instructions can be found in "Ruby, Rails, and Git" on page xxi.

Setup

Before you start using Git, set your name and email address. Open a terminal window and enter the following command to set your name:

```
$ git config --global user.name "Your Name"
```

The --global flag tells Git to apply this change to your global configuration. Without this flag, the change would only apply to the current repository. Also, set your email address:

```
$ git config --global user.email "you@example.com"
```

Now every time you commit a change, your name and email address is included, making it easy to see who made which changes when working with a team.

Getting Started

Now you're ready to create a repository for the blog. Move to your *code/blog* directory and enter this command:

```
$ git init
Initialized empty Git repository in /Users/tony/code/blog/.git/
```

This initializes an empty Git repository in the hidden *.git* subdirectory. Next, let's add all of the application's files to the repository:

```
$ git add .
```

The add command accepts a filename or directory path and adds it to Git's staging area. Files in the staging area are ready to be committed to the repository. The dot in the command represents the current directory. So after you run this command, all files in the current directory and any subdirectories are ready to be committed. When you commit, Git takes a snapshot of the current state of your project and stores it in the repository.

Now commit all staged files to the repository:

```
❶ $ git commit -m "Initial commit"
[master (root-commit) e393590] Initial commit
 85 files changed, 1289 insertions(+)
 create mode 100644 .gitignore
 create mode 100644 Gemfile
--snip--
 create mode 100644 test/test_helper.rb
 create mode 100644 vendor/assets/javascripts/.keep
 create mode 100644 vendor/assets/stylesheets/.keep
```

Note that I specified the commit message "Initial commit" with the -m flag ❶. If you leave off this flag, Git will open your default editor so you can type a commit message. If you do not type a commit message, the commit fails.

If you want to view the current repository's commit history, enter the git log command. The list shows previous commits in order from newest to oldest. Each entry includes who made the commit and when, along with the commit message.

```
$ git log
❶ commit e3935901a2562bf8c04c480b3c5681c102985a4e
Author: Your Name <you@example.com>
Date:   Wed Apr 2 16:41:24 2014 -0500

    Initial commit
```

Each commit is represented by a unique 40-character hexadecimal hash ❶. These hashes can be abbreviated to the first seven characters—in this case, e393590—if you need to refer to this particular commit again.

Basic Usage

As you work on a project using Git, follow this basic workflow:

1. Edit local files as needed.
2. Stage files to be committed with the git add command.
3. Commit the changes to the repository with the git commit command.

You can commit changes to Git as often as you like, but I find it helpful to commit changes related to a single simple feature or bug fix together. That way, all of the changes are tied to one commit, making it easier to revert and remove a feature if necessary. It's also a good idea to commit any outstanding changes at the end of a working session.

Other Useful Commands

Git contains many additional commands; enter git --help to see a list of those you'll use most often. You've already seen the init, add, commit, and log commands, but here are a few more that you'll find particularly useful as you navigate Git.

The git status command displays a list of changed and new files:

```
$ git status
On branch master
nothing to commit, working directory clean
```

In this case, nothing has changed. Edit a file in your project, *README .rdoc*, for example, and then enter the git status command again:

```
$ git status
On branch master
Changes not staged for commit:
  (use "git add <file>..." to update what will be committed)
  (use "git checkout -- <file>..." to discard changes...)

❶    modified:   README.rdoc

no changes added to commit (use "git add" and/or "git commit -a")
```

The git status command shows the current state of your working directory and staging area. Here, it lists all files that have been staged for commit and files with changes that have not been staged for commit ❶.

The git diff command shows detailed changes to files:

```
$ git diff
diff --git a/README.rdoc b/README.rdoc
index dd4e97e..c7fabfa 100644
--- a/README.rdoc
+++ b/README.rdoc
@@ -1,4 +1,4 @@
❶ -== README
+== Blog

 This README would normally document whatever steps are necessary to get the
 application up and running.
```

Here, I changed the word *README* to *Blog* ❶ on the first line of the file. Use this command before git add to see exactly what changes will be staged for commit. You can also pass a filename to this command if you only care about changes to a single file.

The git checkout command can undo changes to a file:

```
❶ $ git checkout -- README.rdoc
$ git status
On branch master
nothing to commit, working directory clean
```

Here, I've discarded the changes to the file *README.rdoc* by using git checkout followed by two dashes and the filename ❶. This command does not produce any output. Then I used git status to confirm that the change had been discarded.

The git clone command makes a local copy of a remote repository:

```
$ git clone url
```

The remote repository is represented by *<url>*. Git is a great tool for collaboration and is used by many open-source projects. This command makes that possible. Before you start working on an existing project, you *clone* a copy of the repository to your computer.

Branches

You may have noticed that the git status command includes the phrase, "On branch master." In Git, a *branch* is a named set of changes. The default branch is called *master*. It represents the main line of development. The changes I've made so far have all been committed to the master branch.

If you're working on a large feature that may take some time to complete, you can create a separate branch to store changes you're working on without affecting the master branch. This way, you can work on your own branch without impacting the rest of your team. Once the new feature is complete, you'll *merge* your new branch back into the master branch.

Use the git branch command followed by a branch name of your choice to create a new branch. In this example, I'll call my branch *testing*:

```
$ git branch testing
```

Enter the git branch command without specifying a name to see a list of the branches that currently exist in the repository:

```
$ git branch
* master
  testing
```

The star shows the currently selected branch. I created a new branch, but I'm still looking at the master branch. To switch to a different branch, use the git checkout command:

```
$ git checkout testing
Switched to branch 'testing'
```

Now I'm on the testing branch. Changes committed here will not affect the master branch. Once you are finished making changes, checkout the master branch and merge your changes into it:

```
$ git checkout master
Switched to branch 'master'
$ git merge testing
Already up-to-date.
```

All of the changes from the testing branch are now also in the master branch. You can confirm this with the git log command. Now that you're finished with the testing branch, add the -d flag to the git branch command to delete it:

```
$ git branch -d testing
Deleted branch testing (was e393590).
```

You don't have to delete branches after they have been merged, but doing so keeps the list of branches clean.

Remotes

So far, all of our changes have been stored locally, but you should store an additional copy of your repository on another server as a backup and to make it easier for others to clone your repository. To do this, you need to set up a remote. A *remote* is simply a nickname for another repository at a specific URL. Use the git remote add command to associate a nickname with a URL:

```
git remote add name url
```

Once you have added a remote, use the git push command to send changes to the URL and the git pull command to retrieve changes made remotely. You'll see a real-world example of this in the next section.

Heroku

Heroku is a cloud application platform for deploying web applications. This type of platform is sometimes referred to as a *Platform as a Service (PaaS)*, meaning Heroku takes care of server configuration and management so you can focus on application development. The service also includes an extensive collection of add-ons. Getting started is free, but large applications requiring more processor resources and memory can get expensive.

After some initial setup, you can use a git push command to deploy your application and access it on the Web.

Getting Started

First, sign up for a free account at *http://www.heroku.com*. Remember the password you select; you'll need it again to log in.

Next, install the Heroku Toolbelt if you haven't already (see *http://toolbelt .heroku.com/* for instructions). The Toolbelt is Heroku's set of tools for deploying your application to its platform.

Now, open a terminal window, navigate to your blog directory, and log in to Heroku:

```
$ heroku login
Enter your Heroku credentials.
Email: you@example.com
Password (typing will be hidden):
Authentication successful.
```

This command prompts you for your email address and the password you created earlier, and then it checks your computer for an existing secure shell (SSH) public key. Your public key is one half of the public/private key pair used to authenticate over SSH. When you attempt to log on, your private key is used to make a cryptographic digital signature. Heroku then uses your public key to verify this digital signature and confirm your identity.

If you don't already have a public key, press **Y** to create one when prompted. Your public key is automatically uploaded to Heroku after it is created. Heroku uses your public key for authentication so you don't have to type your password every time you deploy your application.

Now that you've logged in to Heroku, you need to prepare your application for deployment.

Updating Your Gemfile

No matter what kind of application you're building, you need to install certain gems to interface with Heroku and deploy your application. In this section, we'll look at the two gems you need to add to your application's *Gemfile*.

Heroku's servers use the PostgreSQL database server. Rather than install PostgreSQL locally, we used SQLite for development. You'll need to ensure that the PostgreSQL gem, called simply pg, is installed in the production environment.

Heroku also requires the rails_12factor gem, which ensures that your application's assets can be served by Heroku's servers and that your application's log files are sent to the correct place.

Open the file *Gemfile* in the root of your Rails application and locate the line gem 'sqlite3'. You'll use the PostgreSQL gem in production, but you still need the SQLite gem for development and testing, so update this line by adding group: [:development, :test] as shown here:

```
gem 'sqlite3', group: [:development, :test]
```

This instructs the bundle command to install this gem only in the development and test environments.

Now you need to install the pg and rails_12factor gems just mentioned. You only need these gems in the production environment, so add these next lines below the line you just updated:

```
# gems required by Heroku
gem 'pg', group: :production
gem 'rails_12factor', group: :production
```

Once you've made these changes, save and close the *Gemfile*. Because you've changed your application's *Gemfile*, run the bundle command again to update dependencies.

```
$ bin/bundle install --without production
```

Because you're running this command locally, where you develop and test your application, you don't need to install production environment gems, so add the --without production flag. Bundler remembers flags passed to bundle install, so --without production is assumed every time you run the command from now on.

Finally, you need to add and commit these changes to your Git repository. Enter these commands to update Git with your changes:

```
$ git add .
$ git commit -m "Update Gemfile for Heroku"
[master 0338fc6] Update Gemfile for Heroku
 2 files changed, 13 insertions(+), 1 deletion(-)
```

You could enter any message in place of *Update Gemfile for Heroku*, but commit messages are more helpful when they describe what you've changed.

Now, your account is set up, and your application is nearly ready to deploy. The last step is to create an application on Heroku:

```
$ heroku create
❶ Creating glacial-journey-3029... done, stack is cedar
  http://glacial-journey-3029.herokuapp.com/ | git@he...
❷ Git remote heroku added
```

This command ❶ creates a new application on Heroku's servers with a randomly generated name. You could have specified a name after the create command, but the name must be unique. You can always change the name later if you want. The create command also ❷ sets up a Git remote named heroku for you automatically.

Deploying Your Application

Everything is ready now, so you can finally deploy your application. Use the git push command to push the current state of your master branch to Heroku:

```
$ git push heroku master
Initializing repository, done.
Counting objects: 102, done.
Delta compression using up to 8 threads.
--snip--
-----> Launching... done, v6
       http://glacial-journey-3029.herokuapp.com/ deployed to Heroku

To git@heroku.com:glacial-journey-3029.git
 * [new branch]      master -> master
```

Heroku recognizes this git push command and automatically detects that a Ruby on Rails application is being deployed, installs the production gems specified in your *Gemfile*, updates your application's database configuration, precompiles your application's assets, and launches your application.

When you deploy any application for the first time, you also need to run database migrations to create the database tables needed by your application in Heroku's database server. Use the heroku run command to execute the rake db:migrate command on Heroku's server:

```
$ heroku run rake db:migrate
Running `rake db:migrate` attached to terminal... up, run.1833
Migrating to CreatePosts (20140315004352)
--snip--
```

If you make more database changes to your application, remember to commit the changes to the master branch in Git, push the master branch to Heroku, and run this command again.

Now you can open your web browser to the URL Heroku created for you earlier, or you can let Heroku handle that for you by entering this command:

```
$ heroku open
```

Your default web browser should open and load your blog application automatically.

Now that your application is set up on Heroku, you can deploy any time you want by committing changes to your Git repository and pushing the changes to Heroku.

GITHUB

Any discussion of Git in a Rails book is incomplete without at least a mention of GitHub. *GitHub* is the number one source code host in the world. GitHub provides project management features such as wikis, issue tracking, and code review via pull requests.

The Rails community has embraced GitHub as the best place for collaborating on open-source software. Rails itself is hosted on GitHub at *https://github .com/rails/rails/*. Sign up for a free account, if you don't already have one, and join the community!

Summary

Your blog is now safely stored in the Git distributed version control system. Changes to your source code are being tracked and can be easily undone. You blog is also available to the world via Heroku. Now you can deploy new features with a git push command.

Part I Remarks

This chapter marks the end of the first part of this book. We've covered the fundamentals of Ruby and Rails. Models represent your application's data; views are the user interface for your application; and controllers are the glue that holds them together. You'll use these concepts to build any application you want.

Looking at the application you built in Part I, you'll find plenty of areas to improve. For example, anyone can edit or even delete posts on your blog. Also, what happens if you write thousands of posts? The index page will probably time out before it can display them all! You may not quite have the tools to fix those problems right now, but once you dive into Part II, that will change.

In the next part of this book, we'll build a new social network application and cover advanced topics such as more complex data modeling, authentication, testing, security, performance optimizations, and debugging.

After learning these concepts, you'll be able to solve these problems with the blog and build a variety of other applications.

Exercises

1. Practice making changes to your application, adding and committing those changes to your local Git repository, and then pushing the changes to Heroku. Many Rails developers deploy multiple times per day, so familiarize yourself with this process.

2. Create an account on GitHub, learn how create a new repository on its servers, and push your application. GitHub has an online help area that walks you through the process if you have any trouble. Also, use GetHub's Explore feature to see the repositories of popular projects on its servers.

3. Finally, see if you can "scratch your own itch." Create a simple Rails application based on one of your interests. Create a catalog of your favorite books, or maybe an application to track your vinyl collection.

PART II

**BUILDING A
SOCIAL NETWORKING APP**

7

ADVANCED RUBY

You learned the fundamentals of Ruby back in Chapter 1. This chapter covers some of the language's advanced features, including modules, the Ruby object model, introspection, and a bit of metaprogramming.

Modules are used frequently in Rails applications to group similar functionality and share behavior between classes. The Ruby object model determines how methods are found and called in a hierarchy of inherited classes and shared code from modules. Introspection supports polymorphism by allowing you to look inside a class to see which methods it understands. Metaprogramming lets your classes respond to methods that don't exist by defining methods at runtime.

Open a terminal window and launch IRB to get started. Several of the examples in this chapter are longer than normal. You may find it easier to type the example into your editor, save it as a file with the extension *rb*, and then run the example in your terminal by entering `ruby filename.rb`. Or you can simply copy and paste the code from your editor into IRB.

Modules

As you saw in Chapter 1, a module is a collection of methods and constants that cannot be instantiated. You define modules in basically the same way you define classes. Module definitions begin with the word module, followed by an uppercase name, and continue to the word end.

To demonstrate using modules, we first need a class definition. Let's define a simple Person class:

```ruby
class Person
❶   attr_accessor :name

❷   def initialize(name)
      @name = name
    end
end
```

This class uses attr_accessor ❶ to define getters and setters for the instance variable @name, and sets the value of @name when created ❷.

Class names are usually nouns because they represent objects. Module names are usually adjectives because they represent behavior. Many Ruby modules take this convention a step further and use adjective names ending with *able*, such as Comparable and Forwardable.

Here's a silly example, just to show how it's done:

```ruby
module Distractable
  def distract
    puts "Ooh, kittens!"
  end
end
```

Enter this module in IRB, include it in the Person class you created earlier in this chapter, and see if you can distract someone:

```
irb(main):001:0> class Person
irb(main):002:1>   include Distractable
irb(main):003:1> end
 => Person
irb(main):004:0> p = Person.new("Tony")
 => #<Person:0x007fceb1163de8 @name="Tony">
irb(main):005:0> p.distract
Ooh, kittens!
 => nil
```

In Chapter 5, you also defined a module method while working with Rails helpers. ApplicationHelper is a module that is automatically mixed into all controllers by Rails.

Modules serve two purposes in Ruby:

- Modules are used to group related methods and prevent name conflicts.
- Modules define methods that can be mixed in to classes to provide additional behavior.

Organizing your code becomes more important as your application grows. By providing namespaces and making it easy to share code between classes, modules help you break your code into manageable pieces. Let's look at both of these purposes.

Modules as Namespaces

A Ruby module can be used as a *namespace,* a container for code such as constants or methods with related functionality.

The Math module is an example of a built-in Ruby module used as a namespace. It defines the constants E and PI as well as many common trigonometric and transcendental methods. The double-colon operator (::) is used to access constants in Ruby. The following example accesses the constant PI in the Math module:

```
irb(main):006:0> Math::PI
 => 3.141592653589793
```

Methods defined in a module are accessed with a dot (.), just like methods in a class:

```
irb(main):007:0> Math.sin(0)
 => 0.0
```

Modules as Mixins

A Ruby module can also be used as a *mixin* to provide additional functionality to a class. Ruby only supports single inheritance; that is, a class can only inherit from a single parent class. Modules allow you to implement something similar to multiple inheritance: a class can include several modules, adding each module's methods to its own.

You can add a module's methods to a class in three ways, using include, prepend, or extend. I discuss the effect of each of these keywords next.

include

The include statement adds the methods from a module to a class as instance methods and is the most common way of mixing a module into a class.

The `Comparable` module, included in Ruby, is commonly used as a mixin. It adds comparison operators and the `between?` method to classes when included. The class only needs to implement the `<=>` operator. This operator compares two objects and returns `-1`, `0`, or `1`, depending on whether the receiver is less than, equal to, or greater than the other object.

To use this module as a mixin, add it `Person` class you created previously:

```
class Person
❶   include Comparable

❷   def <=>(other)
      name <=> other.name
    end
end
```

This class now includes the `Comparable` module ❶ and defines the `<=>` operator ❷ to compare the name of this object with the name of another object.

After entering this in IRB, create a few people and see if they can be compared:

```
irb(main):008:0> p1 = Person.new("Tony")
 => #<Person:0x007f91b40140a8 @name="Tony">
irb(main):009:0> p2 = Person.new("Matt")
 => #<Person:0x007f91b285fea8 @name="Matt">
irb(main):010:0> p3 = Person.new("Wyatt")
 => #<Person:0x007f91b401fb88 @name="Wyatt">
irb(main):011:0> p1 > p2
 => true
```

Here `p1` is greater then `p2` because *T* is greater than *M* alphabetically. The `between?` method tells you whether an object falls between two others:

```
irb(main):012:0> p1.between? p2, p3
 => true
```

In this case, `between?` returns `true` since *T* is between *M* and *W* alphabetically, which means it works as expected.

prepend

The `prepend` statement also adds a module's methods to a class, but `prepend` inserts the module's methods *before* the class's methods. This means if the module defines a method with the same name as the class, the module's method will be executed instead of the class's method. Using `prepend`, you can override a method in the class by writing a method in the module with the same name.

One practical use for `prepend` is memoization. *Memoization* is an optimization technique in which a program stores the result of a calculation to avoid repeating the same calculation multiple times.

For example, imagine you wanted to implement the Fibonacci sequence in Ruby. The first two numbers in the Fibonacci sequence are zero and one. Each subsequent number is the sum of the previous two. Here is a method to calculate the *n*th value of the Fibonacci sequence in Ruby:

```
class Fibonacci
  def calc(n)
    return n if n < 2
❶   return calc(n - 1) + calc(n - 2)
  end
end
```

Notice that the `calc` method is recursive. Every call to `calc` with a value of n greater than 1 results in two more calls to itself ❶. Try creating an instance of this class and calculating some small values of n:

```
irb(main):013:0> f = Fibonacci.new
 => #<Fibonacci:0x007fd8d3269518>
irb(main):014:0> f.calc 10
 => 55
irb(main):015:0> f.calc 30
 => 832040
```

As you call the method with larger values of n, the method takes noticeably longer to run. For values of n around 40, the method takes several seconds to return an answer.

The Fibonacci `calc` method is slow because it repeats the same calculations many times. But if you define a module to implement memoization, the calculations should take significantly less time. Let's do that now:

```
module Memoize
  def calc(n)
❶   @@memo ||= {}
❷   @@memo[n] ||= super
  end
end
```

The `Memoize` module also defines a `calc` method. This method has a couple of interesting features. First, it initializes a class variable named `@@memo` ❶ with an empty hash if it is not already initialized. This hash stores the result of the `calc` method for each value of n. Next, it assigns the return value of `super` to `@@memo` at key n ❷ if that value is not already assigned. Because we are using `prepend` to add this module into `Fibonacci`, `super` calls the original `calc` method defined by the class.

Each time the `calc` method is called, `@@memo` stores the Fibonacci number for the value n. For example, after calling `calc(3)`, the `@@memo` hash holds these keys and values:

```
{
  0 => 0,
  1 => 1,
```

```
  2 => 1,
  3 => 2
}
```

On each line, the key (the first number) is the value of n and the value (the second number) is the corresponding Fibonacci number. The Fibonacci number for 0 is 0, 1 is 1, 2 is 1, and 3 is 2. By storing these intermediate values, the calc method never needs to perform the same calculation more than once. Use prepend Memoize to add the Memoize module to the Fibonacci class and try it for yourself:

```
irb(main):016:0> class Fibonacci
irb(main):017:1> prepend Memoize
irb(main):018:1> end
 => Fibonacci
irb(main):019:0> f.calc 40
 => 102334155
```

Now that the values of calc are being memoized, you should be able to call calc for greater values of n and get an answer almost instantly. Try it with n = 100 or even n = 1000. Note that you didn't have to restart IRB or instantiate a new Fibonacci object. Method lookup in Ruby is dynamic.

extend

When you use include or prepend to add a module to a class, the module's methods are added to the class as instance methods. In Chapter 1, you learned that there are also class methods that are called on the class itself instead of on an instance of the class. The extend statement adds the methods from a module as class methods. Use extend to add behavior to the class itself instead of instances of the class.

The Ruby standard library includes a module named Forwardable, which you can use to extend a class. The Forwardable module contains methods useful for delegation. *Delegation* means relying on another object to handle a set of method calls. Delegation is a way to reuse code by assigning the responsibility of certain method calls to another class.

For example, imagine a class named Library that manages a collection of books. We store the books in an array named @books:

```
class Library
  def initialize(books)
    @books = books
  end
end
```

We can store our books, but we can't do anything with them yet. We could use attr_accessor to make the @books array available outside of the class, but that would make all of the array's methods available to users of our class. A user could then call methods such as clear or reject to remove all of the books from our library.

Instead, let's delegate a few methods to the @books array to provide the functionality we need—a way to get the size of the library and add a book.

```
❶ require 'forwardable'
  class Library
❷   extend Forwardable
❸   def_delegators :@books, :size, :push

    def initialize(books)
      @books = books
    end
  end
```

The Forwardable module is in the Ruby Standard Library, not the Ruby core, so we first need to require it ❶. Next, we use extend to add the Forwardable methods to our class as class methods ❷. Finally, we can call the def_delegators method ❸. The first argument to this method is a symbol representing the instance variable to which we're delegating methods.

In this case, the instance variable is @books. The rest of the arguments are symbols representing the methods we want to delegate. The size method returns the number of elements in the array. The push method appends a new element to the end of an array.

In the following example, lib.size initially prints 2 because we have two books in our library. After adding a book, the size updates to 3.

```
irb(main):020:0> lib = Library.new ["Neuromancer", "Snow Crash"]
 => #<Library:0x007fe6c91854e0 @books=["Neuromancer", "Snow Crash"]>
irb(main):021:0> lib.size
 => 2
irb(main):022:0> lib.push "The Hobbit"
 => ["Neuromancer", "Snow Crash", "The Hobbit"]
irb(main):023:0> lib.size
 => 3
```

Ruby Object Model

The *Ruby object model* explains how Ruby locates a method when it is called. With inheritance and modules, you may find yourself wondering exactly where a particular method is defined or, in the case of multiple methods with the same name, which one is actually invoked by a particular call.

Ancestors

Continuing with the simple Person class defined previously, we can find out a lot about this class in IRB. First, let's see which classes and modules define methods for the Person class:

```
irb(main):024:0> Person.ancestors
 => [Person, Distractable, Comparable, Object, Kernel, BasicObject]
```

The class method `ancestors` returns a list of classes that `Person` inherits from and the modules it includes. In this example, `Person`, `Object`, and `BasicObject` are classes, whereas `Distractable`, `Comparable,` and `Kernel` are modules. You can find out which of these are classes and which are modules by calling the class method as explained in the *Class* section below.

`Object` is the default root of all Ruby objects. `Object` inherits from `BasicObject` and mixes in the `Kernel` module. `BasicObject` is the parent class of all classes in Ruby. You can think of it as a blank class that all other classes build on. `Kernel` defines many of the Ruby methods that are called without a receiver, such as `puts` and `exit`. Every time you call `puts`, you're actually calling the instance method `puts` in the `Kernel` module.

The order of this list indicates the order in which Ruby searches for a called method. Ruby first looks for a method definition in the class `Person` and then continues looking through the list until the method is found. If Ruby doesn't find the method, it raises a `NoMethodError` exception.

Methods

You can see a list of the class methods and instance methods defined by a class by calling `methods` and `instance_methods`, respectively. These lists include methods defined by all parent classes by default. Pass the parameter `false` to leave out only these:

```
irb(main):025:0> Person.methods
 => [:allocate, :new, :superclass, :freeze, :===, :==, ... ]
irb(main):026:0> Person.methods(false)
 => []
irb(main):027:0> Person.instance_methods(false)
 => [:name, :name=, :<=>]
```

The `Person` class contains almost 100 different class methods from its ancestors, but it defines none of its own, so the call to `methods(false)` returns an empty array. The call to `instance_methods` returns the `name` and `name=` methods defined by `attr_accessor` and the `<=>` method that we defined in the body of the class.

Class

The last piece of the object model concerns the `Person` class itself. Everything in Ruby is an object, that is, an instance of a class. Therefore, the `Person` class must be an instance of some class.

```
irb(main):028:0> Person.class
 => Class
```

All Ruby classes are instances of the class `Class`. Defining a class, such as `Person`, creates an instance of the class `Class` and assigns it to a global constant, in this case `Person`. The most important method in `Class` is `new`, which is responsible for allocating memory for a new object and calling the `initialize` method.

Class has its own set of ancestors:

```
irb(main):029:0> Class.ancestors
=> [Class, Module, Object, Kernel, BasicObject]
```

Class inherits from the class Module, which inherits from Object as before. The Module class contains definitions of several of the methods used in this section such as ancestors and instance_methods.

Introspection

Introspection, also known as *reflection*, is the ability to examine an object's type and other properties as a program is running. You've already seen how to determine an object's type by calling class and how to get a list of methods defined by an object by calling methods and instance_methods, but Ruby's Object class defines several more methods just for introspecting objects. For example, given an object, you may want to determine if it belongs to a particular class:

```
irb(main):030:0> p = Person.new("Tony")
=> #<Person:0x007fc0ca1a6278 @name="Tony">
irb(main):031:0> p.is_a? Person
=> true
```

The is_a? method returns true if the given class is the class of the receiving object. In this case, it returns true because the object p is a Person.

```
irb(main):032:0> p.is_a? Object
=> true
```

It also returns true if the given class or module is an ancestor of the receiving object. In this case, Object is an ancestor of Person, so is_a? returns true.

Use the instance_of? method if you need to determine exactly which class was used to create an object:

```
irb(main):033:0> p.instance_of? Person
=> true
irb(main):034:0> p.instance_of? Object
=> false
```

The instance_of? method returns true only if the receiving object is an instance of the given class. This method returns false for ancestors and classes inheriting from the given class. This type of introspection is helpful in some situations, but generally you don't need to know the exact class used to create an object—just the object's capabilities.

Duck Typing

In *duck typing*, you only need to know whether an object accepts the methods you need to call. If the object responds to the needed methods, you don't have to worry about class names or inheritance. The name duck typing comes from the phrase, "If it walks like a duck and quacks like a duck, call it a duck."

In Ruby, you can use the respond_to? method to see if an object responds to a particular method. If respond_to? returns false, then calling the method raises a NoMethodError exception as explained earlier.

For example, imagine a simple method to print some information to a file with a timestamp:

```
def write_with_time(file, info)
  file.puts "#{Time.now} - #{info}"
end
```

You can try this method in IRB.

```
❶ irb(main):001:0> f = File.open("temp.txt", "w")
  => #<File:temp.txt>
❷ irb(main):002:0> write_with_time(f, "Hello, World!")
  => nil
❸ irb(main):003:0> f.close
  => nil
```

First, open a File named *temp.txt* in the current directory and store the File instance in the variable f ❶. Then pass f and the message "Hello, World!" to the write_with_time method ❷. Finally, close the File with f.close ❸.

The file *temp.txt* in the current directory now contains a single line similar to the one here:

```
2014-05-21 16:52:07 -0500 - Hello, World!
```

This method works great until someone accidentally passes a value to it that isn't a file, such as nil. Here's a possible fix for that bug:

```
  def write_with_time(file, info)
❶   if file.instance_of? File
      file.puts "#{Time.now} - #{info}"
    else
      raise ArgumentError
    end
  end
```

This fix solves the problem by checking to see if file is an instance of the File class ❶, but it also limits the usefulness of this method. Now it *only* works with files. What if you want to write over the network using a Socket or write to the console using STDOUT?

Instead of testing the *type* of file, let's test its *capabilities*:

```
   def write_with_time(file, info)
❶    if file.respond_to?(:puts)
       file.puts "#{Time.now} - #{info}"
     else
       raise ArgumentError
     end
   end
```

You know that the write_with_time method calls the method puts, so check to see if file responds to the puts method ❶. Now, write_with_time works with any data type that responds to the puts method.

Using duck typing leads to code that can be easily reused. Look for more opportunities to apply duck typing as you build applications.

Metaprogramming

Metaprogramming is the practice of writing code that works with code instead of data. With Ruby, you can write code that defines new behavior at runtime. The techniques in this section can save you time and remove duplication from your code by allowing Ruby to generate methods when your program is loaded or as it runs.

This section covers two different ways of dynamically defining methods: define_method and class_eval. It also covers method_missing, so you can respond to methods that haven't been defined.

define_method

Let's say we have an application with a list of features that can be enabled for users. The User class stores these features in a hash named @features. If a user has access to a feature, the corresponding hash value will be true.

We want to add methods of the form can_*feature*! and can_*feature*? to enable a feature and check if a feature is enabled, respectively. Rather than write several mostly identical methods, we can iterate over the list of available features and use define_method, as shown here, to define the individual methods:

```
   class User
❶    FEATURES = ['create', 'update', 'delete']

     FEATURES.each do |f|
❷      define_method "can_#{f}!" do
         @features[f] = true
       end

❸      define_method "can_#{f}?" do
❹        !!@features[f]
       end
     end
```

```
    def initialize
      @features = {}
    end
end
```

The User class first creates a constant array ❶ of available features named FEATURES. It then iterates over FEATURES using each and calls define_method to create a method of the form can_*feature*! ❷ to allow a user access to a feature. Still inside the each block, the class also defines a method of the form can_*feature*? ❸ that determines whether a user has access to the feature. This method converts the value @features[f] to either true or false by using two NOT operators ❹.

NOTE   *Using two NOT operators isn't strictly necessary because the @features hash returns nil for keys without values and Ruby treats nil as false, but this technique is commonly used.*

Now let's create a new User and try the dynamically defined methods:

```
irb(main):001:0> user = User.new
 => #<User:0x007fc01b95abe0 @features={}>
irb(main):002:0> user.can_create!
 => true
irb(main):003:0> user.can_create?
 => true
irb(main):004:0> user.can_update?
 => false
irb(main):005:0> user.can_delete?
 => false
```

If you want more practice with define_method, see if you can add methods of the form cannot_*feature*!, which disables a feature for the user. More details are provided in Exercise 3 at the end of this chapter.

class_eval

The class_eval method evaluates a string of code as if it were typed directly into the class definition. Using class_eval is an easy way to add instance methods to a class at runtime.

When I discussed attr_accessor in Chapter 1, you learned that it defines getter and setter methods for instance variables in a class, but I didn't discuss exactly how those methods were defined. The attr_accessor method is built in to Ruby. You don't need to define it yourself, but you can learn about class_eval by implementing your own version of attr_accessor.

```
❶ class Accessor
❷   def self.accessor(attr)
      class_eval "
❸       def #{attr}
          @#{attr}
```

```
            end

❹          def #{attr}=(val)
             @#{attr} = val
           end
         "
      end
   end
```

Here, you define a class named Accessor ❶ with a single class method named accessor ❷. This method works like the built-in attr_accessor. It accepts a single parameter representing the attribute for which you're creating getter and setter methods. Pass the string to class_eval, which uses string interpolation to insert the value of attr as needed to define two methods. The first method has the same name as the attribute and returns the value of the attribute ❸. The second method is the attribute name followed by an equal sign. It sets the attribute to a specified value val ❹.

For example, if attr is :name, then accessor defines the methods name and name= by replacing attr with *name* in the specified places. This is a little hard to follow without an example. The following code uses the accessor method in a class:

```
❶ class Element < Accessor
❷   accessor :name

    def initialize(name)
      @name = name
    end
  end
```

First, you have the Element class inherit from the Accessor class ❶ so the accessor method is available. Then, you pass the name of the instance variable to accessor ❷. Here, you pass the symbol :name. When the program runs, the call to class_eval automatically generates this code inside the Element class:

```
❶ def name
     @name
   end

❷ def name=(val)
     @name = val
   end
```

The name method returns the current value of the instance variable @name ❶. The name= method accepts a value and assigns it to @name ❷. Test this by creating an instance of the Element class and trying to get and set the value of name:

```
❶ irb(main):001:0> e = Element.new "lead"
  => #<Element:0x007fc01b840110 @name="lead">
```

```
❷ irb(main):002:0> e.name = "gold"
  => "gold"
❸ irb(main):003:0> puts e.name
  gold
   => nil
```

First, create a new `Element` and initialize its name with "lead" ❶. Next, use the `name=` method to assign the new name "gold" ❷. Finally, use the `name` method to display the value of `@name` ❸. There you have it. With a bit of metaprogramming magic, you turned lead into gold.

method_missing

Whenever Ruby can't find a method, it calls `method_missing` on the receiver. This method receives the original method name as a symbol, an array of arguments, and any block passed to the method call.

By default, `method_missing` calls `super`, which passes the method up the ancestor chain until it finds an ancestor class containing the method. If the method reaches the `BasicObject` class, it raises a `NoMethodError` exception. You can override `method_missing` by defining your own implementation in a class to intercept these method calls and add your own behavior.

Let's start with a simple example so you can see how it works. This class echoes any unknown method calls back to you three times:

```
class Echo
  def method_missing(name, *args, &block)
    word = name
    puts "#{word}, #{word}, #{word}"
  end
end
```

Now that `method_missing` is overridden, if you try to call a nonexistent method on an instance of this class, you'll just see that method's "echo" in the terminal:

```
irb(main):001:0> echo = Echo.new
 => #<Echo:0x007fa8131c9590>
irb(main):002:0> echo.hello
 => hello, hello, hello
```

A real-world use for `method_missing` is the Rails dynamic finder. Using dynamic finders, you can write Active Record queries like `Post.find_by_title("First Post")` instead of `Post.where(title: "First Post").first`.

Dynamic finders can be implemented using `method_missing`. Let's define our own version of dynamic finders. Instead of method names like `find_by_attribute`, we'll use `query_by_attribute` so we can avoid conflicts with the built-in methods.

Open the Post model at *app/models/post.rb* in your blog directory to follow along with this example:

```ruby
class Post < ActiveRecord::Base
  validates :title, :presence => true
  has_many :comments

❶  def self.method_missing(name, *args, &block)
❷    if name =~ /\Aquery_by_(.+)\z/
❸      where($1 => args[0]).first
     else
❹      super
     end
  end
end
```

First, define the `method_missing` class method ❶ because our query _by_*attribute* method will be called on the Post class. Next, test the name against a regular expression ❷.

Finally, call the built-in `where` method ❸ using the string captured by the regular expression and the first argument passed to the method. Be sure to call super ❹ if the string doesn't match; this ensures that unknown methods will be sent to the parent class.

NOTE *The regular expression /\Aquery_by_(.+)\z/ matches strings that start with "query_by_" and then captures the rest of the string using parenthesis. A full discussion of regular expressions is beyond the scope of this book. The website http://rubular.com/ is a great way to edit and test regular expressions online.*

The real dynamic finders also check to make sure the captured string matches an attribute of the model. If you try to call our query_by_*attribute* method with nonexistent column, it raises a SQLException.

```
irb(main):001:0> Post.query_by_title "First Post"
 => #<Post id: 1, ...>
```

Our implementation of query_by_*attribute* has one more problem:

```
irb(main):002:0> Post.respond_to? :query_by_title
 => false
```

Because we're overriding `method_missing` to call this method, Ruby doesn't know that the Post class can respond to it. To fix this, we need to also override the `respond_to_missing?` method in the Post model at *app/models/post.rb*.

```ruby
class Post < ActiveRecord::Base
  --snip--

  def self.respond_to_missing?(name, include_all=false)
❶    name.to_s.start_with?("query_by_") || super
```

```
    end
  end
```

Instead of the regular expression used in method_missing, we just check if the method name starts with "query_by_" ❶. If it does, this method returns true. Otherwise, super is called. Now restart the Rails console and try again:

```
irb(main):001:0> Post.respond_to? :query_by_title
 => true
```

With this change in place, respond_to? returns true as expected. Remember to always override respond_to_missing? when using method_missing. Otherwise, users of your class have no way of knowing which methods it accepts, and the duck typing techniques covered earlier will fail.

Summary

If you write enough Ruby, then you will eventually see all of the techniques covered in this chapter used in real-world programs. When that time comes, you can be confident that you'll understand what the code does, instead of just assuming that metaprogramming is some kind of magic.

In the next chapter, you'll start building a new Rails application from scratch. Along the way I'll cover some advanced data-modeling techniques and you'll learn even more about Active Record.

For now, try these exercises.

Exercises

1. The Rails framework makes extensive use of modules both as namespaces and to add behavior to classes. Open a Rails console inside your *blog* directory and look at the ancestors of Post. How many ancestors does it have? Based on their names, can you tell what some of them do?

2. Update the define_method sample by adding a cannot_*feature*! method. This method should set the value corresponding to the correct key in the @features hash to false.

3. Verify that class_eval created the instance methods you expected inside the Element class by calling Element.instance_methods(false). Then reopen the Element class and call accessor :symbol to add two more methods for an instance variable named @symbol.

8

ADVANCED ACTIVE RECORD

When building a new application, work out the data model first. A *data model* is a description of the models in your program, along with their attributes and associations. First, identify the models needed and the relationships between them, and then create tables for these models and test them in the Rails console. Once the data models are working properly, building the rest of the application is much easier.

Some people think of diagrams with boxes and arrows when they hear the words *data model*. These diagrams are unnecessary if you understand how the models relate without them. This chapter does include some basic diagrams, however, to illustrate different associations. In each diagram, the arrows point from the foreign key in a child model to the primary key in the parent model.

In this chapter, you're going to start building a new application from scratch. The application is a social network in the style of Tumblr. Users create accounts and then post text and images for other users to see. A user can follow other users so their friends' posts appear on the timeline on their home page.

First, I'll discuss several advanced data-modeling techniques. Then we'll work our way through the models needed for your new social networking site.

Advanced Data Modeling

When building the blog, you worked with has_many and belongs_to associations. Real-world applications often require more complex associations.

For example, you sometimes need to model an association between two models of the same type, or you might need to model a many-to-many relationship between models. You also might need to store an object hierarchy in the database, but relational databases don't really support inheritance. Finally, you might need to model a class that can associate with multiple different types of models.

I'll discuss these four situations in this section, starting with modeling a relationship between two models of the same type using a self join association.

Self Join Associations

Imagine an application for managing employees at a company. In addition to data such as each employee's name, job title, and salary, you need to store each employee's manager's name. Each employee belongs_to a manager, and a manager has_many subordinates. A manager is also an employee, so you need to set up an association between two different models of the same type.

Recall that a belongs_to association means the model needs a foreign key to link it to another model. A foreign key is a field that identifies the model on the other side of an association. So the employees table needs a field called manager_id to link each employee to a manager. The diagram in Figure 8-1 shows how this relationship works.

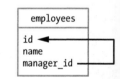

Figure 8-1: Self join association

A *self join association* allows you to model an organizational chart or other tree structure using a single table. The manager_id foreign key points to the id of the employee's manager. This same type of association is also used to model other tree structures such as nested comments, where replies include a parent_id that points to the parent comment.

Once the `manager_id` field has been added to the `employees` table, you can define the associations in the `Employee` model:

```
class Employee < ActiveRecord::Base
❶   has_many :subordinates, class_name: 'Employee',
❷                           foreign_key: 'manager_id'

❸   belongs_to :manager, class_name: 'Employee'
end
```

First, you add a `has_many` association for subordinates. Because this association refers to the `Employee` model, and not a model named `Subordinate`, you must specify `class_name: 'Employee'` ❶. You must also specify the foreign key name, in this case, `manager_id` ❷. Finally, add the `belongs_to` association for the `manager`. Again, you must explicitly state the model's class name because Rails can't figure it out based on the association name ❸.

With these associations in place, you can call the `subordinates` method to get a list of a manager's subordinates. You can also use the methods `manager` and `manager=` to get and set an employee's manager. Almost every employee should have a `manager_id`, as shown in Table 8-1. If your `manager_id` is nil, then you must be the boss!

Table 8-1: The employees Table

id	name	manager_id
1	Alice	NULL
2	Bob	1

Notice that the `manager_id` for Bob is 1. That means Alice is Bob's manager. Alice's `manager_id` is NULL, which is `nil` in Ruby. She's the CEO of this two-person company.

Many-to-Many Associations

Whereas a one-to-many association only involves two tables, a many-to-many association always involves a third table known as a *join table*. The join table stores foreign keys for each side of the association. It `belongs_to` each of the models in the association.

Rails provides two different ways to set up a many-to-many association.

has_and_belongs_to_many

If you're using a join table strictly for the association and need no additional data, then use a `has_and_belongs_to_many` association. You still need to create the join table, but you don't need to define a model for it. The join table must be named after the two models it joins.

For example, authors write many books, and some books have multiple authors. All of the data you need is stored in either the author or book model, so you can create a has_and_belongs_to_many association between authors and books, as in Figure 8-2.

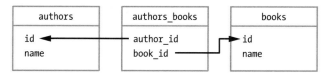

Figure 8-2: has_and_belongs_to_many association

Figure 8-2 shows the Author and Book models with the join table between them. Define the association between these models as shown here:

```
class Author < ActiveRecord::Base
  has_and_belongs_to_many :books
end
```

An author might write many books, but a book can also have many authors:

```
class Book < ActiveRecord::Base
  has_and_belongs_to_many :authors
end
```

For this association to work, the join table between authors and books must be named authors_books and must contain fields author_id and book_id. Use the rails generate command to create an empty migration file:

```
$ bin/rails g migration CreateAuthorsBooks
  invoke  active_record
  create    db/migrate/..._create_authors_books.rb
```

Then edit the migration file to remove the primary key and create the two foreign keys:

```
class CreateAuthorsBooks < ActiveRecord::Migration
  def change
    create_table :authors_books, id: false do |t|
❶     t.references :author, null: false, index: true
      t.references :book, null: false, index: true
    end
  end
end
```

The t.references :author statement ❶ indicates this field is a foreign key that references an Author model. The field is named author_id. The null: false option adds a constraint so NULL values are not allowed, and the index: true option creates a database index to speed up queries on this field. The next line creates the book_id field, also with a NULL constraint and database index.

You can also use the create_join_table method inside the migration to create the join table. This method takes the names of the associations and creates the correct table with no primary key and a foreign key for each association with a NULL constraint. This method does not automatically create indices for the foreign keys. You can add indices as shown here:

```
class CreateAuthorsBooks < ActiveRecord::Migration
  def change
    create_join_table :authors, :books do |t|
      t.index :author_id
      t.index :book_id
    end
  end
end
```

After creating the join table, you don't need to do anything to make the association work. There is no model associated with the join table. With a has_and_belongs_to_many association, Rails manages the join table for you.

has_many :through

If you would like to store additional information in the join table besides the foreign keys of the associated models, use a has_many :through association. For example, you could model the association between bands and venues using a join table named performances. Figure 8-3 shows the relationship among bands, performances, and venues.

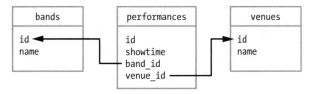

Figure 8-3: has_many :through association

Each performance belongs to a band and a venue. It also has a showtime. The models look like this:

```
class Band < ActiveRecord::Base
  has_many :performances
  has_many :venues, through: :performances
end
```

A band performs many times, and so the band is associated with many different venues through its performances:

```
class Venue < ActiveRecord::Base
  has_many :performances
  has_many :bands, through: :performances
end
```

A venue hosts many performances. The venue is associated with many different bands through the performances it hosts:

```
class Performance < ActiveRecord::Base
  belongs_to :band
  belongs_to :venue
end
```

Performances associate a band with a venue. A venue can also store additional data, such as the showtime of the performance, in the performances table.

Single-Table Inheritance

Sometimes you need to store a hierarchy of classes in the database. Most relational databases don't support inheritance, but you can use *single-table inheritance* to create these models and store the inheritance structure in the database.

For example, imagine you are writing an application to manage a pet store. You need a way to model different types of pets such as dogs and fish. Pet dogs and pet fish share many of the same attributes and methods, so it makes sense for both of them to inherit from a parent class named Pet.

In Rails, you can create a single table for pets and then store records for the two child classes Dog and Fish in the same table. Rails uses a column named *type* to keep track of the type of object stored in each row. In addition to the columns needed by the parent model, you also need to add all columns needed by the child models to the table. You need this because all models are stored in the same table.

The parent model Pet is a normal Active Record model. The Pet model inherits from ActiveRecord::Base:

```
class Pet < ActiveRecord::Base
end
```

The Dog model inherits from Pet:

```
class Dog < Pet
end
```

The Fish model also inherits from Pet:

```
class Fish < Pet
end
```

With these models in place, you can store records of all three types in a single table named pets, shown in Table 8-2.

Table 8-2: The pets Table

id	type	name	cost
1	Dog	Collie	200
2	Fish	Gold Fish	5
3	Dog	Cocker Spaniel	100

These three rows from the pets table hold data for the Dog and Fish models. You can now make calls like Pet.count to count the pets in the table. Calling Dog.count returns 2 and Fish.count returns 1. Because Rails knows teach record type, pet = Pet.find(2) returns an object of type Fish.

You'll look at another example of single-table inheritance in the next section, when you create the post models for your new application.

Polymorphic Associations

With polymorphic associations, a model can belong to more than one other model using a single association. The classic example of a polymorphic association is allowing comments on multiple types of objects. For example, you might want to let people comment on both posts and images. Here is what your comment model might look like using a polymorphic association:

```
class Comment < ActiveRecord::Base
  belongs_to :commentable, polymorphic: true
end
```

Instead of using belongs_to :post or belongs_to :image, you specify that a comment belongs_to something called :commentable. This name can be anything you like, but the convention is to make it an adjective form of the model name.

The comments table will need two fields for this association to work, an integer field named commentable_id and a string field named commentable_type. The commentable_type field holds the class name of the object that owns this comment. This setup is similar to the type column in the single-table inheritance example you saw in the previous section. The commentable_id is a foreign key referring to the id of the object that owns this comment.

Include as: :commentable on the has_many :comments associations in model
that can have comments:

```
class Post < ActiveRecord::Base
  has_many :comments, as: :commentable
end

class Image < ActiveRecord::Base
  has_many :comments, as: :commentable
end
```

The has_many association works the same as always. A method call like
@post.comments returns a list of comments associated with the post. It works
by looking for comments that match both the id of the @post object and the
class name Post.

If your application grows and you need comments on other models, you
can add the same has_many association to the new model without changing
anything in the Comment model.

That's enough theory for now. Let's put some of this knowledge to work.

The Social Application

In this section, you'll build the data model for a social networking service
similar to Tumblr. You need models for users and posts. You also need to
represent a user following another user as well as several different types of
posts, and users should be able to comment on posts.

Start by creating a new, empty Rails application in your code directory:

```
$ cd code
$ rails new social
$ cd social
```

I'm calling my application *social*, but call yours whatever you like. Who
knows, you may launch this app and sell it for a billion dollars someday!

Now let's work through the models needed for this application.

User Model

If this is to be a social site, the first thing you need is a model for users and
the relationships between them. Tumblr, like Twitter, doesn't use the idea of
friendship between users. Instead, you subscribe to another user's updates
by "following" that user.

Start by creating a new resource named User. For now, add string
fields for name and email. You can always add more fields later by creating
another database migration. The following command creates a controller,
model, database migration, and other files for users:

```
$ bin/rails generate resource User name email
```

Create the users table by running this new database migration:

```
$ bin/rake db:migrate
```

Next, you need to create a model to represent the idea of subscriptions. A subscription is a type of self join, but it is a many-to-many association, so you need a join table. What should this model contain? You subscribe to another user's posts by following them. You can call the user you are following a leader. So you need to store a `leader_id` and a `follower_id` in the subscriptions table.

When one user follows another user, the following user's `id` is stored in the `follower_id` field and the other user's `id` is stored in the `leader_id` field. This setup allows you to find a list of a user's followers and leaders easily.

```
$ bin/rails g model Subscription leader:references follower:references
   invoke  active_record
   create    db/migrate/..._create_subscriptions.rb
   create    app/models/subscription.rb
   invoke    test_unit
   create      test/models/subscription_test.rb
   create      test/fixtures/subscriptions.yml
```

Because this is a join table, use the model generator to create a database migration and model for subscriptions. Don't forget to update your database:

```
$ bin/rake db:migrate
```

Now that you've created the tables, you need to update the model files to define the associations. First, open the file *app/models/subscription.rb* in your editor:

```ruby
class Subscription < ActiveRecord::Base
  belongs_to :leader, class_name: 'User'
  belongs_to :follower, class_name: 'User'
end
```

You used `leader:references` and `follower:references` when creating the model, so the Rails model generator added two `belongs_to` associations to the `Subscription` model for you. Both `:leader` and `:follower` actually refer to a `User`, so you need to add the class name `User`. By default, Rails looks for model names that match association names. If you don't specify a class name, Rails looks for models named `Leader` and `Follower`. Figure 8-4 shows the tables for users and subscriptions.

NOTE   *In reality, these tables also include* `created_at` *and* `updated_at` *timestamps, but I left these out of the diagrams in this chapter for brevity.*

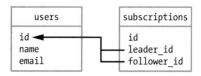

Figure 8-4: Subscription associations

In the subscriptions table, both leader_id and follower_id are foreign keys referring to a user. Now that the Subscription associations are done, let's add the User associations. Open the file *app/models/user.rb* in your editor:

```ruby
class User < ActiveRecord::Base
  has_many :subscriptions, foreign_key: :follower_id,
                           dependent: :destroy
  has_many :leaders, through: :subscriptions
end
```

❶ ❷ ❸

Start with the fact that a user has many subscriptions. In this case, you need to specify the foreign key to use. Normally, you would call this user_id, but you're modeling leaders and followers, so call it follower_id instead ❶. Also specify what happens if this user is deleted with dependent: :destroy ❷. This tells Rails to destroy any associated subscriptions if this user is ever destroyed. Finally, add the has_many:through association to leaders ❸.

Next, add a few methods to the model to make working with the associations easier. You can also use these methods to test the associations in the Rails console:

```ruby
class User < ActiveRecord::Base
  has_many :subscriptions, foreign_key: :follower_id,
                           dependent: :destroy
  has_many :leaders, through: :subscriptions

  def following?(leader)
    leaders.include? leader
  end

  def follow!(leader)
    if leader != self && !following?(leader)
      leaders << leader
    end
  end
end
```

❶

❷ ❸

First, add a *predicate method*, a method returning a true or false value, called following? ❶ to see if the current user is following another user. This method checks to see if the current user's leaders collection includes the leader passed as an argument to the method.

Then, add the `follow!` method ❷ to indicate that the current user is following another user. This method ensures the current user isn't trying to follow himself or herself and isn't already following the other user ❸. If neither case is true, the `leader` passed to this method is inserted into the current user's `leaders` collection with `<<`, the insertion operator.

With these methods in place, you can now launch a Rails console and test your associations:

```
$ bin/rails console
```

Start by creating two users:

```
irb(main):001:0> alice = User.create name: "Alice"
   (0.1ms)  begin transaction
  SQL (0.6ms)  INSERT INTO "users" ...
   (0.8ms)  commit transaction
 => #<User id: 1, name: "Alice", ...>
irb(main):002:0> bob = User.create name: "Bob"
   (0.1ms)  begin transaction
  SQL (0.6ms)  INSERT INTO "users" ...
   (0.8ms)  commit transaction
 => #<User id: 2, name: "Bob", ...>
```

Now, call the `follow!` method on alice and pass in bob. Then call the following? method on alice to confirm that follow worked correctly. Finally, call following? again to see if bob is following alice:

```
irb(main):003:0> alice.follow! bob
  User Exists (0.2ms)  SELECT  ...
   (0.1ms)  begin transaction
  SQL (16.1ms)  INSERT INTO ...
   (20.4ms)  commit transaction
  User Load (0.3ms)  SELECT ...
 => #<ActiveRecord::Associations::CollectionProxy ...>
irb(main):004:0> alice.following? bob
 => true
irb(main):005:0> bob.following? alice
User Exists (0.2ms)  SELECT ...
 => false
```

The call to `alice.follow! bob` adds bob to collection of leaders for alice. Next, the call to `alice.following? bob` checks to see if the `alice.leaders` collection includes bob. It does, so the method returns true. Of course, it doesn't actually look for bob, but the `id` of the `User` referred to as bob. The call to `bob.following? alice` returns false. The `bob.leaders` collection is empty, so bob is not following alice. Tables 8-3 and 8-4 show the users and subscriptions tables after Alice follows Bob, again with the timestamp fields omitted.

Table 8-3: The users Table

id	name	email
1	Alice	NULL
2	Bob	NULL

The users table holds records for alice and bob.

Table 8-4: The subscriptions Table

id	leader_id	follower_id
1	2	1

The subscriptions table holds a single record representing the association between alice and bob. The leader_id is 2, the id of bob; and the follower_id is 1, the id of alice. This means alice is following bob.

At this point, you can get a list of every user that alice is following by calling the leaders method. Having this list is helpful, but it's only half of what you need. You also want to be able to list a user's followers. To do this, use the subscriptions table again, only this time going in the opposite direction.

You need another has_many association on the Subscription model that is the reverse of the existing association. You can then use that association to find followers.

```
class User < ActiveRecord::Base
  has_many :subscriptions, foreign_key: :follower_id,
                           dependent: :destroy
  has_many :leaders, through: :subscriptions

❶ has_many :reverse_subscriptions, foreign_key: :leader_id,
❷                                  class_name: 'Subscription',
                                   dependent: :destroy
❸ has_many :followers, through: :reverse_subscriptions

  def following?(leader)
    leaders.include? leader
  end

  def follow!(leader)
    if leader != self && !following?(leader)
      leaders << leader
    end
  end
end
```

This association is the reverse of the existing :subscriptions association. There's no clever word for the reverse of a subscription, so name the association :reverse_subscriptions. This association uses the leader_id field as the foreign key ❶. Because the association name doesn't match the name of the model, you also need to specify a class name ❷. As with the subscription association, also specify dependent: :destroy so you aren't left with orphan records in the subscriptions table if a user is destroyed. After adding the :reverse_subscriptions association, you can use it to add another has_many :through association for :followers ❸.

Restart the Rails console for these changes to take effect, and then try the new association:

```
❶ irb(main):001:0> alice = User.find(1)
     User Load (0.3ms)  SELECT ...
   => #<User id: 1, name: "Alice", ...>
   irb(main):002:0> bob = User.find(2)
     User Load (0.3ms)  SELECT ...
   => #<User id: 2, name: "Bob", ...>
❷ irb(main):003:0> alice.followers
     User Load (0.2ms)  SELECT ...
   => #<ActiveRecord::Associations::CollectionProxy []>
❸ irb(main):004:0> alice.followers.to_a
   => []
   irb(main):005:0> bob.followers.to_a
     User Load (0.2ms)  SELECT ...
   => [#<User id: 1, name: "Alice", ...>]
```

Because you restarted the console, you first need to find your users in the database ❶. Call the followers method on alice to see if she has any followers ❷. This method returns a type of relation called an ActiveRecord::Associations::CollectionProxy. I made the output a little easier to read by chaining to_a after followers, which converts the output to an array ❸.

The output shows that alice has no followers and bob has a single follower—alice. The User associations and methods are working correctly so far. Now that users can follow each other, let's move on to posts.

Post Models

People don't just want to share plain text on a social network—they also want to share images, links, and videos. We should allow our users to create a different kind of post for each type of content, though the post types will share some common functionality. This sounds like a perfect use for inheritance.

First, create a base model called Post, and then inherit from that class to create models for TextPost, ImagePost, and so on. You can use single-table inheritance to create these models and store the inheritance structure in the database. Because the posts table holds records for all types of posts, you must add columns needed by the other models to the posts table. In addition to the usual title and body fields, add a url field to store the address of an image for image posts and a type field for single-table inheritance.

With those requirements in mind, generate the post resource and update your application's database:

```
$ bin/rails g resource Post title body:text url type user:references
$ bin/rake db:migrate
```

The user:references option adds a user_id field so you can associate post with users. Don't forget to update your application's database.

Now you're ready to create resources for the different types of posts.

```
$ bin/rails g resource TextPost --parent=Post --migration=false
$ bin/rails g resource ImagePost --parent=Post --migration=false
```

Here, I've passed two options to the resource generator. The --parent=Post option indicates that these models inherit from Post and the --migration=false option tells the generator to not create a database migration for this resource. A database migration is not needed because these resources are stored in the posts table you created earlier.

First, let's update the newly created Post model in *app/models/post.rb* to make sure all posts have an associated user and type:

```
class Post < ActiveRecord::Base
  belongs_to :user
❶ validates :user_id, presence: true
❷ validates :type, presence: true
end
```

All posts in our social application belong to an individual user. This validation ensures that a Post can't be created without an associated user_id ❶. The type validation ❷ validates that all records are identified as either a TextPost or an ImagePost.

Now add validations to the TextPost and ImagePost models. First, edit *app/models/image_post.rb* and add a URL validation to the ImagePost model:

```
class ImagePost < Post
  validates :url, presence: true
end
```

The url field holds the address of the image for an ImagePost. Users can copy a URL from an image sharing site such as Flickr or Imgur. The application shouldn't allow an ImagePost to be saved without an image url.

Then update the TextPost model in *app/models/text_post.rb* to check for a post body:

```
class TextPost < Post
  validates :body, presence: true
end
```

The application also shouldn't allow a TextPost to be saved without body text.

While you're editing models, also add the associations for the new post models under the rest of the has_many associations to the User model at *app/models/user.rb:*

```ruby
class User < ActiveRecord::Base
  has_many :subscriptions, foreign_key: :follower_id,
                           dependent: :destroy
  has_many :leaders, :through => :subscriptions

  has_many :reverse_subscriptions, foreign_key: :leader_id,
                                   class_name: 'Subscription',
                                   dependent: :destroy
  has_many :followers, through: :reverse_subscriptions

  has_many :posts, dependent: :destroy
  has_many :text_posts, dependent: :destroy
  has_many :image_posts, dependent: :destroy

  --snip--
```

Now you can restart the Rails console and use these new models:

```
❶ irb(main):001:0> alice = User.find(1)
  User Load (42.0ms)  SELECT ...
  => #<User id: 1, ...>
  irb(main):002:0> post1 = alice.text_posts.create(body: "First Post")
    (0.1ms)  begin transaction
  SQL (0.7ms)  INSERT INTO ...
    (1.9ms)  commit transaction
  => #<TextPost id: 1, ...>
  irb(main):003:0> post2 = alice.image_posts.create(
                              url: "http://i.imgur.com/Y7syDEa.jpg")
    (0.1ms)  begin transaction
  SQL (0.7ms)  INSERT INTO ...
    (1.9ms)  commit transaction
  => #<ImagePost id: 2, ...>
❷ irb(main):004:0> alice.posts.to_a
  Post Load (32.3ms)  SELECT ...
  => [#<TextPost id: 1, ...>, #<ImagePost id: 2, ...>]
❸ irb(main):005:0> alice.text_posts.to_a
  TextPost Load (0.4ms)  SELECT ...
  => [#<TextPost id: 1, ...>]
```

Because you restarted the console, first find the User representing alice ❶. Then create a TextPost and an ImagePost belonging to alice. The posts method on the User model returns all posts associated with that user regardless of type ❷. Note that the TextPost and ImagePost you just created are both returned in the same collection. The text_posts method returns only TextPost objects ❸.

Comment Model

Now that the models for users and posts are in place, create the comments model for the application. Add a text field to hold the body of the comment, a post_id to reference the post that owns this comment, and a user_id to reference the user who left the comment.

Note that I am not using a polymorphic association with these comments. Because my different post types all inherit from the base class Post, I can simply associate Comment with Post, allowing comments on any type of post.

```
$ bin/rails g resource Comment body:text post:references user:references
$ bin/rake db:migrate
```

Also add has_many :comments to the User and Post model to complete the associations among users, posts, and comments. Figure 8-5 shows the tables you created in this chapter and their associations.

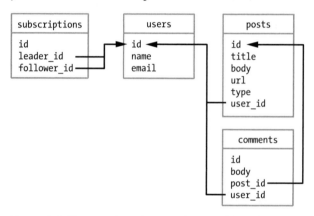

Figure 8-5: The social application data model, with timestamps omitted

With this, you have all of your models and are well on your way to building your new social network.

Summary

I covered some pretty advanced database modeling techniques in this chapter. The User model has several complex associations. The different types of posts demonstrate single-table inheritance. Luckily, the Comment model didn't contain any surprises.

In the next chapter, I'll talk about authentication, and you'll start adding controller actions and views so users can sign up and log in to your social network.

Exercises

1. You specified dependent: :destroy on all has_many associations in this chapter to ensure that dependent models would be removed. For example, because the Post model has a dependent: :destroy association with the User model, if a User is destroyed, then all of the user's posts are also destroyed. What do you think would happen if you specified dependent: :destroy on a belongs_to association?

2. Add validations to the Comment model to ensure that every comment belongs to a User and a Post. Your application shouldn't allow a Comment to be created without a user_id and post_id. You should also ensure that all comments have text in the body field.

3. Use the Rails console to create a new User. Create a TextPost or ImagePost belonging to this User and at least one Comment. Now destroy the User, and make sure the associated Post and Comment are also destroyed.

9

AUTHENTICATION

Identity is a core concept in any social network, and *authentication* is the act of identifying yourself to a system. You want users to be able to sign up for new accounts and log into your application. Although gems like devise and authlogic provide complete authentication systems for Rails applications, in this chapter, you'll get your hands dirty by building your own system instead.

    In addition to the signup, login, and logout actions, you'll also add methods for getting the current logged-in user's identity and redirecting anonymous users to the login page. This authentication system will require controllers and views, so before starting, let's take a moment to add a little style to your site with the Bootstrap framework.

BOOTSTRAP

Bootstrap is an open source frontend framework originally created at Twitter. It provides a collection of CSS and JavaScript files that you can incorporate into a website to provide pleasant typography, a responsive layout that works in both desktop and mobile browsers, and features such as modal dialogs, drop-down menus, and tooltips. Full documentation for Bootstrap is online at *http://getbootstrap.com/*.

You could download the Bootstrap framework and manually integrate the CSS and JavaScript files into your application, but the bootstrap-sass gem can do all of that for you. Since you're already building your own authentication system, save yourself some work here—edit your application's *Gemfile* and add this gem.

```
gem 'bootstrap-sass'
```

Then run the `bin/bundle install` command to update the installed gems. Now that the gem is installed, you need to make a few changes to your CSS and JavaScript files to include Bootstrap. First, update *app/assets/stylesheets/application.css*, as shown here:

```
--snip--
*= require_tree .
*= require bootstrap
*= require_self
*/
```

This code includes the Bootstrap CSS files in your application. Next, include the Bootstrap JavaScript files by editing *app/assets/javascripts/application.js* and adding this line to the end of the file:

```
//= require bootstrap
```

Finally, update the application layout to use Bootstrap styles. Open the file *app/views/layouts/application.html.erb* and change the contents of the body like so:

```
--snip--
<body>
  <div class="container"> ❶
    <%= yield %> ❷
  </div>
</body>
</html>
```

The div with `class="container"` wraps the contents of the page ❶ and provides margins that adjust based on the screen's width, making your site look sharp on both desktop and mobile screens. The `yield` statement ❷ is used by Rails to insert the contents of the view template into the layout.

Now that you have the stylesheets, JavaScript, and basic layout in place, you are all set to start using Bootstrap.

The Authentication System

The purpose of the authentication system is to identify the current user and only display pages the user wants to see or is authorized to see. You'll use a combination of an email address and password to identify users. Email addresses are a good choice because they are globally unique. No two people have the same email address.

In your application, anonymous users are only allowed to see pages for logging in or signing up for a new account. Every other page should be restricted.

Post Index and Show

Before you start building the authentication system, you need data to protect from anonymous users. Let's add the index and show pages for the Post models created in the last chapter. First, you need to add controller actions. Open the file *app/controllers/posts_controller.rb* in your editor and add these index and show methods:

```ruby
class PostsController < ApplicationController
❶   def index
      @posts = Post.all
    end

❷   def show
      @post = Post.find(params[:id])
    end
end
```

These two actions are similar to the index and show actions in the blog from Chapter 4. The index action ❶ retrieves all posts from the database and assigns them to the @posts variable. It then renders the view at *app/views/posts/index.html.erb*. The show action ❷ finds the requested post using the id from the params hash, assigns it to @post, and renders the view at *app/views/posts/show.html.erb*.

Now you need to create corresponding view templates for these actions. Create a new file named *app/views/posts/index.html.erb* and add the following code:

```erb
❶ <div class="page-header">
    <h1>Home</h1>
  </div>

❷ <%= render @posts %>
```

The index view adds a header ❶ using the Bootstrap page-header class and renders the collection @posts ❷ using partials.

Because you're using partials to render the posts, add those next; you'll need a partial for each post type—of which there are two—so you need two partial files.

First, create the file *app/views/text_posts/_text_post.html.erb* and open it
for editing:

```
❶ <div class="panel panel-default">
❷   <div class="panel-heading">
      <h3 class="panel-title">
❸       <%= text_post.title %>
      </h3>
    </div>

❹   <div class="panel-body">
      <p><em>By <%= text_post.user.name %></em></p>

      <%= text_post.body %>
    </div>
  </div>
```

This partial uses Bootstrap's panel component to display a TextPost. The
panel class ❶ adds a gray border around the content. The panel-heading class
❷ adds a light gray background. The title is then rendered inside an h3 element with <%= text_post.title %> ❸. The panel-body class ❹ adds padding to
match the heading. The post author and body are rendered in this section.

Then create the file *app/views/image_posts/_image_post.html.erb* with
the following content. The ImagePost partial is just a slight variation on the
TextPost partial:

```
<div class="panel panel-default">
  <div class="panel-heading">
    <h3 class="panel-title">
      <%= image_post.title %>
    </h3>
  </div>

  <div class="panel-body">
    <p><em>By <%= image_post.user.name %></em></p>

❶   <%= image_tag image_post.url, class: "img-responsive" %>

    <%= image_post.body %>
  </div>
</div>
```

This partial uses the ERB image_tag helper to add an image tag with the
source set to image_post.url ❶, the location of the image. This line also adds
Bootstrap's img-responsive class to the image, which causes it to scale automatically based on the browser width.

With these views in place, start the Rails server and look at the
application:

```
$ bin/rails server
```

Now go to *http://localhost:3000/posts* in your web browser. The Post index view should look similar to Figure 9-1, depending on how many posts you created in the Rails console.

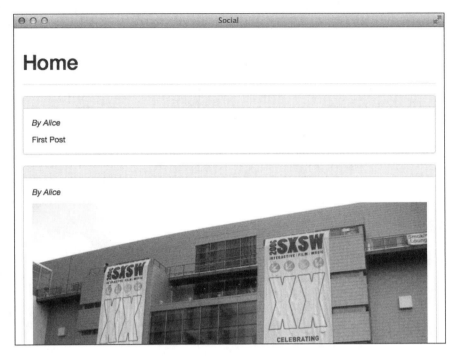

Figure 9-1: The Post index view

You created two posts in the previous chapter, and your application's Post index view currently shows those two posts. You didn't add titles in the last chapter, so the headings are blank.

Now that the Post partials have been created, the Post show view can also use those partials. Create the new file *app/views/posts/show.html.erb* with the following content:

```
<div class="page-header">
  <h1>Post</h1>
</div>
```

❶ `<%= render @post %>`

```
<%= link_to "Home", posts_path,
```
❷ `    class: "btn btn-default" %>`

The show view is similar to the index view with two exceptions. It renders a single post ❶ instead of a collection of posts, and it includes a button ❷ that links back to the posts index page.

Go to *http://localhost:3000/posts/1* to see it in action, as in Figure 9-2.

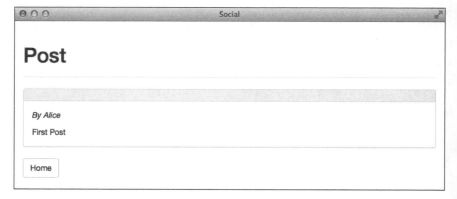

Figure 9-2: The Post show view

Now that the application has actions and views for displaying posts, let's move on to adding authentication to protect these actions from anonymous users.

Sign Up

Here, you'll implement a user sign-up process that asks for an email address, password, and password confirmation. If the user enters an email address that isn't already in the database and provides passwords that match, the system will create a new User and thank the user for signing up.

You can already store the new user's email address because you have a string field named email in the users table. You need to be more careful, however, with passwords. Never store a user's password in plain text. Instead, store a hashed version of the password, known as a *password digest*. The secure password feature in Rails provides built-in support for password hashing, using a hashing algorithm called bcrypt. Bcrypt is a secure one-way hash.

You can enable the secure password feature by calling the method has_secure_password in a Rails model. This method adds the password and password_confirmation attributes to the model and expects the model to have a string field named password_digest. It adds validations that require matching password and password_confirmation attributes on creation. If these attributes match, it automatically hashes the password and stores it in the password_digest field.

First, edit your application's *Gemfile* and add the bcrypt gem. Because many applications include an authentication system, a commented-out line is already available for this gem. Remove the hash mark at the beginning of that line and save the file.

```
gem 'bcrypt', '~> 3.1.7'
```

Anytime you change the *Gemfile*, you also need to run the bin/bundle install command to update the gems installed on your system:

```
$ bin/bundle install
```

The next step is to add the `password_digest` field to the users table and run the database migration with `bin/rake db:migrate` so you can store the user's hashed password:

```
$ bin/rails g migration AddPasswordDigistToUsers password_digest
```

Now you need to turn on the secure password feature for the `User` model. Open *app/models/user.rb* and add the line `has_secure_password` below the `has_many` associations you added in the last chapter. While you're editing that file, also add presence and uniqueness validations for the email field:

```
class User < ActiveRecord::Base
  --snip--

  has_secure_password

  validates :email, presence: true, uniqueness: true

  --snip--
end
```

The default route for creating a new user is *http://localhost:3001/users/new*. That works, but a custom route such as *http://localhost:3001/signup* might be easier to remember.

Edit *config/routes.rb* and add a route for the sign-up page. After a user signs up for an account or logs in to your application, you want to redirect the user to the home page. So set the `root` route to the `posts` index page while you're editing this file.

```
Rails.application.routes.draw do
  resources :comments
  resources :image_posts
  resources :text_posts
  resources :posts
  resources :users

  get 'signup', to: 'users#new', as: 'signup'

  root 'posts#index'
end
```

Open *app/controllers/users_controller.rb* and add the necessary actions to `UsersController` for creating new `Users`:

```
class UsersController < ApplicationController
❶  def new
     @user = User.new
   end

❷  def create
     @user = User.new(user_params)
     if @user.save
```

```
      redirect_to root_url,
        notice: "Welcome to the site!"
    else
      render "new"
    end
  end

  private

  def user_params
    params.require(:user).permit(:name, :email, :password,
                                 :password_confirmation)
  end
end
```

The new method ❶ instantiates an empty new User object and renders the sign-up form. The create method ❷ instantiates a User object using the parameters passed from the form. Then, if the user can be saved, it redirects the user to the root of the site and displays a welcome message. Otherwise, it renders the new user form again.

Now that the controller actions are in place, add the sign-up form in *app/views/users/new.html.erb:*

```
<div class="page-header">
  <h1>Sign Up</h1>
</div>

<%= form_for(@user) do |f| %>
  <% if @user.errors.any? %>
    <div class="alert alert-danger">
      <strong>
        <%= pluralize(@user.errors.count, "error") %>
        prevented you from signing up:
      </strong>
      <ul>
        <% @user.errors.full_messages.each do |msg| %>
          <li><%= msg %></li>
        <% end %>
      </ul>
    </div>
  <% end %>

  <div class="form-group">
    <%= f.label :email %>
    <%= f.email_field :email, class: "form-control" %>
  </div>
  <div class="form-group">
    <%= f.label :password %>
    <%= f.password_field :password, class: "form-control" %>
  </div>
  <div class="form-group">
    <%= f.label :password_confirmation %>
    <%= f.password_field :password_confirmation,
```

❶ (beside `<% if @user.errors.any? %>`)
❷ (beside `<div class="form-group">`)
❸ (beside `<%= f.email_field :email, class: "form-control" %>`)

```
      class: "form-control" %>
  </div>

  <%= f.submit class: "btn btn-primary" %>
<% end %>
```

The first half of this form displays error messages ❶, if any. The form uses a div with the Bootstrap class form-group to group labels and inputs ❷, and adds the class form-control to input controls ❸. Bootstrap uses these classes to apply styles to the form.

Go to *http://localhost:3000/signup* in your web browser to see the sign-up form, as in Figure 9-3.

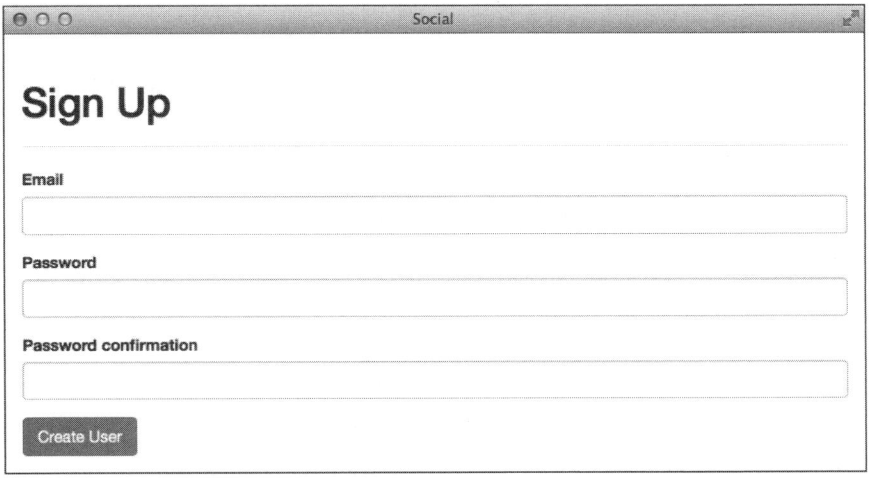

Figure 9-3: The sign-up form

In the create action, you added a flash message to welcome new users, but your views don't have a place for displaying flash messages yet. Bootstrap includes an alert class that's perfect for displaying flash messages. Open the application layout at *app/views/layouts/application.html.erb* and add a section for flash messages, as shown here:

```
--snip--
<body>
  <div class="container">
❶   <% if notice %>
      <div class="alert alert-success"><%= notice %></div>
    <% end %>
❷   <% if alert %>
      <div class="alert alert-danger"><%= alert %></div>
    <% end %>

    <%= yield %>
  </div>
</body>
</html>
```

This application uses two different kinds of flash messages: A notice message ❶ indicates success. A notice is shown in green using Bootstrap's alert-success class. An alert message ❷ indicates an error. An alert is shown in red using the Bootstrap alert-danger class.

In the last chapter, you didn't add email addresses or passwords to the users you created. If you want to log in using alice or bob, you can update their accounts in the Rails console.

```
❶ irb(main):001:0> alice = User.find(1)
  User Load ...
  => #<User id: 1, name: "Alice", ...>
❷ irb(main):002:0> alice.email = "alice@example.com"
  => "alice@example.com"
  irb(main):003:0> alice.password = "password"
  => "password"
  irb(main):004:0> alice.password_confirmation = "password"
  => "password"
❸ irb(main):005:0> alice.save
  --snip--
  => true
```

After starting the Rails console with bin/rails console, find the User by id ❶. Then assign values for the email, password, and password_confirmation ❷. Finally, save the User with alice.save ❸. Repeat these steps for the other User. Make sure the email for each user is unique.

Now that you've seen how to create a form for users to sign up for an account, let's explore how to let them log in.

Log In

A user signing up for an account fills out a form like the one in Figure 9-3 and creates a new user record in the database. On the other hand, there is no model that represents a login, and a login doesn't create a record in the database. Instead, the user's identity is stored in the *session*, a small amount of data used to identify requests from a particular browser to the web server.

Sessions

In general, web servers are *stateless*. That is, they don't remember the identity of a user from one request to the next. You must add this functionality, which you do by storing the currently logged-in user's user_id in the session.

Rails stores session information in a cookie by default. Session cookies are signed and encrypted to prevent tampering. Users can't see the data stored in their session cookie.

Session values in Rails are stored using key-value pairs, and they're accessed like a hash:

```
session[:user_id] = @user.id
```

This command stores @user.id in a cookie on the current user's computer. That cookie is automatically sent to the server with every request to your application.

When a user successfully logs in to your site, you need to store the user_id in the session. Then you look for a user_id in the session on every request. If a user_id is found and a User record matches that id, then you know that user is authenticated. Otherwise, you should redirect the user to the login page.

Implementation

Now let's implement the login process. First, use the Rails generator to create a sessions controller:

```
$ bin/rails g controller Sessions
```

Next, open *config/routes.rb*. Add a new resource called :sessions and add routes for login and logout:

```
Rails.application.routes.draw do
  resources :comments
  resources :image_posts
  resources :text_posts
  resources :posts
  resources :users
  resources :sessions

  get 'signup', to: 'users#new', as: 'signup'

  get 'login', to: 'sessions#new', as: 'login'
  get 'logout', to: 'sessions#destroy', as: 'logout'

  root 'posts#index'
end
```

Now, create a new file named *app/views/sessions/new.html.erb* and add the login form:

```
<div class="page-header">
  <h1>Log In</h1>
</div>
```

```
❶ <%= form_tag sessions_path do %>
    <div class="form-group">
      <%= label_tag :email %>
      <%= email_field_tag :email, params[:email],
        class: "form-control" %>
    </div>
    <div class="form-group">
      <%= label_tag :password %>
      <%= password_field_tag :password, nil,
        class: "form-control" %>
    </div>
    <%= submit_tag "Log In", class: "btn btn-primary" %>
  <% end %>
```

Notice that I'm using form_tag ❶ here instead of form_for. The sign-up process used form_for because that form was associated with the User model. Use form_tag now because the login form is not associated with a model.

The sessions controller handles login and logout. Edit *app/controllers/sessions_controller.rb* to add these actions:

```
  class SessionsController < ApplicationController
❶   def new
    end

❷   def create
      user = User.find_by(email: params[:email])
      if user && user.authenticate(params[:password])
        session[:user_id] = user.id
        redirect_to root_url, notice: "Log in successful!"
      else
        flash.now.alert = "Invalid email or password"
        render "new"
      end
    end

❸   def destroy
      session[:user_id] = nil
      redirect_to root_url, notice: "Log out successful!"
    end
  end
```

The new method ❶ renders the login form. The controller action doesn't need to do anything. Remember that actions render a view file matching their name by default. In this case, the new method renders the view at */app/views/sessions/new.html.erb*. The create method ❷ looks for a user record by email address. If it finds a matching user and that user can be authenticated with the provided password, it stores the user_id in the session and redirects to the home page. Otherwise, it adds an error message to the flash and redisplays the login form. The destroy method ❸ clears the user_id stored in the session and redirects to the home page.

Go to *http://localhost:3000/login* to see the login form shown in Figure 9-4.

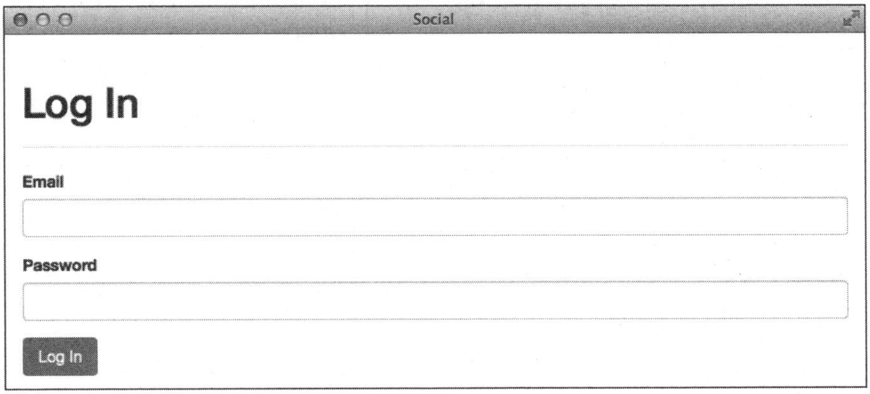

Figure 9-4: The login form

Users can log in and log out now, but the rest of the application has no way to know anything about the current user. As you add features to the application, the identity of the current user will be used frequently. For example, the application uses the current user to decide which posts to display and to assign ownership to any new posts or comments created. Now let's add the methods needed to make the authentication system available to the rest of the application.

Current User

First, you need to be able to identify the currently logged-in user. Add the current_user method to ApplicationController in *app/controllers/application _controller.rb* and make it a helper method. That way, it will be available in all controllers and views, laying the groundwork for other parts of the app to access the currently logged-in user:

```
class ApplicationController < ActionController::Base
  # Prevent CSRF attacks by raising an exception.
  # For APIs, you may want to use :null_session instead.
  protect_from_forgery with: :exception

  private

  def current_user
    if session[:user_id]
      @current_user ||= User.find(session[:user_id])
    end
  end
  helper_method :current_user
end
```

The current_user method returns a User object representing the currently logged-in user. This method returns nil when no one is logged in, so you can also use it in conditional statements that should have different results when no user is logged in.

For example, use the current_user method to add a logout link when a user is logged in or show links to log in and sign up when no one is logged in. Open *app/views/layouts/application.html.erb* and add this code just above the yield statement:

```erb
--snip--
<div class="pull-right">
  <% if current_user %>
    <%= link_to 'Log Out', logout_path %>
  <% else %>
    <%= link_to 'Log In', login_path %> or
    <%= link_to 'Sign Up', signup_path %>
  <% end %>
</div>

  <%= yield %>
  </div>
</body>
</html>
```

Now logged-in users should see a link to log out, and anonymous users should see links to either log in or sign up.

Authenticate User

In any social app, certain pages should not be available to anonymous users. The last thing you need is a way to restrict pages so only authenticated users can view them. You can do this with the Rails before_action method.

A before_action is a method that runs automatically before any other action in the controller. These methods are sometimes used to remove duplication by loading data needed by several different actions. A before_action can also halt the current request by rendering or redirecting to another location.

Create a method named authenticate_user! that redirects to the login page if there is no current user. Add this method to the ApplicationController in *app/controllers/application_controller.rb* so it is available in all controllers:

```ruby
class ApplicationController < ActionController::Base
  # Prevent CSRF attacks by raising an exception.
  # For APIs, you may want to use :null_session instead.
  protect_from_forgery with: :exception

  private

  def current_user
    if session[:user_id]
```

```
    @current_user ||= User.find(session[:user_id])
    end
  end
  helper_method :current_user

  def authenticate_user!
    redirect_to login_path unless current_user
  end
end
```

Because you set the posts index page as the home page of your application, let's try this method in the posts controller. Open the file *app/controllers/posts_controller.rb* and add a before_action:

```
class PostsController < ApplicationController
  before_action :authenticate_user!

  --snip--
end
```

Now if an anonymous user tries to access the home page, he or she should be redirected to the login page automatically. Be sure you don't add this before_action to the sessions page. If you do, anonymous users won't be able to access the login page!

Use Current User

Now that your application knows who's logged in, you can change the home page to display only posts authored by the current user or anyone the current user is following. This type of home page is usually arranged in chronological order and called a *timeline*.

The first thing you need to do is add a method to the User model to return a user_id list that you can use to query posts. Let's call this method timeline_user_ids. Open the file *app/models/user.rb* and add this method near the end:

```
  --snip--

  def timeline_user_ids
❶   leader_ids + [id]
  end
end
```

The has_many :leaders association added in Chapter 8 automatically adds a method called leader_ids that returns an array of the id values of this user's leaders—or the people whose posts the user is following. The timeline_user_ids method adds the current user's id to the array returned by leader_ids and returns the new array ❶, which should contain every user you want to display on the timeline.

Now open *app/controllers/posts_controller.rb* and update the `index` action to use this method:

```
def index
  user_ids = current_user.timeline_user_ids
  @posts = Post.where(user_id: user_ids)
               .order("created_at DESC")
end
```

Instead of just fetching every post with `Post.all`, the `index` action first obtains the list of `user_ids` returned by `current_user.timeline_user_ids`. It then initializes `@posts` to include every post that should be in the timeline based on those ids. Also add an `order` clause because timelines are shown in reverse chronological order.

Log in to see the `Post` index page in Figure 9-5.

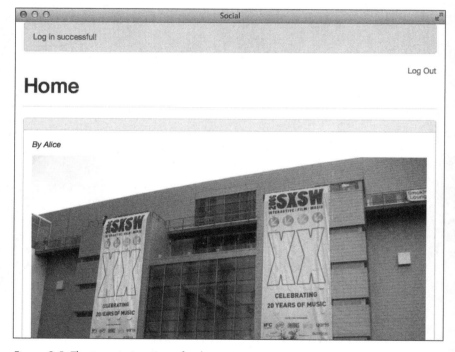

Figure 9-5: The `Post` index view after login

Click the Log Out link and confirm that you're redirected to the Log In page.

Summary

Your application is really starting to take shape now. You have some pretty good-looking styles in place thanks to Bootstrap. Users can now sign up, log in, and log out. You can also restrict access to pages based on whether a user is authenticated.

You've written a lot of code, but so far you've only tested it by clicking around in the browser. This isn't too bad when you only have a few actions to test. As the number of actions in your application grows, however, this sort of testing gets tedious.

In the next chapter, you'll learn about automated testing of models and controllers. We'll look at the default test framework already included by Rails, write tests for various parts of the application, and learn a little about test-driven development.

Exercises

1. You added a post show action and view, but currently you can't get to the page for an individual post without typing in the URL. Use the Rails time_ago_in_words helper to create a link to the post in the TextPost and ImagePost partials based on the created_at field.

2. Add comments to posts. The process is similar to adding comments to the blog at the end of Chapter 5. First, update the post show page at *app/views/posts/show.html.erb* to render a collection of comments and a form for adding a new comment at the bottom as shown here:

```
--snip--

<h3>Comments<h3>
<%= render @post.comments %>

<h4>New Comment</h4>
<%= form_for @post.comments.build do |f| %>
  <div class="form-group">
    <%= f.label :body %><br>
    <%= f.text_area :body, class: "form-control" %>
  </div>
❶ <%= f.hidden_field :post_id %>
  <%= f.submit class: "btn btn-primary" %>
<% end %>
```

The form includes the post_id of the current post in a hidden field ❶. Next, add the create action to CommentsController at *app/controllers/comments_controller.rb*:

```
def create
  @comment = current_user.comments.build(comment_params)

  if @comment.save
    redirect_to post_path(@comment.post_id),
                notice: 'Comment was successfully created.'
  else
    redirect_to post_path(@comment.post_id),
                alert: 'Error creating comment.'
  end
end
```

Also add the private `comment_params` method to `CommentsController`. In addition to the comment body, also permit the `post_id` passed in params:

```
def comment_params
  params.require(:comment).permit(:body, :post_id)
end
```

Make sure only authenticated users can access this controller. Finally, create the comment partial *app/views/comments/_comment.html.erb*. This partial needs to show the name of the user who added the comment and the comment's body.

3. How secure is the authentication system? Look at the `password_digest` field for a `User`. Also, examine the cookie placed on your computer after you log in to the application. Can you figure out the data contained in either of these?

10

TESTING

So far, you've tested your code by typing in the Rails console and clicking links in the web browser. As you add more features to your application, however, this won't scale. And even with more effective test methods, you'll still have to remember to retest everything in the application after you add each feature. Otherwise you might miss a regression.

Rather than manually testing your application, you can write automated tests in Ruby to ensure your code is correct and meets all of your requirements. Once you have a set of automated tests in place, you can run an entire suite of tests to catch regressions, helping you to refactor your code with confidence.

Several different test frameworks are available for Ruby. In this chapter, we focus on the default test framework used by Rails: MiniTest.

Testing in Rails

Basic test skeletons are automatically created in the *test* directory when you generate Rails models and controllers. These are just starting points: They don't really test anything, but having the framework in place makes adding your own tests much easier.

In this chapter, I'll discuss testing models and controllers. You'll learn how to test individual components and the interactions between components. But first, let's prepare your environment for testing.

Preparing to Test

So far you've been working in the Rails development environment while building the application. The Rails test environment is preconfigured for testing, but you still must do a few things before running your tests.

The test environment uses a separate database just for running tests. First, make sure your application's *db/schema.rb* is up to date by running database migrations:

```
$ bin/rake db:migrate
```

The test database is automatically re-created before each test run to ensure that tests don't depend on data already in the database.

Running Tests

Now that the test database is set up, you're ready to run your tests. Rails provides several different rake tasks for running the various types of tests you'll create.

The bin/rake test command runs all tests by default. If you include the name of a test file on the command line, it only runs the tests in that file. While working on a particular model or controller, running the tests associated with that class is faster.

This command runs all of the tests in the file *test/models/user_test.rb*:

```
$ bin/rake test test/models/user_test.rb
```

After a short pause, you should see output like this:

```
Run options: --seed 46676

# Running:

Finished in 0.001716s, 0.0000 runs/s, 0.0000 assertions/s.

0 runs, 0 assertions, 0 failures, 0 errors, 0 skips
```

As the last line indicates, no tests have been defined yet. Open *test/models/user_test.rb* in your editor and let's add some tests.

```
❶ require 'test_helper'

❷ class UserTest < ActiveSupport::TestCase
❸   # test "the truth" do
     #   assert true
     # end
   end
```

This test file first requires the file *test/test_helper.rb* ❶, which holds the configuration for all tests. The test helper also loads all *fixtures*, or sample data, and can include helper methods for tests. Next, the test file defines a *test case* named UserTest by inheriting from ActiveSupport::TestCase ❷. A test case is a set of tests related to a class. Inside the test case, a simple example test ❸ is provided in the comments.

The commented-out test doesn't really test anything even if you uncomment it, so you could remove it. But these lines do show the basic structure of all tests, so let's examine them before moving forward:

```
❶ test "the truth" do
❷   assert true
   end
```

The test method ❶ accepts a test name and a block of code to execute. This block contains one or more assertions ❷. An *assertion* tests a line of code for an expected result. The assert method shown here expects its argument to evaluate to a true value. If the assertion is true, the test passes and a single dot is printed. Otherwise, the test fails and an *F* is printed along with a message identifying the failing test.

Now let's follow this basic test structure to add a real test to this file. I find it helpful to open the model I'm testing, in this case, *app/models/user.rb*, and the test file at the same time. I usually add tests for any custom methods I've added to a model and verify that the model's validations are working as expected. Looking at the user model, you see several has_many associations, followed by the Rails has_secure_password method, a validation, and the methods you've written.

First, let's make sure you can create a valid user. Remember, the has_secure_password method adds validations for attributes named password and password_confirmation. Users are also required to have a unique email address, so to create a valid user, you must provide email, password, and password_confirmation.

```
   test "saves with valid attributes" do
❶   user = User.new(
       email: "user@example.com",
       password: "password",
       password_confirmation: "password"
     )
❷   assert user.save
   end
```

Here, you instantiate a new User object with valid attributes ❶ and assert that it saves ❷.

Run the tests in this file again:

```
$ bin/rake test test/models/user_test.rb
Run options: --seed 40521

# Running:

❶ .

Finished in 0.067091s, 14.9051 tests/s, 14.9051 assertions/s.

❷ 1 runs, 1 assertions, 0 failures, 0 errors, 0 skips
```

The single dot ❶ represents the single test. The last line of output ❷ tells you that you ran one test with one assertion and had zero failures.

You could continue adding tests at this point, but manually creating users for all of your tests will get tedious. Luckily, Rails includes the fixtures I mentioned earlier, which can automatically create as many model objects with sample data as you need.

Using Fixtures

Fixtures provide sample data for tests, and they are written in a format called *YAML*. YAML originally stood for *Yet Another Markup Language*, but is now a recursive acronym for *YAML Ain't Markup Language*. Fixtures are automatically loaded into the test database by the file *tests/test_helper.rb* and are available to all test cases.

User Fixtures

Open the file *test/fixtures/users.yml*, remove its contents, and create two sample users:

```
❶ user1:
❷   email: user1@example.com
❸   password_digest: <%= BCrypt::Password.create "password" %>

user2:
    email: user2@example.com
    password_digest: <%= BCrypt::Password.create "password" %>
```

This code adds sample data for two users. The YAML file begins with the name of the first fixture followed by a colon ❶. In this case, the fixture is named user1. The indented lines under the name specify attributes. The first user has an email address of user1@example.com ❷.

You can even use ERB to help add data to fixtures. Rather than precompute the values for the password_digest field, use the BCrypt::Password.create method to create the password_digest ❸ dynamically . This method is part of the bcrypt gem you installed in Chapter 9.

Refer to one of these users in your tests by calling the users method and passing the name of the user you want. For example, `users(:user1)` returns the first user just defined.

Go back to the user tests in *test/models/user_test.rb* and let's try the new fixtures:

```
    test "validates email presence" do
❶     @user1 = users(:user1)
❷     @user1.email = nil

❸     assert_not @user1.valid?
    end
```

This test uses a fixture to initialize a user ❶, sets the user's `email` to nil ❷, and ensures the user is not valid with the `assert_not` method ❸. The `assert_not` method only passes if its condition is a false value.

This test proves that an email is required; now you'll add a test for email uniqueness.

```
    test "validates email uniqueness" do
❶     @user1 = users(:user1)
      @user2 = users(:user2)

❷     @user1.email = @user2.email

❸     assert_not @user1.valid?
    end
```

This test uses fixtures to initialize two users ❶, sets the first user's `email` equal to the second user's `email` ❷, and asserts ❸ that the first user is no longer valid. The second user is still valid because the first user can't be saved with invalid data. You can look at the test log in *log/test.log* to see the queries being run for each test.

Fixtures have `id` values based on a hash of the fixture name, and those values are always the same. For example, the `id` for `@user1` is 206669143. This value never changes. Associations between fixtures are created by name because the `id` of each fixture is based on its name. The `Post` fixtures discussed next include associations with the `User` fixtures you created earlier.

Post Fixtures

Rails automatically created fixture files for the `TextPost` and `ImagePost` types. You'll include both types of fixtures in the `Post` file. The fixture files for the other types will cause an error, so delete the files *test/fixtures/text_posts.yml* and *test/fixtures/image_posts.yml* before moving on.

Now open the file *test/fixtures/posts.yml* and create some sample posts:

```
post1:
  title: Title One
  body: Body One
```

```
  type: TextPost
  user: user1

post2:
  title: Title Two
  url: http://i.imgur.com/Y7syDEa.jpg
  type: ImagePost
  user: user1

post3:
  title: Title Three
  body: Body Three
  type: TextPost
  user: user2
```

Here, you have three posts. The first two belong to the User named *user1* and the third belongs to *user2*. You'll put these to good use a little later when you add tests for the Post model.

Putting Assertions to Work

Assertions are the building blocks of tests. You've already seen a few assertions, such as assert and assert_not, in the tests you've written so far. The MiniTest library contains more, and Rails adds a few of its own. Here are some of the most commonly used assertions:

assert *test*
>   Passes if the test expression evaluates to true

assert_empty *obj*
>   Passes if obj.empty? is true

assert_equal *expected, actual*
>   Passes if the expected value equals the actual value

assert_includes *collection, obj*
>   Passes if collection.includes?(obj) returns true

assert_instance_of *class, obj*
>   Passes if obj.instance_of?(class) is true

assert_match *regexp, string*
>   Passes if the given string matches the regular expression regexp

assert_nil *obj*
>   Passes if obj.nil? is true

Each of these assertions also comes in a "not" form. For example, assert_not passes if the expression being tested is false and assert_not_equal passes if the expected value is not equal to the actual value. Assertions also accept an optional message parameter, which is a string that prints if the assertion fails.

Let's put our knowledge of assertions to work and add a few more tests to the user model. Here's the first one:

```
    test "should follow leader" do
❶    @user1 = users(:user1)
     @user2 = users(:user2)

❷    @user1.follow!(@user2)

❸    assert_equal 1, @user1.leaders.count
     assert_equal 1, @user2.followers.count
    end
```

This test creates two users using fixtures ❶ and then calls the `follow!` method on `@user1` with `@user2` as an argument ❷. It then ensures that `@user1` has one leader and `@user2` has one follower ❸.

This next test verifies the `following?` method works correctly:

```
    test "following? should be true" do
     @user1 = users(:user1)
     @user2 = users(:user2)

     @user1.follow!(@user2)

     assert @user1.following?(@user2)
    end
```

It again uses fixtures to create two users and then calls the `follow!` method on `@user1` with `@user2` as an argument and finally ensures that `@user1.following?(@user2)` is true.

Eliminating Duplication with Callbacks

The tests you've made should all work correctly, but I've introduced some duplication in the code. Almost every test uses fixtures to create users. Remember, don't repeat yourself. Luckily, test cases include two callbacks that can help eliminate this duplication. *Callbacks* are methods that are called automatically before and after each test.

The setup method is called before each test, and the `teardown` method is called after each test. These methods are commonly used to initialize objects that are employed in multiple tests. You can use the `setup` method to initialize the values of `@user1` and `@user2` automatically.

```
   class UserTest < ActiveSupport::TestCase
❶   def setup
      @user1 = users(:user1)
      @user2 = users(:user2)
     end

   --snip--
```

```
❷   test "following? should be true" do
      @user1.follow!(@user2)

      assert @user1.following?(@user2)
    end
  end
```

Now that `@user1` and `@user2` are being initialized ❶ in the setup method, you can remove the duplication from each of the tests, as shown in the rewritten test for following? ❷.

Model Tests

The tests you've seen so far are model tests. *Model tests* verify the behavior of your application's models. These types of tests were previously called *unit tests*. I typically add tests for validations and for any custom methods I've written.

I've covered both of these for the `User` model, so now let's add tests for the `Post` model. You may also want to refer to the `Post` model in *app/models/post.rb* as you write tests.

```
class Post < ActiveRecord::Base
  belongs_to :user
  has_many :comments, dependent: :destroy

  validates :user_id, presence: true
  validates :type, presence: true
end
```

The `Post` model is still pretty simple. A post belongs to a user and can have many comments. It also validates the presence of a `user_id` and a `type`. Let's add a test to verify that a `Post` has a `user_id`. Open the file *test/models/post_test.rb* in your editor:

```
require 'test_helper'

class PostTest < ActiveSupport::TestCase
❶   def setup
      @post1 = posts(:post1)
      @post2 = posts(:post2)
    end

❷   test "validates user_id presence" do
      @post1.user_id = nil

      assert_not @post1.valid?
    end
  end
```

The setup method ❶ initializes two posts that you can refer to in your tests. The first test ❷ verifies that a Post without a user_id is not valid.

Since you have model tests for the users and posts now, you can use the bin/rake test:models command to run all model tests:

```
$ bin/rake test:models
Run options: --seed 47072

# Running:

......

Finished in 0.234202s, 25.6189 runs/s, 29.8887 assertions/s.

6 runs, 7 assertions, 0 failures, 0 errors, 0 skips
```

If this command results in an error, delete the unused fixture files for the TextPost and ImagePost models as mentioned earlier. Delete *test/fixtures/text_posts.yml* and *test/fixtures/image_posts.yml*.

The other post types have validations of their own. For example, the TextPost validates the presence of a body, and the ImagePost validates the presence of a url. Since we already have TextPost and ImagePost fixtures, let's add tests for both of those validations:

```
      test "TextPost requires body" do
❶       assert_instance_of TextPost, @post1

❷       @post1.body = nil

❸       assert_not @post1.valid?
      end

      test "ImagePost requires url" do
        assert_instance_of ImagePost, @post2

        @post2.url = nil

        assert_not @post2.valid?
      end
```

Both of these tests follow the same pattern. First, verify that @post1 is an instance of TextPost ❶. Next, set the body of @post1 to nil ❷. Finally, verify that @post1 is no longer valid ❸. The ImagePost assertions do the same, but for @post2.

Controller Tests

Controller tests verify the actions of a single controller by simulating requests to your application and validating the responses. Controller tests ensure that a controller action responds successfully to valid requests, and that it renders the correct view or redirects to the correct location. These types of tests were previously called *functional tests*.

Controller Test Helpers

Rails includes several helper methods and variables that make controller tests easier to write.

The methods get, post, put, patch, head, and delete simulate a request to a controller action. These methods can take two optional hashes: one representing request parameters and another representing the current session.

After a request has been made with one of those six methods, the following four hashes become available:

assigns   Contains the instance variables assigned in the controller action

cookies   Contains any cookie values set in the action

flash   Holds the flash values set in the action

session   Contains any session values set by the action

Your tests also have access to three instance variables: @controller contains the controller processing the request; @request is the request being processed; and @response is the controller's response to the request.

Controller Test Assertions

Rails adds several assertions specifically for controller tests in addition to those you've already seen. Controller actions always either render a response or redirect to a different URL.

assert_response *type*
Passes if the HTTP response matches a specific status code. Use a status code or one of the symbols :success, :redirect, :missing, or :error for type.

assert_redirected_to *options*
Passes if the request causes a redirect to the path given in options.

assert_template *expected*
Passes if the request renders the expected template.

These assertions verify that a controller action correctly responds to a request. For a simple GET request, assert_response :success might be the only test needed. If the controller action assigns an instance variable, you should also verify that assignment.

Let's add controller tests for the new and create actions in UsersController. First, test that the new action successfully renders the sign-up form with a newly created instance of the User model. Open the file *test/controllers/users_controller_test.rb* to add the following test:

```
   test "should get new with new user" do
❶    get :new

❷    user = assigns(:user)

❸    assert user.new_record?
     assert_response :success
   end
```

This test issues a GET request for the new user page ❶, gets a copy of the value assigned to the instance variable @user ❷ in the controller, and verifies that user is a new record ❸ and the response was successful.

The next test checks the ability to create new users given valid data:

```
   test "should create user" do
❶    params = {
       user: {
         email: "user@example.com",
         password: "password",
         password_confirmation: "password"
       }
     }

❷    post :create, params

❸    assert_redirected_to root_url
   end
```

This test is a bit more complex because the create action expects a hash of values for the new user ❶. This test issues a POST request to the create action using the params hash ❷ and then verifies that the action redirects to the root_url ❸.

The previous test checks what happens when a User is successfully saved. You should test the other path through the controller action, that is, when the User can't be saved. You could add a test that attempts to create a user with invalid attributes and verifies the new user template is rendered again.

Run the new controller tests with the bin/rake test:controllers command:

```
$ bin/rake test:controllers
```

The UsersController tests should pass successfully, so let's move on to the PostsController. Verify that the before_action method authenticate_user! is working correctly so your application won't show posts to unauthenticated users.

Open the file *test/controllers/posts_controller_test.rb* in your editor and add the following tests:

```
  test "redirects anonymous users to login" do
❶   get :index
❷   assert_redirected_to login_url
  end

  test "get index for authenticated users" do
❸   user1 = users(:user1)

❹   get :index, {}, { user_id: user1.id }
    assert_response :success
  end
```

The first test attempts to GET the post index page ❶ and verifies the action redirects to the login page ❷. The second test initializes a user using a fixture ❸ then issues the GET request for the index page with a user_id in the session ❹. Simulating a logged-in user by including a valid user_id in the session should result in a successful response.

Integration Tests

Integration tests verify the interaction between several different controllers. These are commonly used to test the *flow* between several pages of your application. An example of a flow would be logging in to the application, viewing a page, and then performing some other action. Each of these actions could be covered by controller tests. An integration test ensures that they all work together.

Integration Helpers

Because integration tests generally involve moving between pages in the application, your tests need not only to make requests to actions but also to follow any redirects. The helper methods redirect? and follow_redirect! check to see if the last request resulted in a redirect and follow a redirect response, respectively.

If you know that a request results in a redirect, more specific methods are available. You can use get_via_redirect, post_via_redirect, put_via_redirect, patch_via_redirect, or delete_via_redirect to make the appropriate request and also follow the redirect.

Testing a Flow

Rails doesn't create integration tests automatically like model and controller tests because Rails has no way of knowing which flows you want to test. Although they are not created automatically, Rails does include a generator you can use to create integration tests.

Let's add an integration test to verify that a user can log in to the application, see the home page, and then log out. First, use the bin/rails generate command to create a new integration test:

```
$ bin/rails g integration_test user_flow
```

This command creates a new file named *test/integration/user_flow_test.rb*. Open that file in your editor and let's add a test:

```
require 'test_helper'

class UserFlowTest < ActionDispatch::IntegrationTest

  test "user login, browse, and logout" do
    user = users(:user1)
❶   get "/login"

    assert_response :success

❷   post_via_redirect "/sessions",
        email: user.email,
        password: "password"

    assert_equal "/", path

❸   get_via_redirect "/logout"

    assert_equal "/login", path
  end
end
```

This test looks like an extended controller test. The test requests a page with get ❶ and then verifies a successful response. You know that a user logs in to the application with a POST request to the sessions path and is then redirected to the home page, so you use the post_via_redirect method to submit the user's email address and password and then follow the redirect automatically ❷. Finally, the test issues a GET request for the logout page ❸ and is redirected back to the login page.

Enter the following command to run the integration test:

```
$ bin/rake test test/integration/user_flow_test.rb
Run options: --seed 51886

# Running:

.

Finished in 1.049118s, 0.9532 runs/s, 2.8595 assertions/s.

1 runs, 3 assertions, 0 failures, 0 errors, 0 skips
```

This test confirms that a user can log in to the application, view the home page, and then log out successfully.

This path is basically the only one a user can take through the application at this time. As you add more actions to the application, you can create integration tests to verify that other flows work correctly.

Adding Features with Test-Driven Development

The tests written so far have all verified existing functionality, but some Rails developers use tests to define features before implementing them, a practice called *test-driven development (TDD)*. In TDD, you write a test first and then add code to make the test pass. Once the test passes, you can refactor the code if necessary. If you follow TDD, you won't have to worry about parsing your code later to figure out what functionality to verify.

TDD is usually a three-step process known as red-green-refactor:

1. Write a failing test (red).
2. Write code to make the test pass (green).
3. Refactor as needed (refactor).

By following this process, you can be confident that new functionality meets the requirements specified in the test and that it did not introduce any regressions.

Let's use TDD to add features to our social application. Although many features are still missing, let's focus on these:

- Add a user show page showing a user's posts and a Follow button.
- Give users the ability to create new posts.

For each of these features, you'll first write a failing test and then write code to make the test pass.

Show User

The user show page displays the user's name and posts. It should also include a button to allow other users to follow this user. To add the user show page, you need to add a show method to the user controller and create a corresponding view. You know the controller should assign an instance variable named @user for the view to use and respond with success, so let's add a test for that.

Open the file *test/controllers/users_controller_test.rb* and add this test:

```
test "should show user" do
  user = users(:user1)

  get :show, id: user.id
```

```
  assert assigns(:user)
  assert_response :success
end
```

Now, run the test and make sure it fails:

```
$ bin/rake test test/controllers/users_controller_test.rb
```

Running this test should result in an error. The action show could not be found for UsersController because you haven't created it yet. So let's add the show action to *app/controllers/users_controller.rb*:

```
class UsersController < ApplicationController
  def show
    @user = User.find(params[:id])
    @posts = @user.posts.order("created_at DESC")
  end

  --snip--
```

Save the file and run the tests again. This time you should see a different error. The template is missing. Create a new file named *app/views/users/ show.html.erb*, and add that template now:

```
<div class="page-header">
  <h1>User</h1>
</div>

<p class="lead"><%= @user.name %></p>

<h2>Posts</h2>

<%= render @posts %>

<%= link_to "Home", root_path,
      class: "btn btn-default" %>
```

Save this file and run the tests again. All tests should now pass, but you still have one problem. This page shows the user's email address and the user's posts, but no one can follow the user!

Following a user creates a record in the subscriptions table in the database. Because this has to happen on the server, adding the Follow button requires a controller action and a new route to that action.

Add another controller test to *test/controllers/users_controller_test.rb* to describe this action:

```
  test "should follow user" do
❶   user1 = users(:user1)
    user2 = users(:user2)

❷   get :follow, { id: user2.id }, { user_id: user1.id }
```

❸   assert user1.following? user2

```
      assert_redirected_to user_url(user2)
    end
```

This test first creates two users using fixtures ❶. Next, it issues a GET request for the follow action with the second user's id as a parameter and the first user's id in the session ❷. This simulates user1 following user2. Finally, it verifies that user1 is now following user2 and that the request redirects back to the show page for user2 ❸.

Now open the file *app/controllers/users_controller.rb*, and add the follow action after the other actions, but before the private methods:

```
class UsersController < ApplicationController
  --snip--

  def follow
❶    @user = User.find(params[:id])
❷    if current_user.follow!(@user)
❸      redirect_to @user, notice: "Follow successful!"
    else
      redirect_to @user, alert: "Error following."
    end
  end

  private
  --snip--
```

This method finds the correct user using the id parameter ❶, calls the follow! method on current_user ❷, and then redirects to @user ❸.

Now open *config/routes.rb* and add a route to the new follow action:

```
Rails.application.routes.draw do
  --snip--

  get 'signup', to: 'users#new', as: 'signup'
  get 'follow/:id', to: 'users#follow', as: 'follow_user'

  --snip--
end
```

I added this under the signup route because these actions are both in the user controller. Now, back in *app/views/users/show.html.erb,* you can add the Follow button:

```
--snip--
<p class="lead"><%= @user.name %></p>

<%= link_to "Follow", follow_user_path(@user),
    class: "btn btn-default" %>

<h2>Posts</h2>
--snip--
```

The Follow button is similar to the Home button; it's actually a link with Bootstrap's btn and btn-default styles applied to make it look like a button.

You can now run the controller tests again and verify that they all pass. You can also start the Rails server if it isn't already running and go to *http://localhost:3000/users/1* in your web browser to see the show page for the first user, as shown in Figure 10-1.

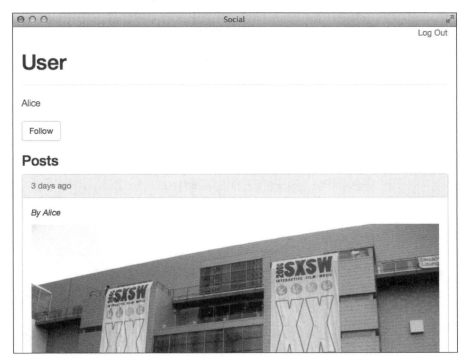

Figure 10-1: The user show page

Figure 10-1 is the show page with the user's name, a button for following this user, and the user's posts.

Create Post

Now let's give users the ability to add posts. Adding posts requires two controller actions: new and create. The new action also requires a matching view. The create action should redirect to the newly created post, so a view isn't needed.

Your application has two different types of posts. Start by adding the ability to create posts of type TextPost. The new action in TextPostsController should instantiate a new TextPost object and render a form for that object. Add a failing test to *test/controllers/text_posts_controller_test.rb* and then get to work:

```
    test "get new with new post" do
❶    user1 = users(:user1)

❷    get :new, {}, { user_id: user1.id }
```

```
  text_post = assigns(:text_post)

  assert text_post.new_record?
  assert_response :success
end
```

The test first creates a new user using a fixture ❶ and then issues a GET request for the new action with user_id set in the session ❷. This step is necessary because the TextPostsController requires an authenticated user. The test then gets the text_post instance variable, verifies it's a new record, and verifies a successful response. Run the tests and watch this one fail:

```
$ bin/rake test test/controllers/text_posts_controller_test.rb
```

The error message should indicate that the new action is missing from TextPostsController. Open *app/controllers/text_posts_controller.rb*, and add the new action:

```
class TextPostsController < ApplicationController
  def new
    @text_post = TextPost.new
  end
end
```

You almost have enough to get the test to pass. The last step is to add the corresponding view. Create the file *app/views/text_posts/new.html.erb*, and add the following content:

```
<div class="page-header">
  <h1>New Text Post</h1>
</div>

<%= render 'form' %>
```

This view is a page header followed by a render command for the form partial. Let's add the partial now. First, create the file *app/views/text_posts/_form.html.erb*, and add this form:

```
<%= form_for @text_post do |f| %>  ❶
  <div class="form-group">
    <%= f.label :title %>
    <%= f.text_field :title, class: "form-control" %>  ❷
  </div>
  <div class="form-group">
    <%= f.label :body %>
    <%= f.text_area :body, class: "form-control" %>  ❸
  </div>

  <%= f.submit class: "btn btn-primary" %>  ❹
  <%= link_to 'Cancel', :back, class: "btn btn-default" %>
<% end %>
```

This partial creates a form for the new TextPost assigned to @text_post ❶. The form includes a text field for the post title ❷, a text area for the post body ❸, and buttons to submit the form or cancel and go back ❹.

While you're editing views, add a button for creating a new text post on the home page. Open *app/views/posts/index.html.erb,* and then add this link under the page header:

```
<p>
  <%= link_to "New Text Post", new_text_post_path,
        class: "btn btn-default" %>
</p>
```

You should now be able to run the TextPostController tests successfully. Now add another controller test to describe creating a TextPost to *test/ controllers/text_posts_controller_test.rb*:

```
    test "should create post" do
❶     user = users(:user1)
❷     params = {
        text_post: {
          title: "Test Title",
          body: "Test Body"
        }
      }

❸     post :create, params, { user_id: user.id }

      text_post = assigns(:text_post)

❹     assert text_post.persisted?
      assert_redirected_to post_url(text_post)
    end
```

As with the previous controller test for the TextPostsController, this test first initializes a new user ❶ from a fixture. Next, it sets up the necessary parameters ❷ for a new TextPost, and then issues a POST request ❸ to the create action with the params hash and the user.id in the session. Finally, it ensures ❹ the new text post was persisted to the database and that the request redirects to the new post's URL.

The first step to making this test pass is to add a create action to the TextPostsController. Open the file *app/controllers/text_posts_controller.rb*, and add the following method:

```
class TextPostsController < ApplicationController
  --snip--

  def create
    @text_post =
❶     current_user.text_posts.build(text_post_params)
```

```
      if @text_post.save
❷      redirect_to post_path(@text_post),
                      notice: "Post created!"
     else
❸       render :new, alert: "Error creating post."
     end
   end
end
```

The create method builds a new text post ❶ for the current user using the params from the form. If it is able to save this new post, it redirects the user ❷ to the newly created post. Otherwise, it renders the new text post form ❸ again with an error message.

Finally, add the text_post_params method for Rails strong params. This method is called in the create action to get the permitted parameters for the new TextPost. Add this private method near the bottom of the TextPostsController class:

```
class TextPostsController < ApplicationController
  --snip--

  private

  def text_post_params
❶    params.require(:text_post).permit(:title, :body)
  end
end
```

This method ensures ❶ that the params hash contains the :text_post key and permits key-value pairs for :title and :body under the :text_post key. With this change, all of your tests should pass again. Click the **New Text Post** button on the home page, as shown in Figure 10-2, to see the form for creating a TextPost.

Figure 10-2: The New Text Post form

The process for creating a new `ImagePost` is similar. Exercise 3 at the end of this chapter walks through the necessary steps.

These new features bring our application much closer to being a fully functioning social network.

Summary

We covered a lot of ground in this chapter. You learned about the MiniTest framework. You wrote model, controller, and integration tests. We discussed test-driven development and then you used it to add features to your social network.

You can write the tests either before or after the code, and you can use any test framework—what matters is that you write tests. The ability to type a single command and verify your application is working correctly is worth the small investment of your time. Over the life of an application, the benefits of a comprehensive set of tests for your application are immeasurable.

Exercises

1. You currently cannot get to the user `show` page without typing in the URL. Update the `TextPost` and `ImagePost` partials so the user's `name` is a link to the user's `show` page. Also, add a link called *Profile* that links to the current user's `show` page next to the *Log Out* link near the top of the application layout.

2. The `follow` action should not be available to anonymous users. Add a call in `UsersController` to `before_action :authenticate_user!` with the `only` option to require authentication before the `follow` action. The following test should pass after you update `UsersController`:

   ```
   test "follow should require login" do
     user = users(:user1)

     get :follow, { id: user.id }

     assert_redirected_to login_url
   end
   ```

   Also, the Follow button on the user `show` page should not appear for anonymous users or if the current user is already following the user being displayed. Update the `show` view to fix this.

3. Add `new` and `create` actions for image posts and the private `image_post _params` method used by the create action in *app/controllers/image_posts_ controller.rb*. Then create a view for the new action at *app/views/image_ posts/new.html.erb* and a partial for the `ImagePost` form at *app/views/ image_posts/_form.html.erb*.

Add the following controller tests to *test/controllers/image_posts_controller_test.rb*. Both tests should pass after you add the actions to ImagePostsController and create the associated views.

```
test "get new with new post" do
  user1 = users(:user1)

  get :new, {}, { user_id: user1.id }

  image_post = assigns(:image_post)

  assert image_post.new_record?
  assert_response :success
end

test "should create post" do
  user = users(:user1)
  params = {
    image_post: {
      title: "Test Title",
      url: "http://i.imgur.com/Y7syDEa.jpg"
    }
  }

  post :create, params, { user_id: user.id }

  image_post = assigns(:image_post)

  assert image_post.persisted?
  assert_redirected_to post_url(image_post)
end
```

Your implementation of these actions and views should be similar to the TextPost new and create actions and views. If you would like to practice TDD, feel free to add these tests and confirm they fail before you start implementing the actions.

11

SECURITY

When users sign up for an account on your website, they trust that you will keep their data safe and secure. Unfortunately, as the popularity of your application increases, so does the likelihood of attack. Even if your application is not popular yet, it can still fall victim to automated systems that scan the web looking for vulnerable sites.

In this chapter, you'll learn about four of the most common security vulnerabilities and how to protect your site from them. We'll discuss authorization, injection, cross-site scripting, and cross-site request forgery attacks.

Authorization Attacks

You created an authentication system in Chapter 9, but authentication is not the same thing as authorization. *Authentication* identifies a user. *Authorization* specifies what a logged-in user can access within your application. Your authentication system uses an email address and a password to identify a user. Authorization systems usually deal with roles or privileges.

At this point, you aren't defining roles for the users in your application, but some privileges should be in place. For example, a user should be able to view and edit his or her own posts but only view posts belonging to another user. A user should also be able to moderate comments on his or her own posts, even if another user added the comment.

An *authorization attack* occurs when a user manages to bypass privileges and access a resource that is owned by another user. The most common type of authorization attack is known as an *insecure direct object reference*, which means the user can manipulate the URL to access a restricted resource in your application.

Let's look at an example from your social app. This code sample creates a method to allow users to edit previously created text posts, but it includes a resource lookup that allows an insecure direct object reference:

```
def edit
  @text_post = TextPost.find(params[:id])
end
```

This method finds the TextPost to edit using the id parameter passed in as part of the URL, regardless of who originally created it. Because this code doesn't check which user is trying to access the post, any authenticated user could edit any post in the application. All the user has to do is open one of his or her posts to edit, work out which part of the URL represents the post id, and change that value to another post's id.

You only want users to be able to edit their own posts. This next listing shows a better way to handle this lookup:

```
def edit
  @text_post = current_user.text_posts.find(params[:id])
end
```

By using current_user.text_posts, the find method is restricted to only posts belonging to the current user. Now if a user changes the id in the URL in an attempt to modify another user's post, the find will fail and the user should see the 404 error page. If a resource is owned by a user, always reference that user when finding the resource in the database.

Now that you know the correct way to find a post to be edited, add the previous method to the text post controller at *app/controllers/text_posts_controller.rb*. When the user submits the edit text post form, the changes are sent to the update action. Use the same authorization idea to add an update method for text posts:

```
  def update
❶   @text_post = current_user.text_posts.find(params[:id])
❷   if @text_post.update(text_post_params)
      redirect_to post_path(@text_post), notice: "Post updated!"
```

```
    else
      render :edit, alert: "Error updating post."
    end
  end
```

This method finds the correct text post ❶ belonging to the current user and calls the update method ❷ using the params from the text post form. If the call to update is successful, the text post is updated in the database and the user is redirected to the updated post. Otherwise, the edit view is rendered again with an error message.

Next, create the file *app/views/text_posts/edit.html.erb* and add the edit view for text posts:

```
<div class="page-header">
  <h1>Edit Text Post</h1>
</div>

<%= render 'form' %>
```

This view is the same as the new view for text posts except for the heading. This view reuses the form partial you created in the last chapter. Finally, add a link to the edit action in the TextPost partial at *app/views/text_posts/_text_post.html.erb*.

```
      <%= text_post.body %>

❶     <% if text_post.user == current_user %>
        <p>
        <%= link_to 'Edit', edit_text_post_path(text_post),
              class: "btn btn-default" %>
        </p>
      <% end %>
    </div>
</div>
```

This link should only appear if the text post belongs to the current user ❶.

Editing image posts follows the same pattern. Add the edit and update methods, complete with authorization, to *app/controllers/image_posts_controller .rb*, create an edit view for image posts at *app/views/image_posts/edit.html.erb*, and add a link to the edit action in the ImagePost partial at *app/views/image _posts/_image_post.html.erb*. These steps are covered in Exercise 1 at the end of this chapter.

Injection Attacks

An *injection attack* occurs when input from a user is executed as part of the application. Injection attacks are extremely common, especially in older applications.

The first rule of avoiding injection attacks is *never trust input from the user.* If an application does not ensure that all data entered by a user is safe, then it is vulnerable to injection attacks. Keep this in mind as we look at two types of injection attacks in this section: SQL injection and cross-site scripting.

SQL Injection

In a *SQL injection* attack, user input is added directly to an SQL statement. If a malicious user provides actual SQL code as input, he or she could bypass your application's authorization system, query your application's database, and obtain or delete restricted information.

For example, consider an application where the Rails built-in secure password feature is not used. Instead, the developer stores usernames and passwords in the database and has written his or her own `authenticate` method to verify a user's credentials. This custom `User.authenticate` method shows what *not* to do, as it's vulnerable to SQL injection:

```
class User < ActiveRecord::Base
❶  def self.authenticate(username, password)
❷    where("username = '#{username}' " +
          "AND password = '#{password}'").first
   end
end
```

This method accepts arguments for `username` and `password` ❶. These values are entered by the user and passed to the controller as parameters. These variables are then added to a `where` call using string interpolation ❷.

This method returns the correct user object for valid username and password combinations. For example, assuming a `User` with `username` tony and `password` secret, this method returns the `User`:

```
User.authenticate("tony", "secret")
 => #<User id: 1, username: ...>
```

The method call then generates the following SQL code:

```
SELECT * FROM "users"
WHERE (username = 'tony' AND password = 'secret')
ORDER BY "users"."id" ASC
LIMIT 1
```

This method also works correctly when passed invalid `username` and `password` combinations:

```
User.authenticate("tony", "wrong")
 => nil
```

In this case, the `password` is not valid so the method returns nil. So far, so good!

Bypassing an Authentication System

Unfortunately, savvy attackers know a handy SQL string that allows them to bypass completely this authenticate method: `' OR '1'='1`. In SQL, the statement `'1'='1'` evaluates to TRUE, so if it is added to any other conditional statement with OR, the entire conditional evaluates to TRUE.

Let's see what happens when this string is passed to the authenticate method for username and password:

```
User.authenticate("' OR '1'='1", "' OR '1'='1")
 => #<User id: 1, username: ...>
```

I didn't pass the method any valid data, so how did the authenticate method succeed? The SQL code generated by the method call shows the trick:

```
SELECT * FROM "users"
WHERE (username = '' OR '1'='1' AND password = '' OR '1'='1')
ORDER BY "users"."id" ASC
LIMIT 1
```

Even though there is no user with an empty string for username and password, the addition of `OR '1'='1'` causes the WHERE clause to evaluate to TRUE and the method returns the first user in the database. The attacker is now logged in as the first user. This attack is made worse by the fact that the first user in the database usually belongs to the application's creator, who might also have special privileges.

Preventing SQL Injection

Thankfully, you can usually find SQL injection errors just by looking at your code carefully. If you see string interpolation inside a where method, assume it is dangerous and needs to be corrected.

If you must build your own query string, switch to hash conditions:

```
def self.authenticate
  username = params[:username]
  password = params[:password]

  where(username: username,
        password: password).first
end
```

Here, the string is completely removed from the call to the where method.

Cross-Site Scripting

Cross-site scripting (XSS) is another common injection attack. In a cross-site scripting attack, an attacker is allowed to enter malicious JavaScript code into your application. Any text field can potentially be used in a cross-site scripting attack. When another user views a page with malicious JavaScript, the user's browser executes the code as if it were part of your application.

Cross-site scripting vulnerabilities can be exploited to deface your website or even display fake log-in forms in an attempt to steal user credentials. The possibilities are almost endless if an attacker is able to inject code into your site.

Built-in Protection

Rails includes protection from cross-site scripting by default. Your application is safe from XSS attacks unless you explicitly bypass this protection. As a quick check, try entering the following JavaScript code in the body of a new text post:

```
<script>alert('XSS');</script>
```

After saving this post, you should see that before displaying text on the page, as shown in Figure 11-1, Rails first *escapes* all HTML tags by replacing special characters with their corresponding character entities.

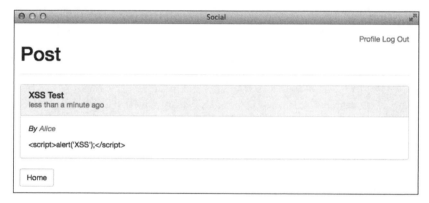

Figure 11-1: Text post with escaped HTML

For example, less-than signs are replaced with < and greater-than signs with >. Instead of being executed, the code is displayed on the page like any other text. So if you never plan to allow users to enter HTML into your site, your application is safe from cross-site scripting.

Unfortunately, users might like to enter HTML tags to format their posts in your application. In this case, your site will need to accept at least a few HTML tags. You can turn off the automatic escaping of HTML tags by using the raw helper method in your view. Open *app/views/text_posts/_text_post.html.erb* and add raw before text_post.body:

```
--snip--
  <%= raw text_post.body %>
--snip--
```

Now when you refresh the page in your browser, the script tag will not be escaped, and you should see a pop-up window with the text "XSS," as shown in Figure 11-2.

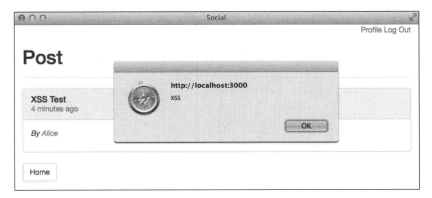

Figure 11-2: Text post with XSS vulnerability

The trick is to let your application only accept safe tags, such as <strong> for bold, <em> for italics, and <p> for marking paragraphs, while rejecting dangerous tags such as <script>. You might be tempted to write your own helper method to deal with these dangerous tags, but thankfully, Rails provides the sanitize helper method to take care of this for you.

The sanitize method

The sanitize helper method removes all HTML tags that are not explicitly allowed by its whitelist. You can see the list of allowed tags by entering `ActionView::Base.sanitized_allowed_tags` in a Rails console.

Try a few examples of the sanitize method in the Rails console to familiarize yourself with how it works:

```
irb(main):001:0> helper.sanitize("<p>Hello</p>")
 => "<p>Hello</p>"
irb(main):002:0> helper.sanitize("<script>alert('XSS')</script>")
 => ""
```

You can specify your own array of allowed tags by including a value for the tags key in the options hash:

```
irb(main):003:0> helper.sanitize("<p>Hello</p>", tags: ["em", "strong"])
 => "Hello"
```

Now that you've seen the sanitize method in action, replace the raw method call with sanitize in the TextPost partial you edited earlier.

```
--snip--
  <%= sanitize text_post.body %>
--snip--
```

Refresh the page again and you should no longer see the alert.

Cross-Site Request Forgery Attacks

A *cross-site request forgery (CSRF) attack* occurs when one of your application's users visits another site that has been modified by an attacker to target your site specifically. The malicious site attempts to use your application's trust in this user to submit requests to your application.

To exploit a CSRF vulnerability, the attacker must first find the vulnerability in your application. Next, he or she must create a page with a link to the vulnerability. Finally, the attacker must trick your application's users into visiting the malicious page and activating the link.

How CSRF Works

Imagine you are building an online payment application. Your application includes a transfer action that accepts amount and to parameters that specify how much money to transfer to another user.

An attacker could study the requests generated by your site and attempt to replicate those requests on his or her own site using something as simple as an HTML image tag:

```
<img src="http://yoursite.com/transfer?amount=100&to=attacker">
```

Every time someone visits this page, the user's browser issues a GET request to your site when it tries to load this image. If the visitor is logged in to your site and your site is vulnerable to CSRF attacks, $100 is transferred from the visitor's account to the attacker's account.

You aren't building a payment site, but your site is vulnerable to a CSRF attack. In Chapter 10, you added a method for one user to *follow* another user on the site. In doing that, you added the following line to *config/routes.rb*:

```
get 'follow/:id', to: 'users#follow', as: 'follow_user'
```

By looking at the request created when I click the Follow button, I can create a malicious link to exploit this vulnerability. Assuming my account's id is 10, the link would look like this:

```
<img src="http://yoursite.com/follow/10">
```

Now all I need to do is convince other users to visit a page containing this image tag and they will follow me automatically.

Preventing CSRF

You can prevent CSRF attacks in two steps. First, include a user-specific token with all requests that change state in your application, and ignore any request that does not include this token. Second, never use a GET request to change state. If a request could create or change data in the database or the session, it should use POST.

Rails takes care of including a secret token and denying requests by default. Open the application layout at *app/views/layouts/application.html.erb* to see the code for including the token:

```
<%= csrf_meta_tags %>
```

Load your site in a web browser and then view source to see the `meta` tags generated by this method in the page's head.

```
<meta content="authenticity_token" name="csrf-param" />
<meta content="KA1Q/JoVfI+aV6/L4..." name="csrf-token" />
```

You can also see the `authenticity_token` in a hidden field included with every form in your application. Every time you submit a form, the value from this hidden field is included with the other parameters. The `authenticity_token` is also automatically included with all POST requests.

Now open *app/controllers/application_controller.rb* to see the code that actually denies invalid requests:

```
protect_from_forgery with: :exception
```

Here, Rails goes one step further and raises an exception for requests that don't include the CSRF token. This exception is logged and can be used to track down attackers.

You must handle the second step yourself. Any time you add a controller action, make sure you do not use a GET request if the action could change data. The `follow` action added in Chapter 10 creates a record in the database, so it should be a POST request. The POST request automatically includes the `authenticity_token`, and Rails verifies the token thanks to the `protect_from_forgery` method in `ApplicationController`.

To correct this vulnerability in your application, open *config/routes.rb* and change the `follow` action to use POST instead of GET:

```
--snip--
post 'follow/:id', to: 'users#follow', as: 'follow_user'
--snip--
```

Now update the link in *app/views/users/show.html.erb* to use the POST method instead of the default GET:

```
<%= link_to "Follow", follow_user_path(@user),
    method: :post, class: "btn btn-default" %>
```

With these two changes, the `follow` action should now be safe from CSRF attacks.

Summary

Malicious users and sites are unavoidable on the Web today. As your application gains popularity, the risk of attack rises. Thankfully, Rails provides the tools you need to protect your application and your users from attacks.

The security vulnerabilities covered in this chapter were taken from the Top 10 list published by The Open Web Application Security Project (OWASP). Visit *http://www.owasp.org/* to find your local OWASP chapter and discuss application security at free meetings in your area.

Now that your application is functional and secure, we'll look at performance in the next chapter. No one likes a slow web application! Here again, Rails provides several tools for improving your application's performance, but you have to put them to use.

Exercises

1. Users should also be able to edit their image posts. Add the edit and update methods to the ImagePostsController at *app/controllers/image_posts _controller.rb*. Also add the ImagePost edit view at *app/views/image_posts/ edit.html.erb*. Finally, add a link to the edit action in the ImagePost partial at *app/views/image_posts/_image_post.html.erb*. The methods and views should be similar to those you added for text posts.

2. Users should be able to moderate comments on their own posts. First, add a @can_moderate instance variable inside the show action in PostsController, as shown here:

```
--snip--

def show
  @post = Post.find(params[:id])
  @can_moderate = (current_user == @post.user)
  end
end
```

This variable is true if the current_user is the author of the post being displayed. Now update the comment partial at *app/views/ comments/_comment.html.erb* to include a link to the destroy action if the value of @can_moderate is true. Finally, add the destroy action to the CommentsController at *app/controllers/comments_controller.rb*. This action should find the correct comment using the id from the params hash, call the destroy method on the comment, and then redirect to the post_path with a message indicating success or failure.

3. You need to correct one more CSRF vulnerability in your application. Open the routes file at *config/routes.rb* and look at the logout route:

```
--snip--
get 'login', to: 'sessions#new', as: 'login'
❶ get 'logout', to: 'sessions#destroy', as: 'logout'

root 'posts#index'
end
```

This route leads to the destroy action in the SessionsController and you're using a GET request ❶ to access it. Change this route from get to delete so a DELETE request is required. Also, add method: :delete to the *Log Out* link in the application layout at *app/views/layouts/application .html.erb*.

12

PERFORMANCE

The relative performance of Ruby on Rails compared
to other languages and web frameworks is still a topic
of debate. A quick Google search reveals that many
people feel Ruby on Rails is slow.

Newer versions of the Ruby interpreter have made great strides where
performance is concerned. Ruby 2.0 included garbage collection optimizations and other improvements that made it much faster than older versions.
Ruby 2.1 introduced a generational garbage collector that was even faster still.

As the Ruby language has improved, so has Ruby on Rails. The Rails
framework now includes several features designed specifically to improve
application performance. This chapter starts with discussions of two of
those built-in features and then moves on to cover some things you can do
to improve performance. Finally, I'll talk about the caching techniques sup-
ported by Rails.

Built-in Optimization Features

The asset pipeline and turbolinks are two built-in Rails performance optimizations you've been using since creating your original blog. Both of these features are enabled by default on new Rails applications, and we'll explore how they work here.

Asset Pipeline

The *asset pipeline* is a Rails feature that combines all of the individual JavaScript and CSS files used by your application into one JavaScript and one CSS file, reducing the number of requests a browser makes to render a web page because your application uses more than one file of each type. Web browsers are limited in the number of requests they can make in parallel, so fewer requests should result in faster loading pages.

The asset pipeline also *minifies*, or compresses, JavaScript and CSS files by removing whitespace and comments. Smaller files load faster, so your web pages load faster.

Finally, the asset pipeline preprocessor also enables you to use higher-level languages such as CoffeeScript instead of JavaScript and Sass instead of plain CSS. Files in these higher-level languages are precompiled to plain JavaScript and CSS using their respective compilers before being served so web browsers can understand them.

Manifests

As you generate controllers for your application, Rails also generates a corresponding JavaScript and CSS file in the *app/assets/javascripts* and *app/assets/stylesheets* directories. Rather than link to each of these files separately in your application, Rails uses a manifest file. As mentioned in Chapter 5, a manifest file is a list of other files needed by your application.

Manifest files use *directives*, instructions specifying other files to include, in order to build a single file for use in the production environment. The require directive includes a single file in the manifest. The require_tree directive includes all files in a directory. The require_self directive includes the contents of the manifest file.

To see an example, open the default CSS manifest at *app/assets/stylesheets/application.css*:

```
/*
 * This is a manifest file that'll be compiled into application.css,
 * which will include all the files listed below.
 *
--snip--
 *
❶ *= require_tree .
❷ *= require bootstrap
❸ *= require_self
 */
```

This file first uses the require_tree . directive ❶ to include all CSS files in the current directory. It then includes the Bootstrap stylesheets using the require bootstrap directive ❷ you added in Chapter 9. Finally, the require_self directive ❸ includes the contents of this file below the comment block. Currently, nothing appears below the comment block.

The asset pipeline searches for assets in three different locations by default. You know about one of them already: The *app/assets* directory is used for CSS, JavaScript, and image files owned by your application.

The *lib/assets* directory is for assets needed by libraries you have written. Because you haven't written any libraries yet, this directory is currently empty. The *vendor/assets* directory is for assets created by third parties, such as code for JavaScript plug-ins and CSS frameworks.

Ruby gems can add their own directories to the list of locations that the asset pipeline searches. You can see this in the JavaScript manifest at *app/assets/javascripts/application.js*:

```
// This is a manifest file that'll be compiled into application.js,
// which will include all the files listed below.
//
--snip--
//
❶ //= require jquery
   //= require jquery_ujs
   //= require turbolinks
❷ //= require_tree .
❸ //= require bootstrap
```

This file uses the require directive ❶ to include the jQuery, jQuery UJS, and Turbolinks libraries that are part of the jquery-rails and turbolinks gems included in your application's *Gemfile*.

It then uses require_tree ❷ to include all JavaScript files in the current directory. Finally, it requires the JavaScript files ❸ needed by the Bootstrap CSS framework.

You won't find *jquery*, *jquery_ujs*, *turbolinks*, or *bootstrap* in the *vendor/assets/javascripts* directory. Instead, the gems that provide these files have updated the asset pipeline search path to include their own directories.

You can see the complete list of asset pipeline search paths by entering Rails.application.config.assets.paths in the Rails console. This statement returns an array of paths. In this list, you should find paths such as *jquery-rails-3.1.0/vendor/assets/javascript*, *turbolinks-2.2.2/lib/assets/javascripts*, and *bootstrap-sass-3.1.1.0/vendor/assets/javascripts*.

Debug Mode

As you've seen, CSS and JavaScript files are served as separate, uncompressed files in the development environment. Your social media application is serving 31 separate CSS and JavaScript files according to the server output. An asset pipeline configuration called *debug mode* controls how assets are handled in each environment.

In the development environment, debug mode is turned on. That means the files referred to in the CSS and JavaScript files are served separately, which is useful if you need to debug an issue with a file using your browser's development tools.

If you want to force assets to be combined and preprocessed so you can see how they are served in the production environment, you can turn off debug mode. Just change the value of `config.assets.debug` near the bottom of the development environment configuration file *config/environments/development.rb*:

```
config.assets.debug = false
```

When debug mode is off, Rails concatenates and runs preprocessors, such as the CoffeeScript or Sass compiler, on all files before serving them. Restart the Rails server after modifying this file, and then check the server output in your terminal to see the difference:

```
Started GET "/login" for 127.0.0.1 at 2014-03-16 20:38:43 -0500
Processing by SessionsController#new as HTML
  Rendered sessions/new.html.erb within layouts/application (1.5ms)
Completed 200 OK in 5ms (Views: 4.5ms | ActiveRecord: 0.0ms)
```

❶ `Started GET "/assets/application.css" for 127.0.0.1 at ...`

❷ `Started GET "/assets/application.js" for 127.0.0.1 at ...`

Only two files (❶ and ❷) are served now—the CSS and JavaScript manifest files. This setting can actually slow down page loads in development because the files are combined for every request, so change `config.assets.debug` back to `true` before continuing.

Asset Precompilation

In the production environment, you should precompile your application's assets and serve them as static files by your web server. You can precompile assets in several ways. When you deployed your blog to Heroku in Chapter 6, you precompiled assets during deployment. Rails also includes a rake task to precompile assets.

The rake task compiles all files from your CSS and JavaScript manifests and writes them to the *public/assets* directory. You can precompile assets for the production environment with the following command:

```
$ RAILS_ENV=production bin/rake assets:precompile
```

During precompilation, an MD5 hash is generated from the contents of the compiled files and inserted into the filenames as the files are saved. Because the filename is based on the contents of the file, you can be sure the correct version of the file is served if you update a file.

For example, after precompilation, the file *app/assets/stylesheets/application*
.css might be named *public/assets/application-d5ac076c28e38393c3059d7167501*
838.css. Rails view helpers use the correct name automatically in production. You don't need the compiled assets for development, so when you're
finished looking at them, remove them using the `assets:clobber` rake task:

```
$ RAILS_ENV=production bin/rake assets:clobber
```

This command deletes the *public/assets* directory and all of its contents.

In Chapter 15, you'll learn how to deploy your application to your own
server using a program called Capistrano. You can configure Capistrano
to precompile assets automatically during deployment just as you did when
you deployed the blog to Heroku.

Turbolinks

The asset pipeline reduces the number of requests the web browser makes
for assets, but the browser still needs to parse and recompile the CSS and
JavaScript for every page. Depending on the amount of CSS and JavaScript
your application includes, this could take a significant amount of time.

Turbolinks is a Rails feature that speeds up the process of following links
in your application by replacing the contents of the current page's body and
the title with the data for the new page instead of loading an entirely new
page. With turbolinks, CSS and JavaScript files are not even downloaded
when a link is clicked.

Turbolinks in Action

Turbolinks is on by default in new Rails applications. You've been using it
without even knowing since you built your first application in Chapter 2.
You can see it working by watching the output from the Rails server. Go to
http://localhost:3000/ in your browser and check the output in your terminal:

```
Started GET "/" for 127.0.0.1 at ...
Processing by PostsController#index as HTML

--snip--

Started GET "/assets/bootstrap.js?body=1" for 127.0.0.1 at ...

Started GET "/assets/application.js?body=1" for 127.0.0.1 at ...
```

After the GET request for the posts index page, the browser fetches all
of the CSS and JavaScript files needed by your application. Now click a link
such as New Text Post on the index page and check the output again:

```
Started GET "/text_posts/new" for 127.0.0.1 at ...
Processing by TextPostsController#new as HTML
  User Load (0.2ms)  SELECT "users".* FROM "users"
    WHERE "users"."id" = ? LIMIT 1  [["id", 7]]
```

```
Rendered text_posts/_form.html.erb (2.4ms)
Rendered text_posts/new.html.erb within layouts/application (3.3ms)
Completed 200 OK in 38ms (Views: 36.5ms | ActiveRecord: 0.2ms)
```

The browser only makes a GET request for the New Text Post page. It does not fetch the CSS and JavaScript files because they are already loaded in memory. Finally, click the Back button in your browser.

This time there is no output in the terminal window. The index page was cached in the browser and no requests were sent to the server. Turbolinks caches ten pages by default.

JavaScript Events

If your application includes JavaScript code that uses jQuery's ready function to attach event handlers or trigger other code, the JavaScript needs to be modified to work with turbolinks. Because turbolinks doesn't reload the entire page when a link is clicked, the ready function is not called.

Instead, the page:load event is fired at the end of the loading process. You can see this in action by adding the following CoffeeScript code to *app/assets/javascripts/posts.js.coffee*:

```
--snip--

  $(document).ready ->
❶   console.log 'Document Ready'

  $(document).on 'page:load', ->
❷   console.log 'Page Load'
```

Unfortunately, CoffeeScript is beyond the scope of this book, but you might recognize what this code snippet does if you're already familiar with JavaScript. It prints "Document Ready" ❶ in your browser's JavaScript console when the page first loads, and "Page Load" ❷ when you click a link that uses turbolinks.

Because you aren't currently using $(document).ready() to trigger any JavaScript code, you don't need to worry about this right now. But you should revisit this section if you ever start using the ready function.

Code Optimizations

Now that you've seen a few of the built-in optimizations provided by Rails, let's look at extra things you can do to improve performance. I'll cover some techniques you can use to reduce the number of database queries your application makes and improve the performance of slow queries.

Reducing Database Queries

Rails models make accessing data so easy that you might forget you're actually querying a database. Luckily, the Rails server shows SQL statements in the terminal. Look at this output as you navigate your application to spot possible inefficiencies.

Examining SQL Output

Make sure your server is running, and keep an eye on your terminal output as I walk you through a few examples. Be sure you are logged out of the application before you start. First, browse to the login page at *http://localhost:3000/login* and check the server output:

```
Started GET "/login" for 127.0.0.1 at 2014-03-18 18:58:39 -0500
Processing by SessionsController#new as HTML
  Rendered sessions/new.html.erb within layouts/application (2.0ms)
Completed 200 OK in 12ms (Views: 11.8ms | ActiveRecord: 0.0ms)
```

This page doesn't produce any SQL queries.

Now log in to the application:

```
Started POST "/sessions" for 127.0.0.1 at 2014-03-18 18:59:01 -0500
Processing by SessionsController#create as HTML
  Parameters: ...
❶ User Load (0.2ms)  SELECT "users".* FROM "users"
    WHERE "users"."email" = 'alice@example.com' LIMIT 1
Redirected to http://localhost:3000/
Completed 302 Found in 70ms (ActiveRecord: 0.2ms)
```

This page produces one SQL query ❶ as Rails loads the user matching the email address you entered on the previous page. The create method in `SessionsController` uses this record to authenticate the password you entered.

After you log in to the application, you should be redirected to the posts index page. Your server output for that page should look something like this:

```
Started GET "/" for 127.0.0.1 at 2014-03-18 18:59:02 -0500
Processing by PostsController#index as HTML
❶ User Load (0.1ms)  SELECT "users".* FROM "users"
    WHERE "users"."id" = ? LIMIT 1  [["id", 1]]
❷ (0.1ms)  SELECT "users".id FROM "users" INNER JOIN
    "subscriptions" ON "users"."id" = "subscriptions"."leader_id"
    WHERE "subscriptions"."follower_id" = ?  [["follower_id", 1]]
❸ Post Load (0.2ms)  SELECT "posts".* FROM "posts"
    WHERE "posts"."user_id" IN (2, 1)
    ORDER BY created_at DESC
❹ User Load (0.1ms)  SELECT "users".* FROM "users"
    WHERE "users"."id" = ? LIMIT 1  [["id", 2]]
  User Load (0.1ms)  SELECT "users".* FROM "users"
    WHERE "users"."id" = ? LIMIT 1  [["id", 1]]
  CACHE (0.0ms)  SELECT "users".* FROM "users"
    WHERE "users"."id" = ? LIMIT 1  [["id", 1]]
  Rendered collection (2.7ms)
  Rendered posts/index.html.erb within layouts/application (3.8ms)
Completed 200 OK in 13ms (Views: 11.0ms | ActiveRecord: 0.6ms)
```

This page produces six queries. It first finds the user with id 1 ❶; this query looks up the current_user inside the authenticate_user! call in PostController. Next, the page finds the ids ❷ of the users the current user is following in the call to current_user.timeline_user_ids. It then finds posts ❸ where the user_id matches the id of the current_user or one of his or her followers.

Finally, the page queries for a user ❹ matching an id with SELECT "users".* FROM "users" three times in a row. That looks a little strange to me. My index page has three posts, but there are three extra queries. Let's look at the index action in *app/controllers/posts_controller.rb* and see what's happening:

```
    class PostsController < ApplicationController
❶     before_action :authenticate_user!

      def index
❷       user_ids = current_user.timeline_user_ids
❸       @posts = Post.where(user_id: user_ids)
                    .order("created_at DESC")
      end

    --snip--
```

This code calls authenticate_user! ❶ before each action. The index action finds the user_ids ❷ that current_user wants to see and then finds the posts ❸ matching those users. You've already accounted for those queries in the previous server output. Since the index action isn't creating the three user queries, they must be coming from the view.

The index view renders the collection of posts. That means the source of these queries must be in the TextPost partial in *app/views/text_posts/_text_post.html.erb*:

```
    --snip--
      <div class="panel-body">
❶       <p><em>By <%= text_post.user.name %></em></p>
    --snip--
```

Here's the problem. The name ❶ of the user who created each post is displayed by calling text_post.user.name. If you check the ImagePost partial, you can verify it does the same thing. For every post displayed, an extra query is generated, which explains the three extra queries you saw in the SQL output.

N + 1 Queries

Code that creates an extra database query for each record in a collection falls into a category of problems called *N + 1 Queries*. These problems are common in Rails applications, and they occur when associations on a collection are referenced without first loading the associated models.

In this case, I loaded a collection of posts into @posts. I then referenced the name for the user who created each post. Because I didn't load all of those users in advance, Rails fetches them one at a time from the database as the page is rendered. These extra queries meant the three posts on the index page resulted in four queries. The number of queries is always one more than the number of items in the collection.

Luckily, this problem is easy to fix. In Rails, you can specify in advance all associations that are going to be needed with the includes method. This technique is called *eager loading*.

Let's update the index action in PostsController to use eager loading now:

```
--snip--
  def index
    user_ids = current_user.timeline_user_ids
❶   @posts = Post.includes(:user).where(user_id: user_ids)
              .order("created_at DESC")
  end
--snip--
```

Here, I chain the includes(:user) method ❶ to the query that sets @posts. The symbol passed to includes must match the name of an association on the model. In this case, post belongs_to :user.

With the includes method, Rails ensures that the specified associations are loaded using the minimum number of queries. After you save this file, refresh the index page in your browser and check the SQL output in your terminal:

```
--snip--
  Post Load (0.3ms)  SELECT "posts".* FROM "posts"
    WHERE "posts"."user_id" IN (2, 1)  ORDER BY created_at DESC
❶ User Load (0.3ms)  SELECT "users".* FROM "users"
    WHERE "users"."id" IN (2, 1)
--snip--
```

The three queries to find each user have been replaced with ❶ a single query that finds all users at once.

Watch out for extra queries as you build applications. Look for calls like text_post.user.name in the view. Notice the two dots in that call. The two dots mean you're accessing data in an associated model, which can introduce an N + 1 Queries problem, so you should preload the association before the view is rendered.

Pagination

You've reduced the number of database queries needed to load posts for the index page, but think about what happens when you have thousands of posts. The index page tries to show them all, increasing your application's load time by a lot. You can use *pagination*, the process of splitting a collection of records into multiple pages, to alleviate this problem.

The will_paginate gem can do all the pagination for you. First, add will_paginate to your application's *Gemfile*:

```
--snip--

gem 'bootstrap-sass'

gem 'will_paginate'

--snip--
```

Remember to always update installed gems after changing the *Gemfile*:

```
$ bin/bundle install
```

Next, update the index action in *app/controllers/posts_controller.rb* to add a call to the paginate method:

```
--snip--
  def index
    user_ids = current_user.timeline_user_ids
    @posts = Post.includes(:user).where(user_id: user_ids)
❶            .paginate(page: params[:page], per_page: 5)
             .order("created_at DESC")
  end
--snip--
```

The paginate method is chained with the other methods that set the instance variable @posts ❶. The will_paginate gem adds params[:page] automatically. I specified per_page: 5 so you can see the pagination working with only 6 posts in your database. The default is 30 records per page.

The paginate method adds the correct limit and offset calls to the database query automatically so the minimum number of records are selected.

Finally, open the index view at *app/views/posts/index.html.erb* and add a call to will_paginate at the end of the page:

```
--snip--
```

```
❶ <%= will_paginate @posts %>
```

The will_paginate view helper ❶ accepts a collection of records, in this case @posts, and renders the correct links to navigate through the pages of this collection.

To see this working, you need to restart your Rails server since you added a new gem. Then create new posts until you have at least six, and browse to a user page. If you click through to the second page, as in Figure 12-1, you should see the new links.

Figure 12-1: Pagination links

The will_paginate view helper added links to *Previous* and *1*, which you can click to go back to the first page from the second.

Check the server output again to see the query used to retrieve posts from the database:

```
Started GET "/posts?page=2" for 127.0.0.1 at 2014-03-26 11:52:27 -0500
Processing by PostsController#index as HTML
  Parameters: {"page"=>"2"}
--snip--
❶  Post Load (0.4ms)  SELECT "posts".* FROM "posts"
    WHERE "posts"."user_id" IN (2, 1)
    ORDER BY created_at DESC LIMIT 5 OFFSET 5
--snip--
```

The query for page two ❶ now includes LIMIT 5 OFFSET 5 as expected. This query only fetches posts that are needed to render the page.

Caching

In programming, *caching* is the process of storing frequently used data so additional requests for the same data will be faster. Rails calls the place where data is stored a *cache store*. Rails applications commonly use two types of caching.

Low-level caching stores the result of time-consuming calculations in the cache—useful for values that are frequently read, but rarely change. *Fragment caching* stores parts of a view in the cache to speed up page rendering. Rendering a large collection of models can be time consuming. If the data rarely changes, fragment caching can increase your application's page load speed.

Caching is disabled, by default, in the development environment, so before you can start learning about it, you need to enable it. Leaving the cache disabled in development is a good idea because you always want to work with the latest version of data while in development. For example, if you store a value in the cache, then change the code that calculates that value, your application could return the cached value instead of the value calculated by the new code.

You'll enable caching in development for this chapter, so you can see how it works and learn about the types of caching used in Rails applications. Open *config/environments/development.rb* and change the value of `config.action_controller.perform_caching` to true:

```
Social::Application.configure do
  --snip--

  # Show full error reports and disable caching.
  config.consider_all_requests_local       = true
  config.action_controller.perform_caching = true

  --snip--
end
```

Once you're finished with this chapter, change this value back to `false` to disable caching in the development environment.

Rails supports several different cache stores. The default, `ActiveSupport::Cache::FileStore`, stores cached data on the filesystem. A popular choice for production applications is `ActiveSupport::Cache::MemCacheStore`, which uses the memcached server to store data. The memcached server is a high-performance cache store that supports distributed caching across several computers.

Now that you've enabled caching, let's specify a cache store for your application to use. Rather than install memcached on your computer, you can use the `ActiveSupport::Cache::MemoryStore` to demonstrate caching. This option also stores cached objects in your computer's memory, but doesn't require the installation of additional software. Add this line to *config/ environments/development.rb* under the line you just changed:

```
Social::Application.configure do
  --snip--

  # Show full error reports and disable caching.
  config.consider_all_requests_local       = true
  config.action_controller.perform_caching = true
  config.cache_store = :memory_store

  --snip--
end
```

Storing the cache in memory is faster than storing it on disk. The memory store allocates 32MB of memory, by default. When the amount of cached data exceeds this amount, the memory store runs a cleanup process that removes the least recently used objects, so you never need to worry about manually removing objects from the cache.

Restart the Rails server for these changes to take effect.

Cache Keys

Everything in the cache is referenced by cache key. A *cache key* is a unique string that identifies a particular object or other piece of data.

Active Record models include the cache_key method for generating a key automatically. You can try it in the Rails console by calling cache_key on an instance of a model:

```
2.1.0 :001 > post = Post.first
  Post Load (0.2ms)  SELECT "posts".* ...
 => #<TextPost id: 1, title: ...>
2.1.0 :002 > post.cache_key
❶ => "text_posts/1-20140317221533035072000"
```

The cache key for this post is the pluralized version of the class name, followed by a slash, then the post id, a dash, and finally the updated_at date as a string ❶.

Using the updated_at date as part of the key solves the cache invalidation problem. When the post is modified, the updated_at date changes, so its cache_key also changes. This way you don't have to worry about getting out of date data from the cache.

Low-Level Caching

Low-level caching is useful when you need to perform a time-consuming calculation or database operation. It is frequently used with API requests that might take a while to return. Low-level caching in Rails uses the Rails.cache.fetch method.

The fetch method takes a cache key and attempts to read a matching value from the cache. The fetch method also takes a block. When given a block of Ruby code, if the value is not already in the cache, the method evaluates the block, writes the result to the cache, and returns the result.

To demonstrate low-level caching, let's show the number of comments for each post on the index page. To do this, first edit *app/views/text_posts/_text_post.html.erb* and add the comment count below the text_post.body:

```
--snip--

    <p><%= sanitize text_post.body %></p>

    <p><%= pluralize text_post.comments.count, "Comment" %></p>

--snip--
```

This new line of code uses the `pluralize` helper method to pluralize the word "Comment" correctly based on the number of comments. For example, if the post has no comments, it prints "0 Comments". Make a similar change to *app/views/image_posts/_image_post.html.erb*, replacing `text_post` with `image_post`.

Now refresh the posts index page in your browser and look at the server output:

```
Started GET "/posts" for 127.0.0.1 at 2014-03-26 15:15:05 -0500
Processing by PostsController#index as HTML
--snip--
❶   (0.1ms)  SELECT COUNT(*) FROM "comments"
      WHERE "comments"."post_id" = ?  [["post_id", 6]]
    (0.1ms)  SELECT COUNT(*) FROM "comments"
      WHERE "comments"."post_id" = ?  [["post_id", 5]]
    (0.1ms)  SELECT COUNT(*) FROM "comments"
      WHERE "comments"."post_id" = ?  [["post_id", 4]]
    (0.1ms)  SELECT COUNT(*) FROM "comments"
      WHERE "comments"."post_id" = ?  [["post_id", 3]]
    (0.1ms)  SELECT COUNT(*) FROM "comments"
      WHERE "comments"."post_id" = ?  [["post_id", 2]]
  Rendered collection (5.4ms)
  Rendered posts/index.html.erb within layouts/application (10.1ms)
Completed 200 OK in 22ms (Views: 16.8ms | ActiveRecord: 1.5ms)
```

This change adds five new queries ❶ to count the number of comments for each post. Those extra queries take up valuable loading time, but you can improve performance by getting rid of them. One way to remove such queries is by caching the values you need (in this case, the number of comments per post) using `Rails.cache.fetch`.

You can perform the caching by adding a method to the `Post` model. Edit *app/models/post.rb* and add the `cached_comment_count` method, as shown here:

```
class Post < ActiveRecord::Base
  --snip--

  def cached_comment_count
❶   Rails.cache.fetch [self, "comment_count"] do
      comments.size
    end
  end
end
```

This method passes the array `[self, "comment_count"]` ❶ to the `Rails.cache.fetch` method. Here, `self` represents the current post. The `fetch` method combines these values into a single cache key. The block still calls `comments.size` as before.

Now update the `TextPost` and `ImagePost` views to use this new method:

```
--snip--

    <p><%= pluralize text_post.cached_comment_count, "Comment" %></p>

--snip--
```

When you refresh the index page in your browser, the six comment count queries are executed one more time and the values are cached. Refresh the page again, watch the server output, and note the queries are no longer executed.

This caching solution has one small problem. The Rails `cache_key` method uses the post id and `updated_at` date to create the cache key, but adding a comment to a post does not change the post `updated_at` date. What you need is a way to update the post when a comment is added.

Rails provides the touch option to associations just for this purpose. When you specify `touch: true` on an association, Rails automatically sets the `updated_at` value of the parent model to the current time when any part of the association changes. This happens when a model is added or removed from the association or when one of the associated models is changed.

Open *app/models/comment.rb* and add `touch: true` to the `belongs_to` association, as shown here:

```
class Comment < ActiveRecord::Base
  belongs_to :post, touch: true
  belongs_to :user

  validates :user_id, presence: true
end
```

Now the `updated_at` value on the post changes whenever one of its comments is updated or deleted or when a new comment is created for it. If you add a comment to a post, then reload the index page, the comment count query is executed for this post again and the new count is cached.

NOTE *You can also solve this problem using a Rails counter cache. With a counter cache, Rails keeps track of the number of comments associated with each post automatically. Enable this feature by adding a column named `comments_count` to the `Post` model and adding `counter_cache: true` to the `belongs_to :post` declaration inside the `Comment` model.*

Fragment Caching

Besides low-level caching of values, you can also use a Rails feature called *fragment caching* to cache parts of a view. Caching the view decreases your application's page load time by storing the rendered view data in the cache. Fragment caching is usually done inside a partial.

To demonstrate fragment caching effectively, I need a slow page. Using a slow page makes the impact of fragment caching obvious. Let's use the Ruby sleep method to render posts more slowly. Obviously, you would never do this in a real application—this is only for demonstration.

Open the *app/views/text_posts/_text_post.html.erb* partial and add the call to sleep on the first line as shown here:

```
❶ <% sleep 1 %>
   <div class="panel panel-default">
     --snip--
   </div>
```

This call to sleep ❶ tells Ruby to pause for 1 second. Make the same change to the ImagePost partial at *app/views/image_posts/_image_post.html.erb*.

Now when you refresh the index page, it should take much longer to display. Check the server output for the exact time:

```
   Started GET "/posts" for 127.0.0.1 at 2014-03-26 16:03:32 -0500
   Processing by PostsController#index as HTML
     --snip--
❶   Rendered collection (5136.5ms)
   Rendered posts/index.html.erb within layouts/application (5191.6ms)
   Completed 200 OK in 5362ms (Views: 5263.1ms | ActiveRecord: 11.8ms)
```

Rendering those five posts took more than five seconds ❶, which makes sense with those five sleep calls.

Now let's add fragment caching to the partials. Edit *app/views/text_posts/_text_post.html.erb* again and add the cache method call and block, as shown here:

```
❶ <% cache text_post do %>
     <% sleep 1 %>
     <div class="panel panel-default">
       --snip--
     </div>
   <% end %>
```

The cache method ❶ calls cache_key on the text_post automatically. I also indented all of the code inside the block. Make the same change to the ImagePost partial.

Now when you refresh the page in your browser, you should see some new output from the Rails server:

```
   Started GET "/posts" for 127.0.0.1 at 2014-03-26 16:18:08 -0500
   Processing by PostsController#index as HTML
     --snip--
❶ Cache digest for text_posts/_text_post.html: 3e...
❷ Read fragment views/text_posts/5-2014... (0.0ms)
❸ Write fragment views/text_posts/5-2014... (0.1ms)
     --snip--
```

```
Rendered collection (5021.2ms)
Rendered posts/index.html.erb within layouts/application (5026.5ms)
Completed 200 OK in 5041ms (Views: 5035.8ms | ActiveRecord: 1.1ms)
```

Rendering the index page now generates several lines of output about the cache. First, a digest is generated ❶ for the partial. This digest is the same every time this partial is rendered. Next, Rails reads the cache ❷ to see if this partial is already there. Finally, since the partial was not found in the cache, it is rendered and then written to the cache ❸.

Refreshing the page again should read all of the partials from the cache, rendering the page much more quickly. Check the server output to be sure:

```
  Started GET "/posts" for 127.0.0.1 at 2014-03-26 16:29:13 -0500
  Processing by PostsController#index as HTML
  --snip--
  Cache digest for text_posts/_text_post.html: 3e...
❶ Read fragment views/text_posts/22-2014... (0.1ms)
  --snip--
❷   Rendered collection (25.9ms)
  Rendered posts/index.html.erb within layouts/application (31.5ms)
  Completed 200 OK in 77ms (Views: 73.1ms | ActiveRecord: 1.0ms)
```

You only see cache reads ❶ now, and the collection renders very quickly ❷, in a fraction of the time it took after you added the sleep calls. Caching can obviously result in dramatic performance improvements.

You should remove the calls to sleep from the TextPost and ImagePost partials now, but leave the caching in place in the views.

Issues

Caching is a great way to make your application faster, but it can also cause some issues. Unless the cache key for a code block or view fragment includes a user id, then the same cached data is sent to every user.

For example, the TextPost and ImagePost partials both contain code that checks to see if the post belongs to the current user. If so, it displays a button linked to the edit action.

```
  <% cache text_post do %>
    <div class="panel panel-default">
      --snip--
❶     <% if text_post.user == current_user %>
        <p><%= link_to 'Edit', edit_text_post_path(text_post),
              class: "btn btn-default" %></p>
      <% end %>
    </div>
  </div>
  <% end %>
```

The conditional statement in the TextPost partial at *app/views/test_posts/_text_post.html.erb* shows the Edit button if the post belongs to current_user ❶.

The owner of a post is probably going to be the first user to view the post. After the owner views the post, the view fragment is cached with the Edit button. When another user views the same post, the fragment is read from the cache and the other user also sees the Edit button.

You can correct this issue in a couple of ways. You could include the user id in the cache key, but that would create a separate copy of the post in the cache for each user and remove the benefit of caching for many users. A simpler solution is to move the button outside the fragment being cached, as shown here:

```
<% cache text_post do %>
  <div class="panel panel-default">
    --snip--
  </div>
<% end %>

<% if text_post.user == current_user %>
  <p><%= link_to 'Edit', edit_text_post_path(text_post),
         class: "btn btn-default" %></p>
<% end %>
```

Once the Edit button is moved outside the cache block, the conditional is evaluated for every user viewing the post and the Edit button is shown only if the current user is the owner of the post. Make the same change to the ImagePost partial at *app/views/image_posts/_image_post.html.erb*.

Remember to edit *config/environments/development.rb*, as shown at the beginning of this section, and disable caching in the development environment after you complete the exercises at the end of this chapter.

Summary

No one likes slow web applications! This chapter covered techniques for speeding up your application, from Rails built-in features like the asset pipeline and turbolinks to database query optimization, pagination, and caching. Now try the following exercises, and make your application even faster.

When you've completed the exercises, change `config.action_controller` `.perform_caching` back to `false` in *config/environments/development.rb*. Leave caching turned off during development. Otherwise you'll need to remember to clear the cache any time you make a change to a cached view partial.

The next chapter covers debugging strategies you can use to track elusive problems with your application. You'll look through server output and logs for clues and finally dive into a running application to see exactly what's happening.

Exercises

1. So far your performance optimizations have focused on the post index page. Open the show page for an individual post, such as *http://localhost:3000/posts/1*. Make sure the post has several comments and then examine the server output. Use eager loading in the `PostsController` at *app/controllers/posts_controller.rb* to reduce the number of queries this page makes.

2. The post show page renders a collection of comments. Add fragment caching to the `comment` partial at *app/views/comments/_comment.html.erb*. You only want the Destroy button to appear if `@can_moderate` is true. In this case, include the value of `@can_moderate` in the cache key by passing the array `[comment, @can_moderate]` to the cache method.

3. You can cache the entire comments collection by wrapping the `render @post.comments` call in the show page in a cache block. Open the show page at *app/views/posts/show.html.erb* and add the cache block. Pass the array `[@post, 'comments', @can_moderate]` to the cache method, ensuring the Destroy button is only shown to users who can moderate comments as mentioned in Exercise 2. The technique of wrapping a cached collection inside another cache block is sometimes called *Russian-Doll* caching because multiple cached fragments are nested inside each other. When an object is added to the collection, only the outer cache needs to be re-created. The cached data for the other objects can be reused and only the new object needs to be rendered.

13

DEBUGGING

I've been told that not all developers are perfect like you and me. We never make mistakes in our code, but sometimes *other* developers make mistakes that we have to clean up. When that happens, the debugging features built into Rails come in handy. This chapter covers those built-in debugging features, starting with the debug helper method, which makes it easier to see the values of variables in your application's views.

We spent some time looking at the Rails log in previous chapters. In this chapter, you'll also see how to add your own messages to that log. Finally, using the debugger gem, you can step inside your application as it's running to track down really tough bugs.

The debug Helper

Rails includes a view helper method called debug that you can use to display the value of an instance variable or method call available inside a Rails view. This helper wraps its output in <pre> tags so it's easier to read.

For example, let's see how the output of the current_user method changes as you move through the application. First edit *app/views/layouts/application.html.erb* and add a call to the debug helper just below the yield method, as shown here:

```
<!DOCTYPE html>
<html>
--snip--

    <%= yield %>

    <%= debug current_user %>
  </div>
</body>
</html>
```

Now start the Rails server, if it's not already running, and go to *http://localhost:3000/login* in your browser. You should see the output from the debug helper just below the Log In button, as shown in Figure 13-1.

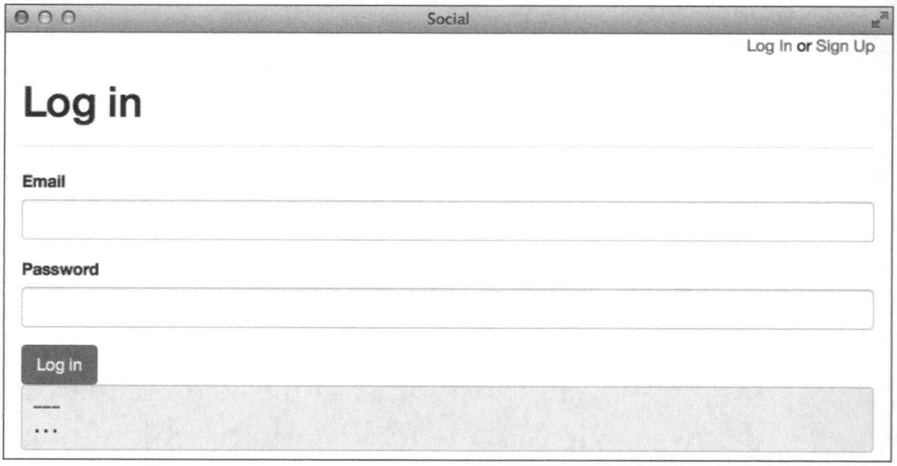

Figure 13-1: Debugging current_user

At this point, the output is simply three dashes on one line followed by three dots on the next line. The debug helper is using YAML to format its output. YAML is a data serialization language used frequently in Rails projects. For example, the Rails database configuration file (*config/database.yml*) is in YAML format. You also used YAML in Chapter 10 to define fixtures that provide default data for tests.

In YAML, the three dashes signify the beginning of a document. Three dots indicate the end of a YAML document. In other words, this is an empty YAML document. On the Log In page current_user is nil, and the empty YAML document reflects that.

Now log in to your application and scroll to the bottom of the posts index page to see how the output from current_user changed.

```
❶ --- !ruby/object:User
❷ attributes:
     id: 1
     name: Alice
     email: alice@example.com
     created_at: 2014-02-26 ...
     updated_at: 2014-02-26 ...
     password_digest: "$2a$10$7..."
```

Now the YAML output is a little more fleshed out. The first line starts with three dashes followed by !ruby/object:User ❶, which represents the type of object being shown. In this case, the object is a Ruby object of class User. The word attributes ❷ represents the start of the object's attributes and their values. Below that, you see the User model attributes: id, name, email, created_at, updated_at, and password_digest.

Displaying this information is a great way to monitor the state of your application as it runs. Unfortunately, using the debug helper limits you to seeing values only for your current session, and if your application renders nothing in the browser window, you won't be able to see any values at all. In those cases, you can rely on the Rails log to track down bugs.

The Rails Logger

Throughout this book, I've talked about Rails server output. As the Rails server runs, it shows a copy of the development log. You can open the file *log/development.log* in your editor to examine that log even when the server is not running.

This file may be quite large depending on how much you've been using the application the log belongs to. You can use the bin/rake log:clear command to clear your application's log files.

Log Levels

The Rails logger uses levels named :debug, :info, :warn, :error, :fatal, and :unknown. These levels indicate the severity of the message being logged. The level is assigned by the developer when a message is logged.

If the level is equal to or higher than the log level configured for the current environment, the message is added to the corresponding log file. The default log level in the development and test environments is :debug and above, and the default log level in the production environment is :info and above.

Because the default log level in production does not display the :debug level, you can leave these debug messages in your code without worrying about cluttering up the logs when your application is deployed and running.

Logging

Each of the log levels has a corresponding method used to print messages. For example, you can call logger.debug "*Message*" to add a message with the level :debug to the log.

You've already seen how to use the debug helper to show values in views. Rails logger messages are typically used in models and controllers.

Let's add the value of current_user to the log and compare it to what is shown in the browser. Open the file *app/controllers/posts_controller.rb* in your editor and add the logger statement shown here to the PostsController:

```
class PostsController < ApplicationController
  before_action :authenticate_user!

  def index
❶   logger.debug current_user

    user_ids = current_user.timeline_user_ids
--snip--
```

This line ❶ adds the output of current_user to the development log every time the posts index action is called. Refresh the page in your browser and examine the log output in your terminal:

```
Started GET "/" for 127.0.0.1 at 2014-04-05 19:34:03 -0500
Processing by PostsController#index as HTML
  User Load (0.1ms)  SELECT "users".* FROM "users"
    WHERE "users"."id" = ? LIMIT 1  [["id", 1]]
❶ #<User:0x007fd3c94d4e10>
  (0.1ms)  SELECT "users".id FROM "users" ...
--snip--
  Rendered posts/index.html.erb within layouts/application (27.1ms)
Completed 200 OK in 61ms (Views: 35.9ms | ActiveRecord: 1.7ms)
```

The logger.debug converts the value of the current_user method to a string and adds it to the log as #<User:0x007fd3c94d4e10> ❶. Unfortunately, when a Ruby object like current_user is converted to a string, the default representation is the object's class followed by its object_id.

What you want to do is inspect the object. The inspect method displays attributes and values when called on a Rails model. Change the call to current_user that you just added to the PostsController to current_user.inspect and refresh the page in your browser again.

```
Started GET "/" for 127.0.0.1 at 2014-04-05 19:34:27 -0500
Processing by PostsController#index as HTML
  User Load (0.1ms)  SELECT "users".* FROM "users"
    WHERE "users"."id" = ? LIMIT 1  [["id", 1]]
```

```
❶ #<User id: 1, name: "User One", ...>
  (0.1ms)  SELECT "users".id FROM "users" ...
--snip--
  Rendered posts/index.html.erb within layouts/application (27.1ms)
Completed 200 OK in 63ms (Views: 40.9ms | ActiveRecord: 1.7ms)
```

This output is much better. The value of current_user is shown ❶ with all attributes, just as it appears in the Rails console. The Rails logger displays any string you send to it. I sometimes label the data that I'm logging and add characters like stars to make the data stand out more:

```
class PostsController < ApplicationController
  before_action :authenticate_user!

  def index
    logger.debug "** current_user = "
    logger.debug current_user.inspect

    user_ids = current_user.timeline_user_ids
--snip--
```

You may have had some trouble locating the value of current_user in output before, but with human-readable labels, it is easier to spot.

Debugger

Sometimes simply seeing the values of variables after the fact is not enough to debug an issue. The Ruby debugger lets you step into your application as it runs. Inside the debugger, you can see code as it is executed, examine the values of variables, and even change values.

First, edit your application's *Gemfile* to add the debugger gem. For Ruby version 2.0 or greater, you should use the byebug gem. Older versions of Ruby should use the debugger gem.

```
--snip--

# Use debugger
gem 'byebug', group: [:development, :test]
```

The correct gem for your Ruby version is commented out at the bottom of the *Gemfile*. Remove the # from the beginning of the line and save the file. The debugger isn't needed in the production environment, so this line only adds it to the development and test groups.

Because you changed the *Gemfile*, remember to update installed gems with the bin/bundle install command. You also need to restart the Rails server:

```
$ bin/rails server
```

Now that you've installed the debugger, let's see what it can do.

Entering the Debugger

If you call the debugger method in your code, your application stops executing when it reaches that call, and Rails launches the debugger. For example, remove the logger statements you added to the posts index action earlier in *app/controllers/posts_controller.rb* and instead use the debugger:

```ruby
class PostsController < ApplicationController
  before_action :authenticate_user!

  def index
    user_ids = current_user.timeline_user_ids

    debugger

    @posts = Post.includes(:user).where(user_id: user_ids)
                 .paginate(page: params[:page], per_page: 5)
                 .order("created_at DESC")
  end
--snip--
```

When the index action is called, execution pauses at the debugger statement, and the debugger is started. Refresh the posts index page in your browser. The page shouldn't finish loading. Check the server output in your terminal, and you should see the debugger prompt:

```
❶ .../social/app/controllers/posts_controller.rb:9
   @posts = Post.includes(:user).where(user_id: user_ids)

   [4, 13] in .../social/app/controllers/posts_controller.rb
❷    4    def index
     5      user_ids = current_user.timeline_user_ids
     6
     7      debugger
     8
  => 9      @posts = Post.includes(:user).where(user_id: user_ids)
    10                   .paginate(page: params[:page], per_page: 5)
    11                   .order("created_at DESC")
    12    end
    13
❸ (rdb:2)
```

In the normal server output, you should see a line indicating the current position ❶ in the source code. In this case, execution is paused at line 9 inside *app/controllers/posts_controller.rb*. Next, the output ❷ shows your place in the code. You should see 10 lines of code with line 9 in the center. Finally, the debugger prompt ❸ is waiting for your input.

Debugger Commands

The debugger accepts a variety of commands for working with your application's code. This section covers the most common commands. Unless otherwise noted, each of these commands can be abbreviated using the first letter of its name.

Start by entering the help command:

```
(rdb:2) help
ruby-debug help v1.6.6
Type 'help <command-name>' for help on a specific command

Available commands:
backtrace  break    catch    condition
continue   delete   disable  display
down       edit     enable   eval
exit       finish   frame    help
info       irb      jump     kill
list       method   next     p
pp         ps       putl     quit
reload     restart  save     set
show       skip     source   start
step       thread   tmate    trace
undisplay  up       var      where

(rdb:2)
```

The help command shows a list of all available debugger commands. You can also follow help with the name of another command for information on a specific command.

When you entered the debugger, you were shown 10 lines of code around your current position. The list command displays the next 10 lines of code inside the debugger.

```
(rdb:2) list
[14, 18] in /Users/tony/code/social/app/controllers/posts_controller.rb
   14    def show
   15      @post = Post.find(params[:id])
   16      @can_moderate = (current_user == @post.user)
   17    end
   18  end
(rdb:2)
```

Each time you enter the list command another 10 lines of code are displayed. In this case, the current file has only five more lines of code, so those five lines are shown. Enter list- to see the previous 10 lines of code, and enter list= to show the code around your current position:

```
(rdb:2) list=
[4, 13] in /Users/tony/code/social/app/controllers/posts_controller.rb
    4    def index
    5      user_ids = current_user.timeline_user_ids
    6
    7      debugger
    8
=> 9      @posts = Post.includes(:user).where(user_id: user_ids)
```

```
 10                     .paginate(page: params[:page], per_page: 5)
 11                     .order("created_at DESC")
 12       end
 13
(rdb:2)
```

Now that you know where you are in the code, you might want to examine the values of some variables. The var command displays currently defined variables and their contents. To see local variables, enter the var local command:

```
(rdb:2) var local
self = #<PostsController:0x007ffbfeb21018>
user_ids = [2, 1]
(rdb:2)
```

Here, only two local variables are defined. The variable self indicates that you are inside the PostsController. The variable user_ids received its contents on line 5 in the previous code.

List instance variables and their values with the var instance command:

```
(rdb:2) var instance
@_action_has_layout = true
@_action_name = "index"
@_config = {}
@_env = {"GATEWAY_INTERFACE"=>"CGI/1.1", "P...
@_headers = {"Content-Type"=>"text/html"}
@_lookup_context = #<ActionView::LookupCont...
@_prefixes = ["posts", "application"]
@_request = #<ActionDispatch::Request:0x007...
@_response = #<ActionDispatch::Response:0x0...
@_response_body = nil
@_routes = nil
@_status = 200
@current_user = #<User id: 1, name: "User 0...
@marked_for_same_origin_verification = true
(rdb:2)
```

Quite a few instance variables are already defined at this point. The only instance variable set by this code is @current_user. This instance variable is defined in the current_user method in ApplicationController. The other variables are defined by Rails. Note that @posts is not defined yet. Your current position is line 9, which defines @posts, but that line has not yet been executed.

The display command adds a variable to the display list inside the debugger. If you are especially interested in the value of user_ids, for example, enter the display user_ids command to add it to the display list, as shown here:

```
(rdb:2) display user_ids
1: user_ids = [2, 1]
(rdb:2)
```

You can also show the contents of the display list and their values with the `display` command, abbreviated `disp`:

```
(rdb:2) disp
1: user_ids = [2, 1]
(rdb:2)
```

To remove a variable from the display list, use the `undisplay` command followed by the number corresponding to a variable in the list. For example, `undisplay 1` removes `user_ids` from the display list.

Use the `eval` command to evaluate any Ruby code you like and print its value. This command is abbreviated `p`, as in print. For example, you might want to print the length of the `user_ids` array or the output from the `current_user` method.

```
(rdb:2) eval user_ids.length
2
(rdb:2) p current_user
#<User id: 1, name: "User One", email: "user...
(rdb:2)
```

The debugger is a Ruby shell, so you can also evaluate Ruby commands by simply entering them at the prompt. The `eval` command is not even necessary. For example, set the value of `user_ids` to an empty array by entering this statement at the debugger prompt:

```
(rdb:2) user_ids = []
[]
(rdb:2)
```

This prints the return value of the expression `user_ids = []` just as if you had typed it in the Rails console.

Several commands are available for executing your application's code inside the debugger. The most commonly used command is `next`, which executes the next line of code. The `next` command executes methods on the next line of code without moving inside the method.

The `step` command is similar, but it also shows you each line that executes inside method calls. The `step` command moves through your application and its dependencies literally one line of code at a time. You can use it to find bugs in the Rails framework or other gems used by your application.

When you are finished moving around in your code, use the `continue` command to resume execution and finish the current request. If you've been following along throughout this section, you may remember you set the value of `user_ids` to an empty array. When you `continue` execution and the posts index page finally renders, no posts are displayed. Because you set `user_ids` to an empty array, the `@posts` instance variable is also empty, and the `render @posts` statement inside the `index` view renders nothing.

The Ruby debugger probably isn't something you'll use every day, and some developers never use it. But if you ever encounter a really hard-to-find bug, the debugger is invaluable.

Summary

This chapter described several debugging techniques. Displaying values in your application's views with the debug helper method or adding data to the log file with logger statements will help you track down most bugs. The interactive debugger provides complete control over your application, allowing you to step through your code and pinpoint bugs that are particularly hard to find.

The next chapter covers web application programming interfaces, or APIs. We'll discuss using other application's APIs and creating your own.

Exercises

1. Using the debug helper method, display the contents of each post as it is rendered on the posts index page. Add a debug call inside the partial for each type of post.

2. Add the id and type of each post in the @posts instance variable to the log using a call to logger.debug in the index action of *app/controllers/posts_controller.rb*.

3. Practice using the debugger to explore your application's code. Use the next command in the debugger to see what happens when a user logs in to the application.

14

WEB APIS

Eventually, you might want to expand your application beyond your website. Popular web applications usually also have a native mobile client and sometimes even a desktop client. You may also want to integrate data from your application with other websites and applications.

A web *application programming interface* (or *API*) makes all of these things possible. Think of an API as a language that applications use to communicate with each other. On the Web, the API is usually a REST protocol using JavaScript Object Notation (JSON) messages.

In this chapter, we'll explore the GitHub API to see how to access detailed information about users and repositories. After discussing GitHub's API, you'll build your own. In the process, I'll cover details such as JSON, the Hypertext Transfer Protocol (HTTP), and token-based authentication.

The GitHub API

The GitHub code-hosting service has an extensive API. Many of its features are even available without authentication. If you want to continue exploring the GitHub API after working through the examples in this chapter, complete details are available online at *https://developer.github.com/*.

The GitHub API provides easy access to data about users, organizations, repositories, and other site features. For example, go to *https://api.github.com/orgs/rails/* in your web browser to see the Rails organization on GitHub:

```
{
    "login": "rails",
❶  "id": 4223,
❷  "url": "https://api.github.com/orgs/rails",
    "repos_url": "https://api.github.com/orgs/rails/repos",
    "events_url": "https://api.github.com/orgs/rails/events",
    "members_url": "https://api.github.com/orgs/rails/me...",
    "public_members_url": "https://api.github.com/orgs/r...",
    "avatar_url": "https://avatars.githubusercontent.com...",
    "name": "Ruby on Rails",
    "company": null,
    "blog": "http://weblog.rubyonrails.org/",
    "location": null,
    "email": null,
    "public_repos": 73,
    "public_gists": 3,
    "followers": 2,
    "following": 0,
    "html_url": "https://github.com/rails",
❸  "created_at": "2008-04-02T01:59:25Z",
❹  "updated_at": "2014-04-13T20:24:49Z",
    "type": "Organization"
}
```

The data returned should be at least partially familiar to anyone who's worked with Rails models. You'll see fields for id ❶, created_at ❸, and updated_at ❹, as seen in all of the models you've created so far. The GitHub API also includes several url fields ❷ that you can use to access more data about the organization.

For example, go to the repos_url (*https://api.github.com/orgs/rails/repos/*) to see a list of source code repositories belonging to the Rails organization. From there, you can access the details of an individual repository by going to its url, such as *https://api.github.com/repos/rails/rails/*.

Go to *https://api.github.com/users/username/* to access information about an individual user. To see my GitHub account, visit *https://api.github.com/users/anthonylewis/* in your browser.

The data returned by these requests is in JavaScript Object Notation (JSON) format, which is based on a subset of the JavaScript programming language. In JSON format, data between curly braces is a single JavaScript object with various named properties. Each property consists of a name, followed by a colon, and the property value. This format is quite similar to a hash in Ruby.

In addition to the simple requests for data you've made so far, the GitHub API also supports creating and updating objects using the appropriate requests. These actions require authentication, of course. But before I can cover API authentication, I need to tell you a little more about HTTP.

HTTP

HTTP is the language of the Web. Web servers and browsers use this protocol to communicate. I've discussed some aspects of HTTP already, such as the HTTP verbs (GET, POST, PATCH, and DELETE), while covering the REST architecture in Chapter 4.

In addition to the data you've seen so far, an HTTP response also contains a header with more detailed information. You're probably familiar with part of the data in an HTTP response header. Anyone who's spent any time on the Web has probably seen a 404 or 500 response from a web server. Status codes such as these are included in every response from a web server.

Status Codes

The first line of every response includes an HTTP status code. This three-digit numeric code tells the client the type of response to expect.

Status codes are broken up into five categories based on their first digit:

- 1*xx* Informational
- 2*xx* Success
- 3*xx* Redirection
- 4*xx* Client Error
- 5*xx* Server Error

You shouldn't encounter any status codes in the 1*xx* range while working with APIs. The original HTTP 1.0 specification did not define any codes in this range, and in my experience, they are rarely used.

Status codes in the 2*xx* range indicate a successful request. Hopefully, you'll encounter many of these. Common codes include *200 OK,* which indicates a successful response, typically to a GET request; *201 Created,* which is returned when an object is created on the server in response to a POST request; and *204 No Content,* which indicates that a request was successful, but there is no additional data in the response.

The *3xx* range of status codes indicates a redirect to a different address. Rails issues a *302 Found* response any time you use `redirect_to` in your application. To see this in action, log in to your application and watch the log for the redirect.

Status codes in the *4xx* range indicate some kind of client error. In other words, the user made a mistake. *401 Unauthorized* is returned in response to a request for a URL that requires authentication. The *403 Forbidden* status code is similar to 401, except the server will not complete the request even if the client successfully authenticates. The *404 Not Found* is sent when a client attempts to access a URL that does not exist. As you work with APIs, you may encounter the *406 Not Acceptable* status code for an invalid request or the *422 Unprocessable Entity* status code, which means the request is valid, but the included data could not be processed.

The *5xx* range of status codes indicates an error on the server. The *500 Internal Server Error* code is the most commonly used. It is a general message that does not provide any additional data. The *503 Service Unavailable* status code indicates a temporary problem with the server.

To see these codes, you need to examine the HTTP header sent with a response. These are not normally displayed by web browsers. Luckily, tools exist that make examining HTTP headers easy. One of the most popular is the command-line program known as Curl.

Curl

Curl is a free command-line tool for network communication. Curl is included with Mac OS X and Linux, and Windows users can download the tool from *http://curl.haxx.se/*. Curl uses URL syntax, making it an ideal tool for testing web APIs.

Open a terminal window and try a few `curl` commands. Let's start with the GitHub API you just looked at.

```
$ curl https://api.github.com/users/anthonylewis
{
  "login": "anthonylewis",
  "id": 301,
  --snip--
}
```

This example shows how to retrieve information about a particular user account from GitHub. Curl only shows the response data by default; enter `curl -i` to include the HTTP headers with the response:

```
$ curl -i https://api.github.com/users/anthonylewis
❶ HTTP/1.1 200 OK
Server: GitHub.com
Date: Thu, 17 Apr 2014 00:36:29 GMT
Content-Type: application/json; charset=utf-8
Status: 200 OK
```

```
❷ X-RateLimit-Limit: 60
   X-RateLimit-Remaining: 58
❸ X-RateLimit-Reset: 1397696651
   --snip--

   {
     "login": "anthonylewis",
     "id": 301,
     --snip--
   }
```

The response headers start with the status code of 200 OK ❶. Also note that GitHub API requests are rate limited. The X-RateLimit-Limit: 60 line ❷ indicates that you are limited to 60 requests over a certain period of time. The next line says you have 58 requests remaining. Your rate limit resets automatically at the time given by the X-RateLimit-Reset: 1397696651 line ❸.

NOTE *The number 1397696651 is a Unix timestamp. You can convert it to a normal time by entering Time.at 1397696651 in an IRB session or Rails console.*

Authentication

So far, you've only read public data from the GitHub API. You can also use the GitHub API to read private data about users and repositories and to create or update information, but these actions require authentication.

I covered user authentication in Chapter 9. Users expect to log in to an application once and then browse a site for some time. You maintain a user's log in state in the session, which is stored in a cookie that the browser automatically includes with every request.

API requests don't maintain a session. Applications accessing an API need to provide authentication credentials with each request. A popular choice for API requests is *token-based authentication*. In token-based authentication, users include a unique API token with each request.

You can use the curl command to test token-based authentication on GitHub. First, you need to generate a personal access token on GitHub's Application Settings page. Log in to GitHub, if necessary, and go to *https://github.com/settings/applications/*. On that page, click the **Generate New Token** button. Next, you provide a description for this token; something like API Testing should be fine. Finally, confirm that the checkboxes beside "repo" and "user" are checked, and click the **Generate Token** Button.

GitHub should take you back to the Application Settings page and present you with a new 40-digit hexadecimal token. Copy your new token and paste it into a text file so you can keep up with it. As the on-screen message says, you won't be able to see it again!

To verify your token is working, enter the following `curl` command in your terminal. Replace the word *token* with your actual token in all of these requests:

```
$ curl -H "Authorization: Token token" https://api.github.com/user
{
  "login": "anthonylewis",
  "id": 301,
  --snip--
```

Here, I've used the -H parameter to `curl` to pass custom header data to the server, and, in this case, that data is the `Authorization: Token` header followed by my token.

You should see information about your own account, even though you didn't specify a username. GitHub uses your personal access token to authenticate the request.

You can now use the token to access private information, such as the list of Git repositories associated with your account.

```
$ curl -H "Authorization: Token token" https://api.github.com/user/repos
[
  {
    "id": 6289476,
    "name": "blog",
    "full_name": "anthonylewis/blog",
    "owner": {
      "login": "anthonylewis",
      "id": 301,
      --snip--
```

GitHub should return an array of repositories created with your account. Depending on how many repositories you've created, this could be a lot of data.

Now that you have a token, you can also add another repository to your account using a POST request. As you learned in Chapter 4, POST means *create* in REST.

```
❶ $ curl -i -d '{"name":"API Test"}' \
          -H "Authorization: Token token" \
          https://api.github.com/user/repos
❷ HTTP/1.1 201 Created
  Server: GitHub.com
  Date: Mon, 21 Apr 2014 23:47:59 GMT
  Content-Type: application/json; charset=utf-8
  Status: 201 Created
  --snip---
❸ {
    "id": 18862420,
    "name": "API-Test",
    "full_name": "anthonylewis/API-Test",
    "owner": {
      "login": "anthonylewis",
```

```
"id": 301,
--snip--
```

The -d option to curl specifies data to be included with the request. Here, you send a JSON string with the name "API Test" for the new repository ❶. Because you're sending data, curl automatically uses a POST request. GitHub responds to the request with headers indicating HTTP status 201 Created ❷, followed by information about the newly created repository ❸.

Now that you have some experience with an existing API, let's create our own API for our social application.

Your Own API

You may remember from Chapter 4 that the Rails scaffold generator used the respond_to method inside the PostsController to return different data based on the type of request. This approach is fine for some applications, but the addition of user authentication and sessions in your application leads to problems.

The existing controllers authenticate users by calling the authenticate_user! method before every action. Your API will use a different method to support token-based authentication. The existing controllers also display data, such as posts, based on the value of current_user. Your API will display all posts when requested.

Rather than use the same controllers for the application and the API, you can build separate controllers for each. Because your application is mainly about posts, you'll start there when building your API.

API Routes

Start by adding routes for API requests. The GitHub API used a subdomain for API requests. Because you haven't set up your own domain, you'll use a separate path for API requests. Open the file *config/routes.rb* and add the following block near the end:

```
Social::Application.routes.draw do
--snip--

❶  namespace :api do
     resources :posts
   end
end
```

The namespace :api block ❶ indicates that all routes created for the resources it contains start with the path *api/*. Additionally, the controller files for those resources should be inside a directory named *api*, and the controller classes should be inside a module named Api.

You can enter the bin/rake routes command in a terminal to see the newly created routes.

API Controllers

Now that you've defined the routes, you need to create a controller to handle these actions. First, create a directory for the API controllers by entering the following command:

```
$ mkdir app/controllers/api
```

Then create a new file named *app/controllers/api/posts_controller.rb* and add the code for the API `PostsController`, as shown here:

```
module Api
  class PostsController < ApplicationController
❶    respond_to :json

❷    def index
       @posts = Post.all
❸       respond_with @posts
     end
  end
end
```

The file starts with `module Api` to indicate this class belongs to the API namespace. Inside the `PostsController` class is a call to the `respond_to` class method. Calling `respond_to :json`, indicates that the actions in this controller return JSON data ❶.

The class then defines the `index` action ❷. The `index` action retrieves all posts and then uses the `respond_with` method to send them to the client ❸. The `respond_with` method automatically formats the data based on the format and HTTP verb used in the request. In this case, it should return JSON data in response to a GET request for the `index` action.

After you save this file, start the Rails server if it isn't already started. Then you can use `curl` to test your API by entering this command:

```
$ curl http://localhost:3000/api/posts
[{"id":1,"title":"First Post","body":"Hello, World!"...
```

The API returns an array of posts in response to the posts `index` action.

The data is compact and on a single line, which can be hard to read, but several free tools can pretty-print JSON data for you. For example, jq is a JSON processor that pretty-prints JSON data and adds syntax highlighting. Download jq from *http://stedolan.github.io/jq/*. Once installed, you can pipe the output through jq's basic filter by adding `| jq '.'` to the end of the command:

```
$ curl http://localhost:3000/api/posts | jq '.'
[
  {
    "id": 1,
    "title": "First Post",
```

```
"body": "Hello, World!",
"url":null,
"user_id":1,
--snip--
```

The remaining examples in this chapter are pretty-printed. I leave off
the | jq '.' for brevity, but you should include it if you want your output to
look like what you see in the book. You can also see JSON output in your
web browser. Entering *http://localhost:3000/api/posts* in your web browser
causes an ActionController::UnknownFormat error. If you check the server
output in your terminal, you'll see this is a *406 Not Acceptable* error, as discussed earlier in this chapter. This error occurs because the controller only
responds to JSON requests, but your web browser asks for HTML by default.

Specify a different content type by adding an extension to the URL
in the address bar. Browsing to *http://localhost:3000/api/posts.json* returns a
JSON array of posts as expected.

Customizing JSON Output

So far your API returns all of the data associated with each post. You may
want to include additional data with each record, and, in some cases, you
may want to exclude data from some fields. For example, including data
about the author of each post is helpful, but you don't want to include the
user's password_digest or api_token.

You can customize the output from your API built in to Rails in a couple
of ways. Which method you use depends on how much customization you
need and your personal preference.

as_json

Because this API returns JSON data, you can easily customize the output
by changing the way Rails converts a model to JSON. Rails first calls the
as_json method on a model to convert it to a hash, which is then converted
to a JSON string.

You can override the as_json method in the Post model to customize the
data returned for each post. Open the file *app/models/post.rb* and add the
as_json method, shown here, to force the method to show only each post's
id and title:

```
class Post < ActiveRecord::Base
  --snip--

❶ def as_json(options={})
❷   super(only: [:id, :title])
  end

  --snip--
end
```

Be sure to include the options parameter with a default value of {} ❶ because the original as_json includes it. You aren't using the options parameter, but because you're overriding an existing method, your definition must match the original. Your as_json method calls super, which invokes the original as_json method defined by Active Record, with the parameter only: [:id, :title] ❷.

With this method in place, your API should only return the id and title of each post. Use the curl command to verify the change:

```
$ curl http://localhost:3000/api/posts
[
  {"id": 1, "title": "First Post"},
  {"id": 2, "title": "Google Search"}
]
```

The as_json method supports several additional options. Instead of specifying fields to include with :only, you could exclude fields with the :except option. You can also include associated models with the :include option. For example, update the as_json method, as shown here, to exclude the user_id field and include the post's associated user model:

```
def as_json(options={})
  super(except: [:user_id], include: :user)
end
```

The :methods option calls a list of methods and includes their return values in the output. For example, you can use this option to call the cached_comment_count method you added in Chapter 12:

```
def as_json(options={})
  super(except: [:user_id], include: :user,
    methods: :cached_comment_count)
end
```

This option will include the cached number of comments associated with this post in the output.

Overriding as_json certainly works, but depending on the level of customization required, this can get a bit messy. Fortunately, Rails provides a way to customize fully the JSON data returned by your API. Remove the as_json method from the Post model and let's cover jbuilder.

Jbuilder

Jbuilder is a domain-specific language for generating JSON output. The jbuilder gem is included by default in the *Gemfile* generated by the rails new command. Using jbuilder, you can create views for each of your API actions, just as you used ERB to create views for web actions.

As with your other views, you need to create a directory for your jbuilder views. The view directory must match the controller name. Enter the following commands to create a directory for API views and a sub-directory for the `PostsController` views:

```
$ mkdir app/views/api
$ mkdir app/views/api/posts
```

With these directories in place, you can create your first jbuilder view. Create a new file named *app/views/api/posts/index.json.jbuilder* and open it in your editor. Add this single line of code and save the file:

```
json.array! @posts
```

The `json.array!` method tells jbuilder to render the value of `@posts` as a JSON array. Use Curl to check the output of the index action:

```
$ curl http://localhost:3000/api/posts
[
  {
    "id": 1,
    "title": "First Post",
    "body": "Hello, World!",
    "url":null,
    "user_id":1,
    --snip--
```

The output is the same as when you started. Now let's see about customizing this output.

The `json.array!` method also accepts a block. Inside the block, you can access each individual record in the array. You can then use the `json.extract!` method to include only certain fields from the post:

```
json.array! @posts do |post|
  json.extract! post, :id, :title, :body, :url
end
```

This example renders the `id`, `title`, `body`, and `url` fields from each post as JSON.

All of the usual view helpers are also available in jbuilder views. For example, you can include a URL for each post using the `api_post_url` helper method:

```
json.array! @posts do |post|
  json.extract! post, :id, :title, :body, :url
❶ json.post_url api_post_url(post)
end
```

The output of method calls, such as api_post_url(post) ❶, are automatically converted to JSON format. The next example adds some data about the author of each post:

```
json.array! @posts do |post|
  json.extract! post, :id, :title, :body, :url
  json.post_url api_post_url(post)

  json.user do
    json.extract! post.user, :id, :name, :email
  end
end
```

Here, I've used the json.extract! method again to include only specific fields for each user. You don't want to make the password_digest for users available through your public API.

Token-Based Authentication

Now let's add authentication so you can also create posts through your API. You'll add token-based authentication, like you used earlier when accessing the GitHub API.

Generating Tokens

First, add a field for the api_token string to the User model by generating a database migration:

```
$ bin/rails g migration add_api_token_to_users api_token:string
```

Remember to enter the bin/rake db:migrate command after generating this migration to update your database.

Now update the User model by opening *app/models/user.rb* in your editor and adding a validation for the api_token field and a before_validation callback to generate the API token:

```
class User < ActiveRecord::Base
  --snip--

❶ validates :api_token, presence: true, uniqueness: true

❷ before_validation :generate_api_token

  --snip--
```

First, you need to validate that the api_token is present and unique ❶. Because you're using this value to authenticate, no two users can have the same api_token.

Next, you use a `before_validation` callback to call a method to generate the api_token if it doesn't already exist ❷. Add the generate_api_token method at the bottom of the User model as shown here:

```
class User < ActiveRecord::Base

  --snip--

  def generate_api_token
❶   return if api_token.present?

    loop do
❷     self.api_token = SecureRandom.hex
❸     break unless User.exists? api_token: api_token
    end
  end

end
```

The generate_api_token method returns immediately if the api_token already has a value ❶. If a value is not present for the api_token, the method calls SecureRandom.hex inside an endless loop to generate a value ❷. The SecureRandom class uses the most secure random-number generator available on your computer to generate values. On Unix computers, it uses the /dev/urandom device; on Windows, it uses the Win32 Cryptographic API. The SecureRandom class also includes several methods for formatting random values. The hex method returns a random 32-character hexadecimal value. Finally, if a user with this api_token doesn't exist, break out of the loop ❸.

Now open a Rails console and update the existing users:

```
❶ irb(main):001:0> user = User.first
   User Load (0.2ms)  SELECT "users".* ...
  => #<User id: 1, ... api_token: nil>
❷ irb(main):002:0> user.save
    (0.1ms)  begin transaction
   User Exists (0.2ms)  SELECT 1 AS one FROM ...
   User Exists (0.1ms)  SELECT 1 AS one FROM ...
   User Exists (0.1ms)  SELECT 1 AS one FROM ...
   SQL (1.3ms)  UPDATE "users" SET "api_token" ...
    (1.7ms)  commit transaction
  => true
```

Because the generate_api_token method is called automatically using a before_validation callback, you simply need to load the user into a variable ❶ and then save it to the database ❷ to update it. Do this for each of your users. If any user doesn't have a value for api_token, it will be created.

Now update the user show view to display the api_token when a user views his or her own account. Update *app/views/users/show.html.erb* as shown here:

```
<div class="page-header">
  <h1>User</h1>
</div>

<p class="lead"><%= @user.email %></p>

❶ <% if @user == current_user %>
  <p class="lead">API Token: <%= @user.api_token %></p>
<% end %>

--snip--
```

Because API tokens are essentially passwords, you want to protect them by only showing them when the user being displayed is equal to the current_user ❶.

Authenticating Requests

Now that all users have an API token, let's put those tokens to use. The process of authenticating with a token is similar to the username and password authentication you already created. Because you may have more than one controller for your API, you should include the authentication method in ApplicationController, which is the parent class of all other controllers.

First, you need a method to authenticate using an api_token. Luckily, Rails has a built-in method called authenticate_or_request_with_http_token to handle the details for you. Open the file *app/controllers/application_controller.rb* and add the following method to see how this works:

```
class ApplicationController < ActionController::Base
  # Prevent CSRF attacks by raising an exception.
  # For APIs, you may want to use :null_session instead.
  protect_from_forgery with: :exception

  private

  def authenticate_token!
    authenticate_or_request_with_http_token do |token, options|
❶     @api_user = User.find_by(api_token: token)
    end
  end

  --snip--
```

This method is named authenticate_token! to match the authenticate_user! method you added in Chapter 9. The authenticate_or_request_with_http_token retrieves the token included in the request's Authorization header and passes it to a block. Inside the block, you try to find a user in the database using the given token ❶. The `find_by` method returns a `User` object if a matching user is found, or `nil` otherwise. This value is assigned to the `@api_user` instance variable and returned from the block. If the block returns a false value, such as `nil`, the method knows that authentication failed and sends a *401 Unauthorized* response to the client.

You wrote a helper method called `current_user` for accessing the authenticated user in Chapter 9. For API requests, the authenticated user is already assigned to the `@api_user` instance variable, so you can use this variable.

Your token-based authentication solution is ready to go now. Let's try it out by adding the ability to create text posts through your API.

Using Token-Based Authentication

First, you need to add routes for text posts, so open *config/routes.rb* and add the `text_posts` resources inside the `:api` namespace:

```
Social::Application.routes.draw do
--snip--

  namespace :api do u
    resources :posts
    resources :text_posts
  end
end
```

Now you need a controller for text posts. Remember, it needs to be inside the *api/* directory because the routes are in the `:api` namespace. Create a file named *app/controllers/api/text_posts_controller.rb* and add the following code:

```
module Api
  class TextPostsController < ApplicationController
    respond_to :json
❶   before_action :authenticate_token!

  end
end
```

This controller starts the same as the API posts controller. The `TextPostsController` class must be inside a module called `Api`. It also includes `respond_to :json`. The first change is the addition of `before_action :authenticate_token!` ❶. The controller calls the `authenticate_token!` method before each action.

You want to create text posts, so add the create method:

```
module Api
  class TextPostsController < ApplicationController
    respond_to :json
    before_action :authenticate_token!
```

```
❶    def create
       @text_post = @api_user.text_posts.create(text_post_params)
       respond_with @text_post
     end
   end
end
```

The create method uses the @api_user instance variable set inside
authenticate_token! to create a new text post ❶. You then use respond_with
to send the new text post back to the client. Note that you don't check to
see whether the text post was actually created. The respond_with method
automatically sends the appropriate error response if @text_post contains
errors.

Because you also want to specify permitted parameter values, your final
addition is a text_post_params method:

```
module Api
  class TextPostsController < ApplicationController
    before_action :authenticate_token!

    respond_to :json

    def create
      @text_post = @api_user.text_posts.build(text_post_params)
      respond_with @text_post
    end

    private

❶   def text_post_params
      params.require(:text_post).permit(:title, :body)
    end
  end
end
```

The text_post_params method permits data for a :title and :body in a
nested hash with the key :text_post ❶. This is the same as the text_post_params
method in the controller for web requests.

Enter the curl command to try out the new API. Make sure to set the
Content-Type header to application/json when you run the command, so Rails
automatically parses the JSON data included with your request. Replace the
word *token* with the actual api_token from one of your application's users.

```
$ curl -i \
       -d '{"text_post":{"title":"Test","body":"Hello"}}' \
       -H "Content-Type: application/json" \
       -H "Authorization: Token token" \
       http://localhost:3000/api/text_posts
❶ HTTP/1.1 422 Unprocessable Entity
  --snip--
```

Something went wrong: The status code *422 Unprocessable Entity* ❶ means the data the client passed to the server is not valid. Check the server output in your terminal for more information.

```
Started POST "/api/text_posts" for 127.0.0.1 at 2014-04-23 19:39:09 -0500
Processing by Api::TextPostsController#create as */*
  Parameters: {"text_post"=>{"title"=>"Test", "body"=>"Hello"}}
❶ Can't verify CSRF token authenticity
Completed 422 Unprocessable Entity in 1ms

--snip--
```

The data passed to the server is valid but didn't include a CSRF token ❶. Remember, this token is not the same as the API token. The CSRF token is another unique token that is sent automatically when you submit form data in your application. Because you aren't submitting a form, you have no way of knowing the correct CSRF token.

When you were updating the ApplicationController earlier, you may have noticed a helpful comment at the top of the class. Rails normally prevents CSRF attacks by raising an exception. This is great for a web application, but it won't work for an API. Instead of raising an exception, you can prevent CSRF attacks by clearing out the user's session data. Now any time the application receives data from a user that does not include the CSRF token, it clears the user's session, effectively logging the user out of the application and preventing the attack.

Fortunately, rather than store authentication data in the session, API clients include the correct API token with each request. So API requests should work fine with a null session. Open *app/controllers/application_controller.rb* in your editor and make the following update:

```
class ApplicationController < ActionController::Base
  # Prevent CSRF attacks by raising an exception.
  # For APIs, you may want to use :null_session instead.
❶ protect_from_forgery with: :null_session

  --snip--
```

In the protect_from_forgery method call ❶, change the value of the :with option to :null_session, and then try the same request again using curl:

```
$ curl -i \
       -d '{"text_post":{"title":"Test","body":"Hello"}}' \
       -H "Content-Type: application/json" \
       -H "Authorization: Token token" \
       http://localhost:3000/api/text_posts
❶ HTTP/1.1 201 Created
  --snip--
```

❷ {
```
    "id":5,
    "title":"Test",
    "body":"Hello",
    "url":null,
    "user_id":1,
    "created_at":"2014-04-24T00:33:35.874Z",
    "updated_at":"2014-04-24T00:33:35.874Z"
}
```

The status code is now *201 Created*, which means success ❶. The HTTP headers are followed by a JSON representation of the new text post ❷. Because you didn't create a jbuilder view for this action, the default JSON representation is used.

You can also open the `posts` index page in your browser, or issue an API request for all posts with the command `curl http://localhost:3000/api/posts`, to verify the text post was created successfully.

Summary

A Web API can open up your application to collaborations from both your customers and third-party applications. With an effective API, you can also build native mobile or desktop clients for your application. You could even use another application's API to integrate its data into yours.

In this chapter, we discussed the GitHub API and used it to access detailed data about users and repositories. After covering the Hypertext Transfer Protocol and token-based authentication, you built your own API for your social network application.

In the next chapter, you'll learn how to set up your own server to host Rails applications and use the Capistrano remote server automation tool to deploy and maintain your applications.

Exercises

1. Verify that your token-based authentication is really working by issuing a POST request with a fake token. Use the `curl` command to send the request, and be sure to check both the status code in the headers and the response body.

2. Try to create a text post with invalid data and see what happens. You can check the validation for text posts in *app/models/text_post.rb*. Again, use the `curl` command to send the request and be sure to check the status code in both the headers and the response body.

3. Extend the API by adding a `show` action to the posts controller. This action should find the correct post using `params[:id]` and then use the `respond_with` method to send the post back to the client. Because this is a GET request, you can check it with `curl` or in your web browser.

15

CUSTOM DEPLOYMENT

Moving your finished application into production and making it available to users requires you to make many choices. You can choose from a variety of web hosting providers, Rails application servers, databases, and automated deployment systems. In Chapter 6, you learned about Heroku, a hosting service that uses Git for deployment.

Most large companies have an operations team to configure servers and deploy applications. But as a beginning Rails programmer, you may not have the luxury of a dedicated operations team to deploy your application.

In this chapter, you'll set up a server to host your application, configure your application's production environment, push your application to GitHub, and finally deploy to your server using Capistrano.

Virtual Private Servers

A *virtual private server (VPS)* is a type of virtual machine sold by web hosting providers. A single physical server can run many virtual private servers. An individual VPS is often referred to as an *instance.*

When you buy a VPS, you get part of the processing power, memory, and disk space of a larger physical server. You get you full access to your part of the server, including the ability to choose your operating system. So you are free to install the software you need and configure the server however you like. Unfortunately, you are also responsible for any installation and configuration errors on the server.

Many different hosting providers offer VPS services. A quick Google search leads to hundreds of competing providers. A popular choice among both startups and established companies is Amazon Web Services (AWS).

NOTE *The rest of this chapter uses AWS to set up a server and deploy your application, but the instructions are not AWS specific. If you would rather use a different service, create an instance running Ubuntu Linux 14.04 LTS, and you should be able to follow along with no problem. Ubuntu Linux 14.04 LTS is a long-term support release with guaranteed support until April 2019.*

Amazon AWS Setup

In addition to being a popular choice, Amazon also provides an AWS free usage tier for new users. You can read more about the free usage tier at *http://aws.amazon.com/free/* to see if you qualify. Even if you don't qualify for the free usage tier, you can still get an AWS Micro instance for a few cents an hour.

Amazon calls their VPS service *Amazon Elastic Compute Cloud (Amazon EC2)*. Rather than cover the details of setting up your Amazon account here, please refer to the Amazon EC2 documentation at *http://aws.amazon.com/documentation/ec2/*.

Click the **User Guide** link, and follow the instructions, starting with Setting Up. This section walks you through the process of signing up for AWS, creating a user account in the AWS Identity and Access Management (IAM) system, creating a key pair, and creating a security group. Be sure you store your IAM credentials and private key—you'll need them for this chapter.

Then move on to Getting Started. In this section, you should launch an EC2 instance, connect to your instance, add a storage volume, and finally clean up your instance and volume. The EC2 user guide uses an Amazon Linux machine image that we won't be using again, so be sure to follow the clean-up instructions in the User Guide when you're done with this section.

Once you're up to speed on Amazon EC2, you can set up your production server as described in this section. I recommend Ubuntu Linux, so the instructions that follow are Ubuntu specific. From the EC2 Management Console, click the **Launch Instance** button to create a new server instance, and choose the Ubuntu Server 14.04 LTS (PV) Amazon Machine Image in the Quick Start section. Because this is a web server, you need to configure the security group to allow HTTP traffic. Click the **Next** button in the Launch Instance wizard until you reach Step 6: Configure Security Group. Now click the **Add Rule** button, select **HTTP** from the Type drop-down menu, and click the **Review and Launch** button. Finally, click the **Launch** button.

Once the instance is running, make note of the public DNS name displayed in the EC2 Management Console, and then connect to the instance with SSH in a terminal window. Using the following command, replace *your_key_file* with the full path to the private key file you created in the Setting Up section of the EC2 User Guide and *your_instance_name* with the public DNS name of your instance:

```
$ ssh -i your_key_file ubuntu@your_instance_name
Welcome to Ubuntu 14.04 LTS...
--snip--
```

The default user account on the Ubuntu AMI is named *ubuntu*. So this command connects to the user named ubuntu at your instance.

Ubuntu Linux Setup

Once you're connected, you can configure the instance for hosting Ruby on Rails applications. Enter all of the commands in this section on your instance over the SSH connection.

Ubuntu uses a system called apt-get for installing software from online repositories. The first thing you need is Ruby. Unfortunately, the default repositories often contain an older version of Ruby, but you have a way around that.

Installing Ruby

The developers at a hosting company called Brightbox have set up their own Ubuntu repository with the latest version of Ruby and made it available to the public. This repository is known as a *Personal Package Archive (PPA)*. You can add this repository to your instance and get the latest version of Ruby using these commands:

```
$ sudo apt-get install python-software-properties
Reading package lists... Done
--snip--
Setting up python-software-properties (0.92.36) ...
$ sudo apt-add-repository ppa:brightbox/ruby-ng
Next generation Ubuntu packages for Ruby ...
--snip--

http://brightbox.com
 More info: https://launchpad.net/~brightbox/+archive/ruby-ng
Press [ENTER] to continue or ctrl-c to cancel adding it
```

Press ENTER when prompted, and then wait for the word OK to appear. After you add the Brightbox repository, update the apt-get package lists so it can find the newer versions of the Ruby packages.

```
$ sudo apt-get update
Ign http://us-east-1.ec2.archive.ubuntu.com trusty ...
--snip--
Fetched 13.7 MB in 9s (1,471 kB/s)
Reading package lists... Done
```

Now install Ruby version 2.1. The following command installs both the Ruby interpreter and the development headers needed to compile additional gems:

```
$ sudo apt-get install ruby2.1 ruby2.1-dev
Reading package lists... Done
--snip--
Do you want to continue? [Y/n]
```

Press ENTER to continue. Once the installation completes, check the Ruby version.

```
$ ruby -v
ruby 2.1.1p76 (2014-02-24 revision 45161) [x86_64-linux-gnu]
```

Since Ruby is frequently updated, you'll probably see a newer version number than the one shown here. Now that Ruby's installed, you need a web server for Ruby on Rails applications.

Installing Apache and Passenger

A variety of web servers are available today. The most popular web server is Apache, and that's what we'll use. Install the Apache HTTP Server version 2 with this command:

```
$ sudo apt-get install apache2
Reading package lists... Done
--snip--
Do you want to continue? [Y/n]
```

Press ENTER to continue.

Once you've completed this, open your web browser and go to the public DNS name of your instance to see the default Ubuntu website. Although you can't see your application yet, you're making progress.

Apache is great for serving web pages, but you need an application server to run your Ruby on Rails application. A popular application server that integrates with Apache is Phusion Passenger.

Phusion provides the Passenger application server through its own apt-get repository. It's not a PPA like the Brightbox repository you used earlier, however, so the setup has a few more steps.

First, enter the apt-key command to import Phusion's RSA key for the Ubuntu key server:

```
$ sudo apt-key adv --keyserver keyserver.ubuntu.com \
                   --recv-keys 561F9B9CAC40B2F7
Executing: gpg --ignore-time-conflict ...
--snip--
gpg:                      imported: 1  (RSA: 1)
```

The apt-get program uses this key to ensure that packages you install are really coming from Phusion. Phusion's repository uses an encrypted HTTP connection (HTTPS) to communicate with your instance.

First, you need to add the Phusion Passenger repository to your instance. Enter the following command to open a new file in the nano editor on your instance. (Or, if you're more comfortable with another command-line editor, use that instead.)

```
$ sudo nano /etc/apt/sources.list.d/passenger.list
```

Enter **deb https://oss-binaries.phusionpassenger.com/apt/passenger trusty main** on the first line to add the address of the Phusion Passenger repository to your instance. Then, if you're using nano, press CTRL-O followed by ENTER to save the file and CTRL-X to exit the editor.

Now update the apt-get package lists again:

```
$ sudo apt-get update
Ign http://us-east-1.ec2.archive.ubuntu.com trusty InRelease
--snip--
Reading package lists... Done
```

Then install the Apache 2 Phusion Passenger module:

```
$ sudo apt-get install libapache2-mod-passenger
Reading package lists... Done
--snip--
Do you want to continue? [Y/n]
```

Press ENTER to continue. Once the installation completes, your instance should be set up to serve both standard web pages and Ruby on Rails applications.

With your web server installed, create a directory for your application. The default directory for regular HTML web pages is */var/www/html*. Because you're deploying a Ruby on Rails application, create a separate directory with these commands.

```
$ sudo mkdir /var/www/social
$ sudo chown ubuntu /var/www/social
$ sudo chgrp ubuntu /var/www/social
```

The first command creates a directory named */var/www/social*. The next two commands assign ownership of that directory to your ubuntu user and group, allowing you to write files to that directory as needed.

Now you need to install and set up a database for your application.

Installing PostgreSQL

This chapter uses the PostgreSQL database, but which database software you choose is mostly up to you. MySQL is another popular, open source option you might consider.

Install PostgreSQL with this command:

```
$ sudo apt-get install postgresql postgresql-contrib
Reading package lists... Done
--snip--
Do you want to continue? [Y/n]
```

Press ENTER to continue. Now that the database software is installed, let's add a user account and create a few databases. The default user account for PostgreSQL is named *postgres*, so you need to issue the createuser command as the postgres user with the sudo -u postgres command:

```
$ sudo -u postgres createuser --superuser ubuntu
```

This command creates a new user named *ubuntu* with superuser access to the database. This user has full access to all database commands. PostgreSQL is configured with an authentication system known as *ident sameuser,* by default, in Ubuntu. This means if your Ubuntu username matches your PostgreSQL username, you can connect without a password.

Now that you've created a PostgreSQL account for yourself, add a database and then see if you can connect to it:

```
$ createdb ubuntu
$ psql
psql (9.3.4)
Type "help" for help.

ubuntu=# help
You are using psql, the command-line interface to PostgreSQL.
Type:  \copyright for distribution terms
       \h for help with SQL commands
       \? for help with psql commands
       \g or terminate with semicolon to execute query
       \q to quit
ubuntu=#
```

Your account can now log in to PostgreSQL and run commands. Enter \q to quit. Now add a production database for your social application by entering this command:

```
$ createdb social_production
```

You won't need to enter any other PostgreSQL commands on your instance. Now that you've created the production database, the migrations in your application create the tables needed by your application. You'll configure the application to use this database before you deploy to your instance.

Installing Build Tools

Your instance is almost ready to go! Before you can deploy your application, however, you need to install a few more tools. Some of the gems your application uses need to be compiled, and to do so, you need build tools such as a C compiler. You also need Git for retrieving code from repositories and header files for PostgreSQL to compile the PostgreSQL database gem.

Fortunately, this single command should install all of the build tools you need:

```
$ sudo apt-get install build-essential git libpq-dev
Reading package lists... Done
--snip--
Do you want to continue? [Y/n]
```

The build-essential package is a collection of common build tools needed to compile many different types of software. You're already familiar with Git from Chapter 6. The libpq-dev package is needed to compile PostgreSQL client applications such as the pg gem.

Installing Gems

The last setup step is to install the gems your application needs. As you'll learn in the next section, the bundle command runs automatically when you deploy, but installing gems while you're connected to the server helps to verify everything is working.

Gems normally generate documentation during installation. On the server, this documentation just takes up space and slows down the installation. You can tell the gem command to not generate documentation by adding gem: --no-document to your *.gemrc* file:

```
$ echo "gem: --no-document" >> ~/.gemrc
```

Now that you've turned off gem documentation, install Rails:

```
$ sudo gem install rails
Fetching: thread_safe-0.3.3.gem (100%)
Successfully installed thread_safe-0.3.3
Fetching: minitest-5.3.3.gem (100%)
Successfully installed minitest-5.3.3
--snip--
```

Because you're using the PostgreSQL database, also install the pg gem. Parts of this gem are written in C, and they'll be compiled automatically during the installation.

```
$ sudo gem install pg
Building native extensions.  This could take a while...
Successfully installed pg-0.17.1
1 gem installed
```

Finally, you need a gem called therubyracer. This gem embeds Google's V8 JavaScript interpreter into Ruby. Rails uses this gem to compile assets on the server. Parts of this gem must also be compiled.

```
$ sudo gem install therubyracer
Building native extensions.  This could take a while...
Successfully installed therubyracer-0.12.1
1 gem installed
```

With these gems in place, your instance is ready to run Rails applications. Now that the VPS setup is complete, let's learn about Capistrano and the changes you need to make to your application to deploy and run it in production.

Capistrano

Capistrano is an open source tool for automating the process of running scripts and deploying applications on remote servers over an SSH connection. Capistrano extends the rake tool that you've used already. Just like rake, Capistrano uses a simple DSL to define *tasks*, which are applied to different servers based on their *role*.

Tasks include things such as pulling code from a Git repository, running bundle install, or running database migrations with rake. Roles are different types of servers such as web, application, or database. Currently, these are all on the same server, but when your application gets too big for a single server, Capistrano makes splitting the work among multiple servers easy.

Capistrano also supports deploying an application to different *stages*. Capistrano stages are sets of servers, such as staging servers and production servers. Both of these servers run your Rails application in the production environment, but the staging server is probably used only for testing, whereas the production server is accessible by your users.

Getting Started

Exit the SSH session on your VPS or open another terminal window on your local computer to set up Capistrano. Because Capistrano is a gem, you first need to update your application's *Gemfile*. Capistrano is already in the file, but it's commented out. Remove the pound sign from the beginning of the line for the capistrano-rails gem to install both Capistrano and the Rails-specific tasks you need.

While you're editing the *Gemfile*, also make the changes needed for running in production:

```
--snip--

# Use sqlite3 as the database for Active Record
❶ gem 'sqlite3', group: [:development, :test]

--snip--

# See https://github.com/sstephenson/execjs#readme...
❷ gem 'therubyracer', platforms: :ruby, group: :production

--snip--

# Use Capistrano for deployment
❸ gem 'capistrano-rails', group: :development

❹ # Use PostgreSQL in production
  gem 'pg', group: :production

# Use debugger
gem 'byebug', group: [:development, :test]
```

These changes first specify that the SQLite gem is only needed in the development and test environments ❶. Next, therubyracer gem is needed to compile assets in production ❷ as mentioned in the last section. The capistrano-rails gem is only needed in development ❸. Finally, you also need the PostgreSQL gem in production ❹.

Now update the installed gems on your computer:

```
$ bin/bundle install --binstubs --without production
Fetching gem metadata from https://rubygems.org/........
Fetching additional metadata from https://rubygems.org/..
Resolving dependencies...
--snip--
```

The --binstubs option tells bundler to also install the executable files in the *bin/* directory. For example, Capistrano includes the cap command that you'll use to deploy your application, and you'll run that from *bin/*. The --without production option tells bundler to install only gems for the development and test environments.

Next, you need to install Capistrano in your application:

```
$ bin/cap install
mkdir -p config/deploy
create config/deploy.rb
create config/deploy/staging.rb
create config/deploy/production.rb
mkdir -p lib/capistrano/tasks
Capified
```

This process generates the files you need to configure Capistrano to deploy your application. Let's dig into those next.

Configuration

Now that your application has been Capified, you may notice some new files. The first of these is named *Capfile* and is located in the root of the application. You need to make one small change to that file:

```
# Load DSL and Setup Up Stages
require 'capistrano/setup'

# Includes default deployment tasks
require 'capistrano/deploy'
```
❶ ```
Include all Rails tasks
require 'capistrano/rails'
```

*--snip--*

As the comment says, the new require line includes Capistrano's Rails-specific tasks in your application ❶. After you save this file, you can see a list of Capistrano tasks by entering the bin/cap -T command in your terminal.

Next, you need to edit the file *config/deploy.rb*. This file contains configuration that is shared by all deployment stages, such as the name of your application and the address of your Git repository.

```
config valid only for Capistrano 3.1
lock '3.2.1'
```
❶ ```
set :application, 'social'
set :repo_url, 'https://github.com/yourname/social.git'

# Default branch is :master
# ask :branch, proc { `git rev-parse --abbrev-ref HEAD`.chomp }.call

# Default deploy_to directory is /var/www/my_app
```
❷ ```
set :deploy_to, '/var/www/social'
```

*--snip--*

```
namespace :deploy do
```
```

```
      desc 'Restart application'
      task :restart do
        on roles(:app), in: :sequence, wait: 5 do
          # Your restart mechanism here, for example:
❸         execute :touch, release_path.join('tmp/restart.txt')
        end
      end

      after :publishing, :restart

      --snip--

end
```

First, set the name of your application to social and specify the URL of
your Git repository ❶. Replace *yourname* with your GitHub username. Next,
set the *deploy* directory to the */var/www/social* directory that you created on
your instance ❷. Finally, uncomment the execute line ❸ in the restart task.
This line executes the touch tmp/restart.txt command. This command is
needed to restart the Passenger application server after deployment.

Now that the shared settings are updated, edit the *config/deploy/
production.rb* file. This file contains settings specific to the Capistrano
production stage. Replace the existing code in this file with the following code:

```
      server 'your_instance_name',
❶           user: 'ubuntu', roles: %w{web app db}

❷ set :ssh_options, {
        keys: 'your_key_file'
      }
```

First, Capistrano needs the address of your servers, along with the
username and roles of each server ❶. Your instance is fulfilling all three
roles, and the username is ubuntu. Replace *your_instance_name* with your
server's public DNS name. Next, specify the SSH options needed to connect to your instance ❷. Capistrano needs the path to your private key to
connect. Replace *your_key_file* with the full path to your private key file.

Database Setup

Next, configure your application to use the PostgreSQL database you created earlier. Database configuration is in the file *config/database.yml*. Update
the production section, as shown here:

```
      --snip--

      production:
        adapter: postgresql
        encoding: unicode
❶       database: social_production
        pool: 5
```

```
❷   username: ubuntu
❸   password:
```

This code tells Rails to use the PostgreSQL database named
social_production ❶ in the production environment. Rails will connect
to the database with the username ubuntu ❷ and no password ❸, thanks to
the Ubuntu's ident sameuser authentication setup mentioned earlier.

Secrets Setup

The last thing you need to set up is the secret key used to sign your application's cookies. This value is stored in the file *config/secrets.yml*. This file can
also be used to store other secret information such as passwords or API keys
needed by your application.

```
--snip--
development:
  secret_key_base: 242ba1d...

test:
  secret_key_base: 92d581d...

❶ # Do not keep production secrets in the repository,
  # instead read values from the environment.
  production:
❷   secret_key_base: <%= ENV["SECRET_KEY_BASE"] %>
```

As mentioned in the comment, you shouldn't keep production secrets
in this file ❶. If the code for your application is stored in a public Git repository, these secrets would then be publicly available. Instead, this file uses an
ERB tag to read the value of the SECRET_KEY_BASE environment variable ❷.

Before you can set this environment variable on your server, generate a
value using the following command:

```
$ bin/rake secret
a3467dbd655679241a41d44b8245...
```

Copy the value output by this command and save it in a safe place.
You'll need it again when you set up the virtual host for your application
later in this chapter.

Add to Git

With Capistrano configured and the database configured, you're ready to
create a Git repository for your application and push your code to GitHub.
Capistrano runs git commands on your instance to pull changes to your
application from GitHub during deployment.

First create a Git repository on your local computer with the following
commands. (Refer back to Chapter 6 if you need a refresher on Git.)

```
$ git init
Initialized empty Git repository in ...
$ git add .
$ git commit -m "Initial commit"
[master (root-commit) 1928798] Initial commit
 123 files changed, 1826 insertions(+)
--snip--
```

Now log in to your GitHub account and create a new public repository named *social*. Once the repository is created, add a remote to the local repository you just created and push the code up to GitHub.

```
$ git remote add origin https://github.com/yourname/social.git
$ git push -u origin master
Counting objects: 141, done.
--snip--
Branch master set up to track remote branch master from origin.
```

Once Capistrano is configured and your application is on GitHub, you're ready to deploy.

Deployment

First, test the connection to your instance and check if the instance is ready to receive a deployment from Capistrano. The deploy:check task ensures everything on the instance is set up correctly:

```
$ bin/cap production deploy:check
 INFO [722a06ac] Running /usr/bin/env ...
--snip--
 INFO [5d3c6d3e] Finished ... exit status 0 (successful).
```

Note that I specified the production stage in the command. You must include the stage with every Capistrano command.

If the deploy:check task finishes successfully, you're ready to deploy your application for the first time:

```
$ bin/cap production deploy
 INFO [e6d54911] Running /usr/bin/env ...
--snip--
 INFO [3cb59e26] Finished ... exit status 0 (successful).
```

The deploy task not only checks out the latest code from GitHub but also runs bundle install to update installed gems, compiles your application's assets, and migrates the database. Even once your application is installed on your instance and running, however, you still need to make one more configuration change to see your application on the Internet.

Adding a Virtual Host

A *Virtual Host* is a way to host multiple sites on the same server or instance. The Apache web server allows you to set up many different sites on the same physical server. It then uses the DNS name of each site to serve the correct site for each incoming request. You currently have only a single site running on your instance, but you still need to set it up as a Virtual Host.

You perform this step one time. You won't need to do this again unless you decide to add another site to the same server. You needed to wait until after your application was deployed since the directory names you're going to specify didn't exist before.

First, connect to your instance with SSH, and then create a configuration file for the social application in the */etc/apache2/sites-available* directory:

```
$ sudo nano /etc/apache2/sites-available/social.conf
```

The previous command opens the new file in the nano editor. Enter the following Apache configuration code in the new file:

```
❶ <VirtualHost *:80>
❷   ServerName your_instance_name
❸   DocumentRoot /var/www/social/current/public
❹   SetEnv SECRET_KEY_BASE a3467dbd65...
❺   <Directory /var/www/social/current/public>
      Allow from all
      Options -MultiViews
    </Directory>
  </VirtualHost>
```

The first line means this Virtual Host responds to all requests (indicated by the star) on port 80 ❶. Next, specify the server name of this Virtual Host ❷. Replace *your_instance_name* with the public DNS name of your instance.

Then set the document root for this Virtual Host ❸. The document root is normally the location of the site's HTML files, but here, you set it to your application's public directory. This configuration is specific to the Passenger application server.

The next line sets the SECRET_KEY_BASE environment variable ❹. Replace the partial key shown here with the complete 128-digit key generated by the bin/rake secret command you entered earlier.

Finally, set options for the document root directory ❺. The Allow from all line means that all hosts and IP addresses are allowed access to the files in this directory. The Options -MultiViews line turns off the MultiViews feature in Apache. This feature uses automatic content negotiation, which can cause Apache to serve files to a client even if the file extension is not specified, which you don't want.

Press CTRL-O followed by ENTER to save the file, and then press CTRL-X to exit the editor.

Now that the new site is configured in Apache, you need to disable the default site that comes with Apache and enable the social site:

```
$ sudo a2dissite 000-default
Site 000-default disabled.
To activate the new configuration, you need to run:
  service apache2 reload
$ sudo a2ensite social
Enabling site social.
To activate the new configuration, you need to run:
  service apache2 reload
```

Once this is done, reload Apache to activate the changes:

```
$ sudo service apache2 reload
 * Reloading web server apache2
 *
```

Now open your web browser and go to the public DNS name of your instance. Your application should be available to the world, running in production on your own virtual private server.

Summary

In this chapter, you learned how to set up a Linux server for hosting Rails applications. You installed and configured the Apache web server, the Phusion Passenger application server, and the PostgreSQL database server.

You also learned how to integrate the remote server automation tool Capistrano in your Rails application. You configured your Rails application for production and used Capistrano to deploy it to your instance.

With this done, you are well on your way to becoming a professional Rails developer!

Exercises

1. Make a small change to your application, such as updating the title of each page. Commit the change to your local Git repository, push the changes to GitHub, and then deploy the change to your instance.

2. Learn about other gems you can use to add features to your Rails applications easily. For example, you might want to allow users to upload images to your site instead of using a third-party image-hosting service. Hundreds of open source projects are available for adding this and other features to your application. Find one you like and try it out. If you find a bug, fix it and send the developer a pull request on GitHub.

3. Get to know the Ruby on Rails community and get involved. Follow Rails development on GitHub. Check out the official Ruby on Rails website and blog. Find out about Ruby and Rails conferences and try to attend; make yourself known at your local Ruby or Rails User Group.

SOLUTIONS

Chapter 1

1. Exercise 1 is about learning to read a file and exploring the array
    methods using the contents of the file. I'd expect to see something
    like this in the console after completing the exercise:

```
irb(main):001:0> file = File.read("test.txt")
 => "Call me Ishmael..."
irb(main):002:0> puts file.split
Call
me
Ishmael
--snip--
 => nil
irb(main):003:0> puts file.split.length
 => 198
irb(main):004:0> puts file.split.uniq.length
 => 140
```

The output depends on the text you used.

2. The second exercise requires writing a little code. The following sample solves the problem using only methods covered so far:

```
file = File.read("test.txt")
counts = {}
file.split.each do |word|
  if counts[word]
    counts[word] = counts[word] + 1
  else
    counts[word] = 1
  end
end
puts counts
```

This solution should print something like this:

```
=> {"Call"=>1, "me"=>3, "Ishmael."=>1, ...
```

The word "Call" appears once in the paragraph; the word "me" appears three times; and so on.

3. Using the sample code provided in Exercise 3, the complete solution looks like this:

```
class WordCounter
  def initialize(file_name)
    @file = File.read(file_name)
  end

  def count
    @file.split.length
  end

  def uniq_count
    @file.split.uniq.length
  end

  def frequency
    counts = {}
    @file.split.each do |w|
      if counts[w]
        counts[w] = counts[w] + 1
      else
        counts[w] = 1
      end
    end
  end
end
```

This combines the solutions to the first two exercises, wrapping them in a Ruby class.

Chapter 2

1. The first exercise is about familiarizing yourself with a simple Rails application and the functionality provided by default. The address of the home page is *http://localhost:3000/posts*. As you move around the application, that address changes. The new post form is at */posts/new*; the first post is at */posts/1*; and the form for editing the first post is at */posts/1/edit*. These paths and their meaning are covered in Chapter 4.

2. If you've never worked on a large application before, the number of files in a typical Rails application can seem daunting. Most editors contain some type of project list for opening files, as well as keyboard shortcuts for quickly searching for files by name. These features are invaluable when working on larger projects.

Chapter 3

1. The following commands generate and run the migration to add an email address to comments:

```
$ bin/rails g migration add_email_to_comments email:string
    invoke  active_record
    create    db/migrate/20140404225418_add_email_to_comments.rb
$ bin/rake db:migrate
== 20140404225418 AddEmailToComments: migrating...
--snip--
```

   You can then launch a Rails console with `bin/rails console` and create a new comment with an email address.

2. Open *app/models/comment.rb* and add the validation as shown here:

```
class Comment < ActiveRecord::Base
  belongs_to :post
  validates :author, :body, presence: true
end
```

   Note that I added the validation for both fields on a single line. You could do this, however, with two separate calls to the `validates` method.

3. You can't write a single query to determine the number of comments for each post, but you can iterate over all posts and count the comments. Enter something like this in the Rails console:

```
2.1.0 :001 > Post.all.each do |post|
2.1.0 :002 *   puts post.comments.count
2.1.0 :003 > end
```

   This code first finds all of the posts and then makes a count query on the comments table for each one.

Chapter 4

1. Open the file *app/controllers/comments_controller.rb*, and find the create method.

```
class CommentsController < ApplicationController
  def create
    @post = Post.find(params[:post_id])

    if @post.comments.create(comment_params) ❶
      redirect_to @post,
                  notice: 'Comment was successfully created.'
    else
      redirect_to @post,
                  alert: 'Error creating comment.'
    end
  end
--snip--
```

Note that it currently uses `@post.comments.create(comment_params)` ❶ to initialize and save the new comment as part of the if statement. You need to store the new comment in a variable so you can use the errors method to get a list of errors when the save fails. Update the create method as shown here:

```
class CommentsController < ApplicationController
  def create
    @post = Post.find(params[:post_id])
    @comment = @post.comments.build(comment_params)

    if @comment.save
      redirect_to @post,
                  notice: 'Comment was successfully created.'
    else
      redirect_to @post,
                  alert: 'Error creating comment. ' +
                         @comment.errors.full_messages.to_sentence ❶
    end
  end
--snip--
```

This code adds the errors to the existing alert. Notice I used the to_sentence method ❶ to convert the array of error messages to a sentence like this: "Author can't be blank and Body can't be blank."

2. Edit *app/controllers/comments_controller.rb*, and find the comment_params method. Add :email to the call to the permit method:

```
class CommentsController < ApplicationController
--snip--

  private
```

```
  def comment_params
    params.require(:comment).permit(:author, :body, :email)
  end
end
```

Now if a user enters an email address when adding a new comment, the address should be stored in the database. Without this change, the email field is simply ignored.

Chapter 5

1. Remove the h1 element from *app/views/posts/index.html.erb* and update *app/views/layouts/application.html.erb,* as shown here:

```
--snip--
<body>
<h1>Listing posts</h1>

<%= yield %>

</body>
</html>
```

Also change the headings in *app/views/posts/new.html.erb* and *app/views/posts/edit.html.erb* to h2 headings:

```
<h2>New post</h2>

<%= render 'form' %>

<%= link_to 'Back', posts_path %>
```

2. First, add a label and text field for :author to the *app/views/posts/_form.html.erb* partial:

```
--snip--
  <div class="field">
    <%= f.label :title %><br>
    <%= f.text_field :title %>
  </div>
  <div class="field">
    <%= f.label :author %><br>
    <%= f.text_field :author %>
  </div>
  <div class="field">
    <%= f.label :body %><br>
    <%= f.text_area :body %>
  </div>
--snip--
```

Then add `:author` to the list of permitted parameters in the `post_params` method at the bottom of *app/controllers/posts_controller.rb*:

```
--snip--
    def post_params
      params.require(:post).permit(:title, :author, :body)
    end
end
```

3. Make the changes to *config/routes.rb* and *app/views/comments/_comment .html.erb* as described in the question. Here is how I would write the destroy action in *app/controllers/comments_controller.rb*:

```
--snip--
  def destroy
    @post = Post.find(params[:post_id])
    @comment = @post.comments.find(params[:id])

    @comment.destroy
    respond_to do |format|
      format.html { redirect_to @post }
      format.json { head :no_content }
    end
  end
--snip--
```

Chapter 6

1. After editing files in your application, stage your changes in Git with **git add .**, then commit these changes with **git commit -m "Commit Message"**, and finally push the changes to Heroku with **git push heroku master**.

2. If you don't already have a GitHub account, go to *https://github.com/* and complete the sign-up form. Next you'll need to choose a plan. The free plan includes unlimited public repositories. Once you finish the sign-up process, you should see the GitHub Bootcamp screen. Follow the instructions there to create a repository and upload your application.

3. Create your new application in the *code* directory you created in Chapter 2, not inside the *blog* directory. Use the rails new command followed by the name of your new application. For example, to create an application to track your record collection, type this command:

```
$ rails new vinyl
```

Next think about the models your application needs. In this case, you probably need a Record or Album model. The model needs fields such as title, artist, and release_date. Move to the *vinyl* directory, and use the rails scaffold command to generate some code to get started:

```
$ cd vinyl
$ bin/rails generate scaffold Album title artist release_date:datetime
```

Now start the Rails server and work with your new application.

Chapter 7

1. In my version of Rails, the Post class has 58 ancestors.

```
irb(main):001:0> Post.ancestors.count
=> 58
```

Using the Ruby pretty-print method (pp), you can list each ancestor on a separate line:

```
irb(main):012:0> pp Post.ancestors
[Post(id: integer, title: string, body: text, created_at: datetime,
updated_at: datetime, author: string),
 Post::GeneratedFeatureMethods,
 #<Module:0x007fabc21bafd8>,
 ActiveRecord::Base,
 --snip--
 ActiveRecord::Validations,
 --snip--
 Kernel,
 BasicObject]
```

As you scroll through the list of ancestors, you should see some names you recognize, such as ActiveRecord::Associations and ActiveRecord::Validations. Also, notice that Post inherits from BasicObject, just like every other class in Ruby.

2. The cannot_*feature*! method should be the same as the can_*feature*! method except it assigns false to the @features[f] instead of true.

```
class User
  FEATURES = ['create', 'update', 'delete']

  FEATURES.each do |f|
    define_method "can_#{f}!" do
      @features[f] = true
    end
```

```
      define_method "cannot_#{f}!" do
        @features[f] = false
      end

      define_method "can_#{f}?" do
        !!@features[f]
      end
    end

  def initialize
    @features = {}
  end
end
```

After adding this method, create another instance of the User class and make sure the new method works as expected:

```
irb(main):001:0> user = User.new
 => #<User:0x007fc01b95abe0 @features={}>
irb(main):002:0> user.can_create!
 => true
irb(main):003:0> user.can_create?
 => true
irb(main):004:0> user.cannot_create!
 => false
irb(main):005:0> user.can_create?
 => false
```

3. First, look at the instance methods defined by the Element class:

```
irb(main):001:0> Element.instance_methods(false)
 => [:name, :name=]
```

The methods name and name= are defined as expected. Now reopen the Element class and add a call to accessor :symbol:

```
irb(main):002:0> class Element
irb(main):003:1>   accessor :symbol
irb(main):004:1> end
 => :symbol=
```

This should create two new methods named symbol and symbol=. You can verify that the methods were created by calling instance_methods again:

```
irb(main):005:0> Element.instance_methods(false)
 => [:name, :name=, :symbol, :symbol=]
```

You can verify that the methods work as expected by creating an instance of the Element class and assigning a symbol with e.symbol = "Au".

Chapter 8

1. Specifying `dependent: :destroy` on the `belongs_to` side of the association causes the parent model to be destroyed when any child model is destroyed. In this example, destroying any `Post` also destroys the associated `User`. This mistake is fairly common.

2. The completed `Comment` model should look like this:

```
class Comment < ActiveRecord::Base
  belongs_to :post
  belongs_to :user

  validates :post_id, presence: true
  validates :user_id, presence: true
end
```

The Rails generator adds `belongs_to` associations automatically, but it does not add validations.

3. Launch the Rails console with **bin/rails console**. Create a new `User`, `TextPost`, and `Comment`. Verify that all of the models were created. Then call `destroy` on the new `User` and verify that the associated `TextPost` and `Comment` records are also destroyed.

```
irb(main):001:0> carol = User.create name: "Carol"
 => #<User id: 3, name: "Carol", ...>
irb(main):002:0> post = TextPost.create user: carol, body: "Testing"
 => #<TextPost id: 3, body: "Testing", ...>
irb(main):003:0> comment = Comment.create post: post, user: carol, \
                                  body: "Hello"
 => #<Comment id: 1, body: "Hello", ...>
irb(main):004:0> carol.posts.count
 => 1
irb(main):005:0> carol.comments.count
 => 1
irb(main):006:0> carol.destroy ❶
--snip--
 => #<User id: 3, name: "Carol", ...>
irb(main):007:0> carol.posts.count
 => 0
irb(main):008:0> carol.comments.count
 => 0
irb(main):009:0> carol.reload ❷
ActiveRecord::RecordNotFound: Couldn't find User with id=3
--snip--
```

Note that calling `destroy` on the model does not remove it from memory ❶. The variable carol still refers to the model even though it has been deleted from the database. Attempting to reload the model from the database raises an `ActiveRecord::RecordNotFound` exception because the record for carol has been deleted ❷.

Chapter 9

1. First, edit the text post partial at *app/views/text_posts/_text_post.html.erb*, as shown here:

```erb
<div class="panel panel-default">
  <div class="panel-heading">
    <h3 class="panel-title">
      <%= text_post.title %>
    </h3>
    <%= link_to(
          "#{time_ago_in_words text_post.created_at} ago",
          post_path(text_post)) %>
  </div>
  --snip--
```

This creates a link to the text_post with the time in words such as "5 days ago." Edit the image post partial at *app/views/image_posts/_image_post.html.erb* with a similar change.

```erb
--snip--
  </h3>
  <%= link_to "#{time_ago_in_words image_post.created_at} ago",
        post_path(image_post) %>
</div>
--snip--
```

The only difference here is the word text_post is replaced with image_post. Now load the posts index page and make sure the links work correctly.

2. The most important part of this exercise is restricting access to the controller to authenticated users. Add before_action :authenticate_user! in *app/controllers/comments_controller.rb*, as shown here:

```ruby
class CommentsController < ApplicationController
  before_action :authenticate_user!

  --snip--
end
```

The comment partial at *app/views/comments/_comment.html.erb* shows the name of the user that created the comment and the body of the comment.

```erb
<p><em><%= comment.user.name %> said:</em></p>
<p><%= comment.body %></p>
```

This partial is rendered once for each comment by render @post.comments in the post show view.

3. First, start a Rails console with **bin/rails console** to see the **password_digest** for a user.

```
irb(main):001:0> alice = User.find 1
  User Load ...
 => #<User id: 1, name: "Alice", ...>
irb(main):002:0> alice.password_digest
 => "$2a$10$NBjrpHtfLJN14c6kVjG7sety1N4ifyuto7GD5qX7xHdVmbtweL1Ny"
```

The value of alice.password_digest that you see will be different. Bcrypt automatically adds a salt to the password before generating the hash digest. I can't tell the password for alice by looking at that value. Bcrypt seems pretty secure!

You can see the cookies for a site by looking at resources in your browser's Developer Tools or Page Info. According to the Chrome developer tools, my current _social_session cookie is 465 bytes of alphanumeric digits like this "M2xkVmNTaGpVaFd...". Again, I'm not able to decipher that information.

Chapter 10

1. Open the TextPost partial at *app/views/text_posts/_text_post.html.erb*. It already displays the user's name. Add a call to the link_to helper method before the text_post.user.name and also pass the text_post.user to the helper:

```
--snip--
<div class="panel-body">
  <p><em>By <%= link_to text_post.user.name, text_post.user %></em></p>

  <%= text_post.body %>
</div>
--snip--
```

Then update the ImagePost partial at *app/views/image_posts/_image_post.html.erb*:

```
--snip--
<div class="panel-body">
  <p><em>By <%= link_to image_post.user.name, image_post.user %></em></p>

  <%= image_tag image_post.url, class: "img-responsive" %>

  <%= image_post.body %>
</div>
--snip--
```

Finally, update the application layout at *app/views/layouts/application .html.erb*:

```
--snip--
<div class="pull-right">
  <% if current_user %>
    <%= link_to 'Profile', current_user %>
    <%= link_to 'Log Out', logout_path %>
  <% else %>
--snip--
```

The application layout already has a check for current_user. Add the *Profile* link inside this conditional.

2. Open UsersController at *app/controllers/users_controller.rb*. Requiring authentication before the follow action is a one-line change using the authenticate_user! method you wrote in Chapter 9.

```
class UsersController < ApplicationController
  before_action :authenticate_user!, only: :follow

  --snip--
```

The only: :follow option means anonymous users can still access the show, new, and create actions. Now update the user show view at *app/ views/users/show.html.erb*. I used two if statements to first verify that current_user is not nil, and then to verify that current_user is not equal to or already following the user being displayed.

```
--snip--
<p class="lead"><%= @user.name %></p>

<% if current_user %>
  <% if current_user != @user && !current_user.following?(@user) %>
    <%= link_to "Follow", follow_user_path(@user),
          class: "btn btn-default" %>
  <% end %>
<% end %>

<h3>Posts</h3>
--snip--
```

You could have also done this with a single if combining all three of the conditional statements.

3. First, open *app/controllers/image_posts_controller.rb*, and add methods for the new and create actions and the private image_post_params method. These are similar to the corresponding methods in TextPostsController.

```
class ImagePostsController < ApplicationController
  def new
    @image_post = ImagePost.new
  end
```

```
  def create
    @image_post = current_user.image_posts.build(image_post_params)
    if @image_post.save
      redirect_to post_path(@image_post),
                    notice: "Post created!"
    else
      render :new, alert: "Error creating post."
    end
  end

  private

  def image_post_params
    params.require(:image_post).permit(:title, :url, :body)
  end
end
```

Next, add the new view at *app/views/image_posts/new.html.erb*:

```
<div class="page-header">
  <h1>New Image Post</h1>
</div>

<%= render 'form' %>
```

Then add the form partial at *app/views/image_posts/_form.html.erb*:

```
<%= form_for @image_post do |f| %>
  <div class="form-group">
    <%= f.label :title %>
    <%= f.text_field :title, class: "form-control" %>
  </div>
  <div class="form-group">
    <%= f.label :url %>
    <%= f.text_field :url, class: "form-control" %>
  </div>
  <div class="form-group">
    <%= f.label :body %>
    <%= f.text_area :body, class: "form-control" %>
  </div>

  <%= f.submit class: "btn btn-primary" %>
  <%= link_to 'Cancel', :back, class: "btn btn-default" %>
<% end %>
```

Finally, add a button to the home page at *app/views/posts/index.html. erb* that links to the New Image Post form:

```
--snip--
<p>
  <%= link_to "New Text Post", new_text_post_path,
        class: "btn btn-default" %>
```

```
      <%= link_to "New Image Post", new_image_post_path,
          class: "btn btn-default" %>
</p>
--snip--
```

Refer back to "Create Post" on page 153 if you have any questions about these actions or views.

Chapter 11

1. First, add methods for the edit and update actions to the ImagePostsController at *app/controllers/image_posts_controller.rb*, as shown here:

```
  --snip--

  def edit
    @image_post = current_user.image_posts.find(params[:id])
  end

  def update
    @image_post = current_user.image_posts.find(params[:id])
    if @image_post.update(image_post_params)
      redirect_to post_path(@image_post), notice: "Post updated!"
    else
      render :edit, alert: "Error updating post."
    end
  end

  private

  def image_post_params
    params.require(:image_post).permit(:title, :body, :url)
  end
end
```

Next, create the edit view at *app/views/image_posts/edit.html.erb*:

```
<div class="page-header">
  <h1>Edit Image Post</h1>
</div>

<%= render 'form' %>
```

This view uses the form partial you created in Chapter 10. Finally, add a link to the edit action in the ImagePost partial at *app/views/image _posts/_image_post.html.erb*:

```
  --snip--
  <%= image_post.body %>
```

```
    <% if image_post.user == current_user %>
      <p>
      <%= link_to 'Edit', edit_image_post_path(image_post),
            class: "btn btn-default" %>
      </p>
    <% end %>
  </div>
</div>
```

This link is wrapped in a conditional so it only appears if this image post was created by the current user.

2. Update the PostsController at *app/controllers/posts_controller.rb,* as shown in the question.

```
--snip--

def show
  @post = Post.find(params[:id])
  @can_moderate = (current_user == @post.user)
end
end
```

Now edit the comment partial at *app/views/comments/_comment .html.erb* and add a link to destroy the comment when the @can_moderate instance variable is true:

```
<p><em><%= comment.user.name %> said:</em></p>
<p><%= comment.body %></p>
<% if @can_moderate %>
  <p>
  <%= link_to 'Destroy', comment_path(comment),
        method: :delete, class: "btn btn-default" %>
  </p>
<% end %>
```

Be sure to add method: :delete to the link so the destroy action is called. Finally, add the destroy action to the CommentsController at *app/ controllers/comments_controller.rb:*

```
--snip--

def destroy
  @comment = Comment.find(params[:id])

  if @comment.destroy
    redirect_to post_path(@comment.post_id),
                notice: 'Comment successfully destroyed.'
  else
    redirect_to post_path(@comment.post_id),
                alert: 'Error destroying comment.'
  end
end
```

```
    private

    def comment_params
      params.require(:comment).permit(:body, :post_id)
    end
  end
```

This method finds the comment, calls destroy, and redirects back to the post with a message indicating success or failure.

3. Open the routes file at *config/routes.rb* and edit at the logout route:

```
    --snip--
    get 'login', to: 'sessions#new', as: 'login'
    delete 'logout', to: 'sessions#destroy', as: 'logout'

    root 'posts#index'
  end
```

Edit the application layout at *app/views/layouts/application.html.erb* and add method: :delete to the *Log Out* link.

```
    --snip--

    <div class="pull-right">
      <% if current_user %>
        <%= link_to 'Profile', current_user %>
        <%= link_to 'Log Out', logout_path, method: :delete %>
      <% else %>
    --snip--
```

Now the link issues a DELETE request to log out of the application.

Chapter 12

1. The show page loads the collection of comments to render and then loads the owner of each comment individually as the comments are rendered. You can eager load the comments and the owners for a post by adding includes(comments: [:user]) in the show method in the PostsController at *app/controllers/posts_controller.rb*:

```
    --snip--

    def show
      @post = Post.includes(comments: [:user]).find(params[:id]) ❶
      @can_moderate = (current_user == @post.user)
    end
  end
```

Adding includes(comments: [:user]) tells Rails to eager load the comments for this post and all users associated with those comments.

2. Open the Comment partial at *app/views/comments/_comment.html.erb* and add the cache block:

```
<% cache [comment, @can_moderate] do %> ❶
  <p><em><%= comment.user.name %> said:</em></p>
  <p><%= comment.body %></p>
  <% if @can_moderate %>
    <p>
      <%= link_to 'Destroy', comment_path(comment),
            method: :delete, class: "btn btn-default" %>
    </p>
  <% end %>
<% end %>
```

Passing an array to the cache method creates a cache key that combines the elements in the array ❶. In this case, the cache key contains the values of the comment's id and updated_at fields and the value of @can_moderate, either true or false.

3. Open the show page at *app/views/posts/show.html.erb* and add the cache block.

```
--snip--

<h3>Comments</h3>
<% cache [@post, 'comments', @can_moderate] do %> ❶
  <%= render @post.comments %>
<% end %>

--snip--
```

This creates a cache key that is a combination of the cache key for @post, the word "comments," and the value of @can_moderate ❶. Now the comments collection is displayed after a single read from the cache.

Chapter 13

1. You need to update the view partials for both types of posts for this exercise. First, edit the file *app/views/text_posts/_text_post.html.erb* and add a debug call near the bottom, as shown here:

```
<div class="panel panel-default">
  --snip--

    <%= debug text_post %>
  </div>
</div>
```

Then edit *app/views/link_posts/_link_post.html.erb* and add a debug call near the bottom:

```
<div class="panel panel-default">
  --snip--

    <%= debug link_post %>
  </div>
</div>
```

2. The easiest way to add the id and type of each post to the log is by iterating over the contents of the @posts instance variable. Edit *app/controllers/posts_controller.rb* and update the index action.

```
class PostsController < ApplicationController
  before_action :authenticate_user!

  def index
    user_ids = current_user.timeline_user_ids
    @posts = Post.includes(:user).where(user_id: user_ids)
               .paginate(page: params[:page], per_page: 5)
               .order("created_at DESC")

    @posts.each do |post|
      logger.debug "Post #{post.id} is a #{post.type}"
    end
  end
--snip--
```

Now when you refresh the posts index page, you should see five lines similar to "Post 5 is a TextPost" in the log.

3. To debug what happens when a user logs in to the application, you need to add a debugger call to the create action in *app/controllers/sessions_controller.rb*:

```
class SessionsController < ApplicationController
  --snip--

  def create
    debugger
    user = User.find_by(email: params[:email])
    if user && user.authenticate(params[:password])
      session[:user_id] = user.id
      redirect_to root_url, :notice => "Logged in!"
    else
      flash.now.alert = "Invalid email or password"
      render "new"
    end
  end

  --snip--
```

With this line in place, you can examine the `params` sent to this action, the current contents of the session, and the value of user as you move through this action.

Chapter 14

1. This curl command is the same one you used earlier to create a new post, except I replaced the *token* with the word fake.

```
$ curl -i \
       -d '{"text_post":{"title":"Test","body":"Hello"}}' \
       -H "Content-Type: application/json" \
       -H "Authorization: Token fake" \
       http://localhost:3000/api/text_posts
HTTP/1.1 401 Unauthorized
--snip--

HTTP Token: Access denied.
```

Note that the status code is *401 Unauthorized* and the body contains the text `"HTTP Token: Access denied."`

2. Text posts validate the presence of a body, so use curl to attempt to create a text post without specifying a body.

```
$ curl -i \
       -d '{"text_post":{"title":"Test"}}' \
       -H "Content-Type: application/json" \
       -H "Authorization: Token token" \
       http://localhost:3000/api/text_posts
HTTP/1.1 422 Unprocessable Entity
--snip--

{"errors":{"body":["can't be blank"]}}
```

Note that the status code is *422 Unprocessable Entity* and the body contains a JSON representation of the errors.

3. Add the `show` method to *app/controllers/api/posts_controller.rb*:

```
module Api
  class PostsController < ApplicationController
    respond_to :json

    --snip--

    def show
      @post = Post.find(params[:id])
      respond_with @post
    end
  end
end
```

This method finds the requested post and assigns it to the @post instance variable and then responds with that post. The following curl command verifies that this action is working:

```
$ curl http://localhost:3000/api/posts/1
{
  "id":1,
  "title":"First Post",
  "body":"Hello, World!",
  "url":null,
  "user_id":1,
  "created_at":"2014-04-22T00:56:48.188Z",
  "updated_at":"2014-04-22T00:56:48.188Z"
}
```

Because you didn't create a jbuilder view for this action, the default JSON representation for posts is returned.

Chapter 15

1. Edit the file *app/views/layouts/application.html.erb* to change the title of each page:

```
<!DOCTYPE html>
<html>
<head>
  <title>My Awesome Site</title>
  --snip--
```

After you save this change, add it to your local Git repositories staging area, and then commit the change with an appropriate commit message.

```
$ git add .
$ git commit -m "Update title"
```

Now deploy your change by entering bin/cap production deploy in your terminal.

2. The Ruby Toolbox at *https://www.ruby-toolbox.com/* lists hundreds of gems you can use to add features to your application. For example, you can let users upload files to your application. Check the Rails File Uploads category to find several choices, including Paperclip and CarrierWave. From there, you can visit the website, read the documentation, and see the source code for each project.

3. Go to *https://github.com/rails/rails/* to join the discussion on open issues and pull requests, and see previous commits. Ruby on Rails has a page at *http://rubyonrails.org/community/* for those looking to get involved online. You can learn about upcoming Ruby and Rails conferences at *http://rubyconf.org/* and *http://railsconf.com,/* respectively. I hope to see you there!

INDEX

/etc/apache2/sites-available directory, 236–237

eval command (debugger), 203

exclamation mark (!), at end of method name, 7

:exclusion validation, 38

exit command, 4, 30

extend statement, 94

F

favcon.ico file, 25

features, enabling and checking for, 99–100

fetch method, 187

Fibonacci sequence, 93–94

Fielding, Roy, 43

field_with_errors class, 71

file.open method, passing block to, 13

file.read method, 18

file.split method, 18

find_by method, 219

find method, 32, 164

first method, 32

fixtures, 144–146, 156

flags, in Bundler, 82

flash hash, 150

flash messages, 52
     displaying, 131–132

floating-point math, 5

flow between pages, testing, 152

follow action, safety from CSRF attacks, 171

following? method, 114

following! method, 115

follow_redirect! method, 152

foreign key, 106
     in migration file, 108

for loop, 12–13

form builder object, 71

form_for method, 71, 72

forms, 69–72
     for comments, 72–73

form_tag, 134

Forwardable module, 94–95

Fowler, Martin, *Patterns of Enterprise Application Architecture*, 30

fragment caching, 185, 189–191

friendly_date helper method, 61

full-stack web framework, 19

functional tests, 150

G

garbage collection, optimization, 175

gem command, 25, 229

Gemfile
     adding debugger gem, 199
     updating for Heroku, 81–83

gems, 20, 258
     bcrypt, 128
     bootstrap_sass, 124
     byebug, 199
     capistrano-rails, 231
     directories in asset pipeline searches, 177
     documentation from, 229
     installing, 229–230
     jbuilder, 214–216
     updating installed, 124, 128, 199
     will_paginate, 184

generate_api_token method, 217

generate command, 26

get method, 150

GET request, 44, 46, 60
     and state change, 170
     test issuing, 151

getter methods, 16

get_via_redirect method, 152

git add command, 77

git branch command, 79

git checkout command, 79, 80

git commit command, 77–78

git diff command, 78–79

git --help command, 78

GitHub, 84
     account, 244
     pushing code to, 234–235

GitHub API, 205, 206–207
     authentication with, 209–211
     token generation, 209–210

git log command, 77

git pull command, 80

git push command, 80, 83

git remote add command, 80

git status command, 78, 79

Git version control system, 75
     basic usage, 77–80
     branches, 79–80
     getting started, 76–77
     remotes, 80
     repository, creating, 234–235
     setup, 76
     staging area of, 77

greater than (>) operator, 9

greet method, 15–16

H

Hansson, David Heinemeier, 19
hashed version of password, 128
hashes, 8–9
    for commit, 77
    iteration over, 13
hash rocket (=>), 8–9
has_many association, 106, 107, 112, 116, 143
has_many :leaders association, 137
has_many method, 40
has_many :through association, 109–110, 117
has_secure_password method, 128, 143
head element (HTML), 64
head method, 150
help command, for debugger, 201
--help command (Git), 78
helpers, 22, 59–61
    adding methods, 61
    for controllers, 47–48
    controller test, 150
    integration, 152
    methods for form controls, 69–70
helpers directory, 23
Heroku cloud application platform, 75,
        81–84
    deploying application, 83–84
    Gemfile update for, 81–83
heroku run command, 83
Heroku Toolbelt, installing, xxi, 81
hex method, 217
home page
    root route setting for application, 47
    timeline for, 137
HTML, partials for shared code, 67–69
HTML5 field types, helper
                methods for, 72
HTML page
    Rails layout for, 64
    Ruby code and, 22
HTTP, 207–209
    status codes, 207–208
HTTP verbs, 60
    for database actions, 44

I

identifiers, symbols as, 7
id field, 28
    retrieving record by, 32
if statement, 11, 250
ImagePost
    editing, 165
    fixture files for, 145–146
    validation test, 149

image_post_params method, 250–251
image_tag helper, 126
img-responsive class (Bootstrap), 126
include statement, for methods, 91–92
:inclusion validation, 38
index action, 44, 48, 125, 212
index for array, 8
index page
    for post model, 125
    for posts, 61–63
indices, creating for foreign keys, 109
inheritance, 17–18
    in Ruby, 91
    single-table, 110–111
initialize statement, 15
injection attacks, 165–169
insecure direct object reference, 164
inspect method, 198
installing
    Apache, 226–228
    build tools, 229
    gems, 229–230
    Heroku Toolbelt, xxi, 81
    PostgreSQL, 228–229
    Rails, xxi–xxiii, 230
    Ruby, xxi–xxiv, 225–226
instance, 224
    of class, creating, 16
instance methods, 17
instance_methods method, 96
instance_of? method, 97
instance variables
    accessing, 16
    assigning value to, 15
instantiating objects, 31
integer division, 5
integration tests, 152–154
Interactive Ruby interpreter (IRB), 4
Internal Server Error code, 208
introspection, 97
IRB (Interactive Ruby interpreter), 4
irb command, 4
is_a? method, 97
is-a relationship, 17
:is validation, 38
iteration, 12–13

J

JavaScript
    asset pipeline and, 176
    events, 180
    including in application, 124
    list of files in use, 65
javascript_include_tag method, 66

UPDATES

Visit *http://nostarch.com/railscrashcourse/* for updates, errata, and other information.

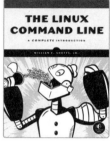
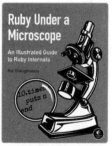